DREAMING WITH BEES

SACRED MEDICINE FROM BEYOND THE VEIL OF GRIEF

Dasha Allred Bond

Featuring: Jill "GiGi" Austin, Batsheva, Christina Marta Beebe, Leah Benjamin, Maria Brannon, Kristin Clark, Emilie Collins, Kim Collins, Elizabeth DeVaughn, Angelica Dunsavage, Kim Louise Eden, Lilly Emerson, Leslie Garbis, Jennifer Harvard, Jan Hatcher, Wendy House, Hope Kernea, Sonia Fernández LeBlanc, Paula Martens, Dusty Rose Miller, Shelby Reardon, Lauren Russell, Carrie Elizabeth Wilkerson

Dreaming with Bees

SACRED MEDICINE FROM BEYOND THE VEIL OF GRIEF

Dasha Allred Bond

Featuring: Jill "GiGi" Austin, Batsheva, Christina Marta Beebe, Leah Benjamin, Maria Brannon, Kristin Clark, Emilie Collins, Kim Collins, Elizabeth DeVaughn, Angelica Dunsavage, Kim Louise Eden, Lilly Emerson, Leslie Garbis, Jennifer Harvard, Jan Hatcher, Wendy House, Hope Kernea, Sonia Fernández LeBlanc, Paula Martens, Dusty Rose Miller, Shelby Reardon, Lauren Russell, Carrie Elizabeth Wilkerson

Dreaming with Bees

Sacred Medicine from Beyond the Veil of Grief

Dasha Allred Bond

Copyright © 2024 Dasha Allred Bond

Published by Brave Healer Productions

All rights reserved. No part of this book may be used or reproduced by any means, graphic, electronic, or mechanical, including photocopying, recording, taping, or by any information storage retrieval system without the written permission of the publisher, except in the case of brief quotations embodied in critical articles and reviews.

Paperback ISBN: 978-1-961493-30-8

eBook ISBN: 978-1-961493-29-2

EARLY PRAISE

"What a delight to find a hive of twenty-four women healers, artists, and dreamers telling the bees the deepest stories of their lives and weaving magic to bring us up from the dark places on shining wings. The humming of the bees, familiar not only in nature but in the shift to a shamanic state of consciousness, stirs the pages. We are encouraged to find the gifts in our wounds and rescue the inner children who went away when the world got too cold and cruel. We are given keys for ancestral healing. We are shown how we can journey to meet wounded ancestors in the time and place of their own wounding and become the soul friends who can help them through. To create - which means to bring something new into our world - is always healing and *Dreaming with Bees* - will inspire you to write and draw, to sing and dance, to embrace the wind and commit poetry. May the bees bless you as you find and follow your path of honey."

~ **Robert Moss**, author of
Conscious Dreaming and *Dreaming the Soul Back Home*

"*Dreaming with Bees* is not simply a collection of compelling stories but feels more like the casting of a great spell—a communal invitation to heal generations of unresolved trauma. The raw intimacy shared within each of these women's stories is not only courageous and inspiring it is also *addictively readable*. And I absolutely love the touch of "medicine" that follows each chapter, almost like a spiritual antidote to each wound being exposed. What an extraordinary tapestry of creativity and wisdom. Bravo!"

~ **Michael Goorjian**, author/filmmaker
What Lies Beyond the Stars, Illusion, Amerikatsi

"This book reads like sitting in a women's circle, hearing the brave and tender stories of loss, grief, and the landscape of our very human headlines. A beautiful read for anyone seeking to navigate through the sacred realms grief can take us to."

~ **Ariella Daly**, bee guardian,
dreamwork guide, founder of Honey Bee Wild

"Dasha Bond is a most incredible woman with a vision to help create a small conscious community where women and children with no funds or family assistance who are in need of hospice have a safe place to transition while being held in love. She wrote *Dreaming with Bees: Sacred Medicine from Beyond the Veil of Grief*, an amazing book on how to work with bee allies and the wisdom held in our dreams to help process various stages of grief.

Dreaming with Bees is filled with heartwarming stories of women who suffered different types of loss – whether it was through health challenges, the loss of loved ones, traumatic events in life, and so on. The book includes grieving over our mothers and grandmothers.

Dasha Bond and her bee sisters give readers empowering tools of how nature and the universe are always talking to us and offering guidance. Each chapter ends with a spiritual tool, practice, and meditation. There are links provided for a long list of practices that are empowering and healing.

Combining working with nature and death, Dreaming with Bees shows us how we can foster an environment that will help the dying transition with peace and a deeper connection to their soul purpose while feeling so much love, which heals the personal and collective.

Dreaming with Bees is really a must read for our times! Caring for the dying with compassion creates a beautiful transition and brings healing back to the collective. This book will touch the deepest reaches of your soul."

~ **Sandra Ingerman**, MA, international shamanic teacher and
award-winning author of 13 books including
Soul Retrieval: Mending the Fragmented Self

"*Dreaming with Bees* is a rare treasure. The soul-stirring stories of 24 accomplished women show us how to be courageous, resilient, compassionate, and hopeful through life's daunting tests and trials. They mine the delicate territory of loss and grief while expressing the urgent need for self-love and a supportive community. Each woman's "medicine" offering, whether through sacred plants, sound, meditation, or a shamanic journey, inspires ongoing healing and self-discovery. This deeply personal, transformational book helps us to find our way home to our truest selves. With a poignant blend of grit and grace, and a refreshing dose of raw honesty, Dreaming with Bees reminds us of the healing power of story and that one woman's story is, in some way, everywoman's story."

~ **Dana Micucci**, author of
The Third Muse and *Sojourns of the Soul:
One Woman's Journey around the World and into Her Truth*

"This compilation of stories offers a distinctive phenomenological experience. In the unique voice of each contributor, the reader absorbs the breadth as well as the deep essence of the countless faces of grief. Most importantly, each story describes how the author walked through her grief and includes "Medicine"—meaningful suggestions for others to heal. Thus, these are not just first-person stories but a sharing of a diverse compilation of approaches for healing: rituals, breathwork, writing, fiber and expressive arts, somatic work, plant healing, birthing new bodies and identities, to note a few; all realigning oneself into a richer existence. To say the very least, these stories are REAL. Hear the bees buzz as you integrate the voices of the subconscious coming through to consciousness. Each story is transformative in its own space – together they speak for healing our collective feminine."

~ **Deborah W Tegano**, PhD, University of Tennessee,
retired Professor, Department of Child & Family Studies

"Bee-ware. This book will immediately draw you in. Dasha Bond is a gifted writer who magically sets the stage for each of her sister pilgrims to enter. Each one shares her unique and sacred story of transformation through experiences of grief. An audible buzz of love, compassion, and divine guidance surrounds the reader. Asking you to revisit your own story from a new perspective, helping you to become more aware of the necessity and importance of being seen, heard, and nurtured by women. After reading *Dreaming with Bees*, you may even bee-inspired to create your own sacred circle."

~ **Marsha Parsons**, PhD, Licensed Psychologist

"*Dreaming with Bees* - A hive of honey for the soul. Transcendent words of wisdom and wonder, grit, grief, and grace. Storytelling that will crack open your heart and have you crying and cheering through the bittersweet beauty of it all. This book is a voice for generations of women who came before and brave new ones coming forward now."

~ **Stephanie Urbina Jones**, bestselling author, recording artist and co-founder of Freedom Folk & Soul

"Dasha Allred Bond's chapters sizzle with pain and grief but also with compassion and even joy as she reflects on leading a group of like-minded women, all bearing their own trauma and practicing their own spirituality, toward the healing and power of community. I love that this book's proceeds go toward caring for the unhoused, a beautiful way of channeling personal brokenness from the past into present-day caring for the overlooked."

~ **Joy Jordan-Lake**, bestselling author of
A Tangled Mercy, Under a Gilded Moon,
and the Christy Award winning *Blue Hole Back Home*.

"True medicine for your soul, *Dreaming with Bees* is a beautiful compilation of stories, wisdom, and transformational moments to help us remember who we really are."

~ **Rea Frey**, Book Doula,
#1 Bestselling Author of *Don't Forget Me* and *The Other Year*

"Dasha Bond, along with a sacred circle of twenty-three women, discover their individual paths to healing mind, body, soul, and spirit in lessons learned from the sacred medicine of bees and the healing hive, beginning with the dreams and stories that must be told and shared so that each one remembers who they are and why they are here. The stories are both painful and elegant. They are stories of medical crises, abandonment, abuse, immense grief, anger, and the loss of "voice," made whole in the exploration of personal and community dreaming and in the sacred support of the "hive." Dreams need action. These dreams and stories become the catalyst for giving back as each person in the sacred circle finds their individual gifts, courage, hope, and the resilience to pick themselves up, dust themselves off, and get on with dreaming bigger and better, ultimately embodying the ways of hope, that place where you know that the impossible is just personal magic waiting to find its voice in you."

~ **Wanda Burch**, historian/writer and member of the National Coalition of Independent Scholars. Her published works include *She Who Dreams: A Journey into Healing through Dreamwork* and *The Home Voices Speak Louder than the Drums: Dreams and the Imagination in Civil War Letters and Memoirs*.

"This book represents a sisterhood of trauma survivors coming together for the purpose of healing. In their stories of vulnerability and pain are tools and hope. What I admire in these chapters is each woman's willingness to embrace the transformative powers of imagination and intuition and to take the risk of voicing her experience in a supportive community. Honoring the richness of dreaming is a shared passion. Yet even so, this is not a book that emphasizes just one path to wellness. Many of the storytellers have worked in a variety of healing modalities. I hope you'll find what sparkles for you here and receive it as a catalyst for your own reflection and creative renewal."

~ **Robin Blackburn McBride** - Novelist, Poet, Life Coach

"The stories in this book are so beautifully written, so powerful, so healing; I urge you to buy it and then make the space to sit down and savor every word, every bit of healing medicine. You will be changed. Dasha Bond, the lead writer, is an exquisite storyteller with a powerful, touching message. She has chosen her collaborators with such care. They are offering the beauty and sustenance of the sisterhood of the beehive. Incredible beauty, incredible medicine. Thank you all so much for this extraordinary gift."

~ **Iva Enright**, M.A, healer, writer, equine collaborator, and founder of The Dreaming Horse Ranch

"*Dreaming with Bees* is a sacred book. Led by master dreamer Dasha, each of the collaborating authors weaves their personal story into a honeycomb of healing and builds a hive of precious words where each heart can be held in the reading. Wisdom from the bees is shared between each chapter, while trauma and grief find transformation and peace in the warm drip of honey, the dusting of pollen, and the shaping of propolis and wax. This book shines light into dark corners and awakens love for those who need it most."

~ **Emily K. Grieves**, Visionary Artist and Healer

"A truly powerful read! I felt honored to peek into the deeply intimate details of these women's experiences of pain and suffering. They all showed, in commanding and important ways, how adversity can be overcome by believing their resoluteness will show them a better way. I was inspired to tears more than once. And I really appreciated how each shared their unique medicine with the reader. I've already recommended Dreaming with Bees to friends."

~ **Juliana Ericson**, Rebirthing Breathwork Life Coach, Ordained Presbyterian Elder, Founder of The Joyful Life Project, and Author of *The Other F Word: 7 Days to Forgiving Anyone*

Dreaming with Bees, by Dasha Bond and her Bee Sisters, is not just a great read; it's a transformative journey. This book is a powerful message in words and energies that draws us into a deeper understanding of our relationships. Beyond the authors' extraordinary bond with bees and the presence of the Holy Mother, they unveil the essence of those seemingly "normal" relationships, revealing their profound meanings and the dimensions that often go unnoticed.

Reading *Dreaming with Bees* ignited a spark in my heart as the authors shared the mystery and magic of their lives, experiences that resonated deeply with my own. We are all "dreamers" navigating our unique human journey through this world. Life holds so much more than the narrow lens we've been conditioned to see through, and it's truly invigorating to delve into the sweetness, challenges, and revelations of another's journey.

Embark on your own transformative journey. Buy this book and allow yourself to relax and dream your way through Dasha and the Bee sister's stories. Immerse yourself in the journey of *Dreaming with Bees* and discover the magic that awaits you."

~ **Lee McCormick**, founder of three paradigm-shifting mental health and addiction treatment programs, author of *Dreaming Heaven* – a book and film documentary, *Spirit Recovery Meditation Journal, Spirit Recovery Medicine Bag, The Heart Reconnection Guidebook*, and creator of Spirit Recovery Inc., a program dedicated to working with indigenous teachers and medicine people in Mexico and Peru.

DEDICATION

This book is dedicated, first and foremost, to my loving husband, Kenny. He has been at my side every step of the way. Whether helping to transport food and supplies for Dreaming with Bees circles and retreats or talking me off the ledge when I wasn't sure I could tell my real story. He has been my constant and steady North Star, and I couldn't have pulled this project off without his love and support.

I also owe gratitude to my children, Lilli and Avery. You two have taught me so much about what it means to be a mother. I am grateful for your patience, kindness, and willingness to allow me to share parts of my story that are also yours. I am thankful for the wisdom and courage of your generation. I believe in you. The bees believe in you.

To my mother, I love you to the moon and back, plus one more. You have taught me so much about resilience and having the courage to pick myself up from the ground, dust myself off, and get back out there. Thank you for gifting me life and pushing me to dream bigger and own my weirdness. Telly, thank you for your love and guidance over the years. Go Tigers!

In memory of the late David Philpo, my buddy and neighbor, thank you for standing in as a father figure when my own Father(s) couldn't. I am grateful for the way you and Barbara adopted me and the kids like we were your own. Dave, you were the first to show a genuine interest in my writing and push me to keep telling my stories. I still cherish all my old drafts with your red pencil edit markings. I have felt your presence crafting this book and am grateful for your support even from beyond the veil.

To my bee sister, Kristin Clark, my twin, my wombmate from many lifetimes. You SEE me even when I am trying to hide with the snails in the dream garden. You KNOW my heart and always manage to find me when I feel most lost. May we always play in our Dreaming Tree, sister.

To my sacred Sister Circle of Seven: Kristin Sentman Clark, Jennifer Harvard, Dusty Rose Miller, Leslie Garbis, Shambia Ananda Prem, and Carrie Wilkerson, I am so thankful for the many ways you show up. Our constellation shines bright, sisters!

To my bee sister, Beverly Bain, I owe you so much gratitude. You have been a source of strength for me on so many occasions—literally the "B" in my buzz.

I am grateful to my sister, Shelley, for our bond and commitment to challenge and heal our ancestral wounds. I'm grateful the Universe stepped in to ensure we would be in each others lives. I love you more than you know. I couldn't ask for a better warrior of a sister to break down the walls.

To my brothers Daniel, Paul, and Mason, I'm grateful for your love, honor, and respect and for all the ways you have tried to protect me and all the women in your lives. You three beautifully represent the Divine Masculine.

To Florence, Ken, and Annie, I couldn't ask for better in-laws. I feel like we have been together for many lifetimes, and I love you so much.

Laura Di Franco, Stephanie Urbina Jones, Jeremy Pajer, and Tina Green, thank you for believing in the healing power of stories and showing us a pathway to share our sacred words.

Finally, I want to honor three special bee sisters:

Brianna Mortimer, Deanna "Daisy" Grimes, and Sandy Hutchins.

These women came into our circle of dreaming bees in beautiful, mystical ways. I am forever grateful for their love, wisdom, and inspiring stories over the last year. Our circle continues to honor and pray for them and their families as they continue their battles with cancer.

DISCLAIMER

This book offers health and nutritional information and is designed for educational purposes only. You should not rely on this information as a substitute for, nor does it replace professional medical advice, diagnosis, or treatment. If you have any concerns or questions about your health, you should always consult with your own physician or other healthcare professional. Do not disregard, avoid, or delay obtaining medical or health-related advice from your healthcare professional because of something you may have read in this publication. The opinions, ideas, and recommendations contained in this publication, do not necessarily represent those of the Publisher. The use of any information provided in this book is solely at your own risk.

Developments in medical research may impact the health, fitness, and nutritional advice that appears in this publication. The publisher makes no assurances that the information contained in this book will always include the most relevant findings or developments with respect to the particular field.

The experts featured in this publication have shared their tools, practices, and knowledge with you with a sincere and generous intent to assist you on your health and wellness journey. Please contact them with any questions you may have about the techniques or information they provided. They will be happy to assist you further!

THE BEE PRAYER

- Anonymous

Winged Spirit of Sweetness, I call on you.

Teach me the ways of Transformation and Fertilization.

The path from pollen to sweetest honey.

Teach me to taste the essence of each place I alight,
carrying that essence with me to continue creation's cycle.

Teach me the ways of hope, reminding me
that what seems impossible may yet be achieved.

The flowing tears of the Gods draw me ever closer to the wisdom
hidden within beauty. Give me flight and sunlight,
passion and productivity, cooperation with those around me,
and sharpened strength to defend my home.

May I ever spiral out from my heart, searching for what I need, and
return there once again to turn those lessons into nourishment.

Bee Spirit, I call to you.

OH BLESSED BEE

Song Channeled by Dasha - Playa De Los Muertos - Mexico

Salt of my Body

Salt of the Sea

Milk of Pachamama

Honey from the Bees

Maria, Maria. . .Keeper of the Veil

Maria, Maria. . .Please deliver up our Prayers.

Maria, Maria. . .We open our hearts to Thee

Maria, Maria. . .Oh Blessed Bee

Repeat all. End with "Oh Blessed Bee" three times.

TABLE OF CONTENTS

INTRODUCTION | i

CHAPTER 1
THE LOST YEARS | 1
RECLAIMING THE LOST VOICES OF THE GRANDMOTHERS

By Dasha Allred Bond

CHAPTER 2
COMING HOME TO MYSELF | 11
AN ADOPTEE'S JOURNEY FROM ABANDONMENT TO BELONGING

By Jennifer Harvard, LMT

CHAPTER 3
WATER IN THE DESERT | 20
GROUNDING MEDITATION FOR THE LOSS OF A LOVED ONE

By Angelica Dunsavage

CHAPTER 4
THE VOICE MAGNETIC | 29
ALCHEMIZE WOUNDS INTO WISDOM
By Maria Brannon, Vocal Embodiment Guide, Sound Healing Practitioner

---

CHAPTER 5
BREAKING FREE FROM EXPECTATIONS | 39
THE POWER OF FINALLY BEING WHO YOU ARE
By Christina Marta Beebe

CHAPTER 6
ADULT FRIENDSHIPS | 51
FIND YOUR SOUL BESTIES WITH A SIMPLE BODY-CENTERED PRACTICE
By Elizabeth DeVaughn, LPC-MHSP

CHAPTER 7
GRIEF AND GRATITUDE | 61
HOW PLANT MEDICINE HELPED ME HEAL
By Kim Louise Eden

CHAPTER 8
THE GIFTS YOU WERE BORN WITH | 70
EXPLORING PURPOSE THROUGH DREAM TRAVELING
By Jan Hatcher

CHAPTER 9
AUTHENTIC SELF-MOTIVATION FOR BUSINESS LEADERS | 79
A SHAMANIC CEREMONY TO UNWIND YOUR RELENTLESS ACHIEVER
By Jill "GiGi" Austin, MBA

CHAPTER 10
THE FATHER WOUND | 93
MANIFESTING THE LOVE THAT'S MISSING
By Emilie Collins, RN, AS, BSN, MSN

CHAPTER 11
WHAT'S YOUR VOICE STORY? | 106
A PATH TO LOVING AND FREEING YOUR TRUE VOICE
By Leslie Garbis

CHAPTER 12
EPIPHANIES OF A MOTHERLESS MOTHER | 115
MY JOURNEY THROUGH THE WOUND
By Wendy House, Certified Reiki Practitioner

CHAPTER 13
INSTRUCTIONS FOR BEING BORN: | 123
AN INVITATION TO SEE AND BE SEEN
By Dusty Rose Miller, PhD

CHAPTER 14
THE LIGHT SHE BRINGS | 135
MOVING FORWARD WITH GRIEF THROUGH THE GUIDANCE OF AYAHUASCA

By Kim Collins, C.C.H., Medicine Woman

CHAPTER 15
HOMEBODY: LOST AND FOUND | 148
USING THE SENSORY WISDOM OF PLANTS TO GUIDE US HOME

By Lauren "Elle" Russell, MA LPC

CHAPTER 16
PROCESSING PAIN THROUGH POETRY | 158
WRITING AT NIGHT NEVER FELT SO RIGHT

By Lilly Emerson

CHAPTER 17
FORGED IN FIRE | 179
A HEROINE'S JOURNEY FROM DARKNESS TO LIGHT

By Paula Martens

CHAPTER 18
BEHELD BY BODIES OF LISTENING IN ALTARED STATES OF GRIEF | 188
AN OFFERING TO THE MOUNTAINS OF OUR GREAT BODY

By Leah Benjamin, LMT

CHAPTER 19
ESCAPING THE BELLY OF THE BEAST | 202
FINDING YOUR WAY THROUGH THE NIGHTMARE OF TRAUMATIC GRIEF

By Carrie Elizabeth Wilkerson, M.A., M.MFT, O.M.

CHAPTER 20
SAFE IN THE WORLD | 211
HEAL ANCESTRAL TRAUMA AND FREE YOUR MAGICAL CHILD

By Kristin Clark

CHAPTER 21
FOLDING TIME | 222
OUR STORIES THAT HEAL LINEAGE FORWARD AND BACKWARD

By Sonia Fernández LeBlanc, M.Ed

CHAPTER 22
WISDOM OF YOUR MOTHERS | 232
WEAVING ANCESTRAL GRIEF AND HOPE INTO YOUR OWN STORY

By Shelby Reardon, LMFT

CHAPTER 23
TWO MOONS | 244
A MOTHER'S JOURNEY

By Hope Kernea, Author and Mother

CHAPTER 24
INRAVELING | 251
FINDING YOUR WAY THROUGH THE SHADOW MAZE OF TRAUMA AND ADDICTION

By Batsheva

CONCLUSION | 261

POSTSCRIPT | 263

ARTIST STATEMENT | 266

INTRODUCTION

PART 1

THE CALLING

"In the beginning was the Word, says the Gospel of John. But the truth is, words came later. In the beginning, was the rose."

~ Perdita Finn

In August 2019, My husband, Kenny, and I traveled through Southern France for almost three weeks, pilgrimaging through the mountains and holy ruins in search of the secrets of a distant past. I was studying many texts describing a very different history of Mary Magdalene than what I was taught in my Sunday School lessons as a child. My channeled prayers with her and Mother Mary opened my heart to the deep call to go to the very lands where she lived the last 30 years of her life.

    I didn't want to go as part of any organized group. I needed to make this journey alone, with just my husband at my side. We had yet to travel through Europe, and neither one of us spoke French. It was all new terrain, but I had to go. I planned the entire three weeks, mapping our way from the Alps to the Pyrenees and all points in between that held some clue to the real story of Mary Magdalene.

My own bloodline traces back to this region. Something in my DNA was intensely activated as I walked the beaches of Saintes-Maries-de-la-Mer and began climbing Mount Bugarach and many other sacred places that seemed to quake with ancestral stories. I swear there were corners I turned down cobbled streets, and I knew in my bones that I'd been there in a past lifetime. We visited three points of interest that I previously saw in my dreams. To say, "I felt at home" was an understatement. I was home.

I remember sitting on the steps going down into the vault where the gold-encased skull of Mary Magdalene is kept and feeling dizzy with nausea from the intense energy vibrations entombed in the space. My mind spun, and I found myself pulled into a vision. I felt myself dream walking into the energy field of Mary Magdalene, standing at the foot of the cross where Yeshua was crucified. I felt waves of grief, her grief, flooding my body. I felt the immensity of her love for him and the rage and gut-wrenching despair as she watched her beloved suffer and die.

The vision shifted back in history, where I found myself this time in the energy field of Isis. Once again, I felt the absolute horror and devastation as she watched the crucifixion of Horus.

While in France, I walked through the many valleys of lavender-laced ancient secrets for three weeks. I lit ruby-red votive candles in caves and monasteries in honor of the dead —the literally hundreds of thousands silenced and murdered during the Albigensian Crusade. I felt my own throat constrict as my mind flashed to the thousands of screams burning in flames that reached clear up to the heavens—tortured in the name of God.

Touring the old ruins of those cities, with their ancient stone structures and collections of relics and bones left me feeling utterly haunted. A million past lives and timelines were screaming, "Remember me?" And "Don't forget about me!"

When my husband and I toured the catacombs below the city of Paris, I couldn't help but wonder who each skull, vertebrae, mandible, etc. belonged to. *Who were they? How did they die? What was their story?*

Three weeks later, we were in the cab on our way to Charles de Gaulle Airport to catch our departing flight when I started heaving with tears.

I was on my way to a full-blown panic attack. I sobbed so hard I could barely breathe. Snot ran down my face as I irrationally explained to my husband, "We can't go back! We have to stay! I belong here! Please just ship our things and the kids and the pets here! I can't leave!"

The energy of Mary Magdalene opened me up in incredible ways. The exposure to a new language, new flavors and smells, and the nudges to trust what only my senses could translate rather than just how to read and write words awakened something primal in me. It was like my intuition expanded threefold. I intensely sensed the guidance of the Divine, and I think I was afraid that if I got on that plane and left, the connection would be lost.

Just as the cab was turning onto the freeway to the airport, I heard a woman's voice in my mind's eye. *Please stop crying. You must go back, but know that in time, you will return. You have work to do in your own city now. I have shared with you the beauty of this land. Now, you must see its underbelly. These are my children, too. This is who I need you to love.*

Outside my window, the very last image I saw, the final impression on this pilgrimage to connect with Mary Magdalene, was not the crisp cold blues of the Mediterranean where she first stepped foot on that land, but instead, a sea of homeless men, women, and babies. It was a cardboard tent camp that went on for miles. *Oh God! Who are they? What are their names? What are their stories?*

A quick Google search estimates there are currently over 50,000 homeless individuals living on the streets in this area.

Many of the texts I read about Mary Magdalene explained that she was a midwife who also worked with the dying, often tending to the marginalized, the outcasts. Mother Theresa followed in her first steps, caring for thousands of dying individuals on India's street corners and back alleyways.

When I heard those words that day in the cab, they confirmed a deep knowing I was already awakened to. And this wasn't the first time I heard this woman's voice.

One year prior, I was on a walk near my home. No one else was in the park at that hour; however, it felt like I was being followed, like someone was moving close behind me. I jumped and turned, but no one was there.

Spooked, I started a slow jog's pace towards home. Suddenly, the feeling of another ran up close, nipping at my heels. I stopped again and turned. No one. But a voice did come through my mind's eye. *Go home and watch the movie your mom's been asking you to watch.*

I shook my head, rubbed my eyes, and stood there, questioning my sanity. Again, the voice came through. *Don't be afraid. Go home and watch the movie The Letters.*

And so I did. The Letters is the story of Mother Theresa and her work with the dying. Right before one scene, the voice came to me again. *Pay attention. This is important.*

In the scene, Mother Theresa explains to a young nun that every person deserves the right to die with dignity and that no one should die alone. The voice called, *Go look inside your writing desk. In the back corner.*

The desk the voice was referring to was one my father crafted. Beautiful hardwood, roll-top design, just like the one Nathaniel Hawthorne used to write many of his grief-stricken tales. When I reached into the darkest corner of the bottom drawer, I found something I had never seen before. It was a small book of Mother Theresa's prayers and speeches. *This doesn't belong to me. I'm the only person in the family to have been a practicing Catholic, yet this isn't mine. This doesn't make sense. Dad could barely read or write and hated all religions. So Strange.*

However, when I opened the tiny book, I saw his name scrolled in his handwriting. Then I noticed underlined and highlighted the same quote I heard Mother Theresa say in the film minutes prior. "No one should die alone."

My hands began to shake, and I almost dropped the book. In 2012, my father took his own life, and the thought that haunted me up until this point was how lonely and lost he must have felt those last few minutes before he moved the barrel of the shotgun into his mouth and pulled the trigger.

Later that night, I dreamed of seeing my father with my grandmother and his favorite aunt. I knew it was a visitation. A Divine allowance to bring some peace to my own grieving heart. He appeared shy, hanging back, but waved and smiled, and I knew he was safe and not alone.

The following day, I walked into the hospital where I was working and was shocked to find a flyer from our hospital chaplain on my desk, announcing he was starting a NODA program—No One Dies Alone. At the center of the flyer was the quote again from Mother Theresa.

I ran to Chaplain Tim and signed up immediately.

March 14th, 2018, I was driving to work when I heard the sad news that physicist and cosmologist Stephen Hawking had died. I immediately started thinking about my father because his name was also Stephen, and he and I, even though we disagreed on many subjects, would talk for hours about space and time and the cosmos.

One of my favorite memories from my youth was snuggling with my dad on our black leather couch, watching episodes of Nova, and listening to Carl Sagan's theories.

That morning, I walked into work, thinking about the death of Stephen Hawking and my father, Stephen, and my phone received a text message from Chaplain Tim asking me if I was available to sit with a hospice patient who had no family or friends. He was my first NODA program patient, and he, too, was named Stephen.

After that day, I began noticing Divine signs and synchronicities almost daily that I needed to somehow work with the dying who were also experiencing homelessness.

A year later, COVID was peaking across our planet, and working at a hospital as the Staffing Officer during the first big wave and then the Ethics and Compliance Officer for the second wave, I witnessed and experienced the full brunt of burnout and grief directly impacting my community. The NODA calls came more frequently.

This was the year I decided to complete certification in the End of Life Doula program offered by the University of Vermont. Throughout my studies in the program, I started noticing individuals moving through what looked like the grief process. And it wasn't just those struggling with the death of loved ones. It seemed like everyone was grieving a multitude of losses. The entire planet was grieving. I believe it is still grieving.

PART 2

THE DREAMS

". . .There's nothing you keep; there's only your reflection."

~ Manchester Orchestra

My professional dream work journey started in 2008. I was an adult student at Belmont University in Nashville and signed up for a Dream Work course as an elective. My instructor opened me up to a world I had no idea existed.

Even as a young child, I've always felt a solid connection to my dreams. As a writer, I've always been drawn to metaphor and symbolism hidden in myths, fairy tales, songs, and films. The Bible and Torah are filled with stories highlighting the importance of dreams. During this class, I was equipped with the language needed to crack the code, so to speak, to the "collective universal unconscious."

I've never viewed the world the same since completing that course of study. During this study, I started a dream group that met once a month in my home. We started with four close friends but grew to 15-20 folks coming regularly. It has been a fantastic experience watching diverse individuals often walk in, afraid to share something so profound with the group—something literally from their soul. Then, as the group begins sharing their intuitive responses, seeing the spark of light as the dreamer starts to make what I can only describe as Divine connections.

Over the years, I've been fortunate to have the opportunity to study and work alongside several global dream masters and acquired a wide array of techniques and tools to work within the Dreamtime. The study of dreams is ancient. The study of the collective unconscious has been shared across all cultures and time. I believe the Dreamtime to be a sacred space where you can intimately become one with the Divine Source, bringing back wisdom that can heal the mind, body, and Spirit.

PART 3

THE BEES

"Stories have to be told, or they die, and when they die, we can't remember who we are or why we're here."

~ The Secret Life of Bees ~ Sue Monk Kidd

In 2022, I was asked to co-facilitate a Divine Feminine Rosary workshop in Teotihuacan, Mexico, as part of a week-long women's retreat led by my close friends, Jennifer Harvard of Gaia Sisterhood and Stephanie Urbina Jones of Freedom Folk & Soul.

Before COVID, I was leading a Way of the Rose Rosary circle in addition to Dream circles, so my plan was to introduce some of the same teachings I was offering, including the legendary story and medicine of Our Lady of Guadalupe.

Well, a strange thing started happening leading up to this trip. Every night, out of the blue, I started dreaming about bees. They taught me how the Sacred Medicine of Mother Mary is the same medicine as the bees and the healing hive. Every night for months, they came. During the day, I started noticing bee imagery everywhere, messages on walls about bees, and actual live bees began flying into my field.

Before I went to sleep at night, I felt their little energy bodies lit on my skin. I thought I was really losing my mind. Around a week before my trip to Mexico, I learned about a training session with Ariella Daly, who teaches bee shamanism. *They are already talking to me, so I should check this out.*

The coursework was fascinating and completely aligned with what the bees shared with me in my dreams. I felt like I found my true shamanic path. I flew to Mexico and presented my first Dreaming with Bees Rosary workshop. I felt the energy of the bees and Guadalupe coursing through our meeting space. The women in the circle were resonating deeply with the wisdom coming from this energy. The room buzzed.

Emily Grieves, the owner of the casita where we stayed, is an amazing artist attuned to the vibration of Our Lady. So, being in her home, surrounded by her gorgeous paintings depicting this energy I also felt, was otherworldly.

The next day, we were to tour the Basilica of Our Lady of Guadalupe and see the famous Tilma of Roses. I was just blessed by the Priest and was about to enter the area where the shrine is located when, up ahead, I heard all the women in our group who were seeing it before me say, "Dasha, oh my gosh, look up! Look up!"

I enter the space and look up. I'm shocked to find the entire chapel is shaped like the inside of a beehive. The lights are shaped like golden chunks of honeycomb with honey dripping down the sides. The baptismal font is also the same honeycomb shape, with honey dripping down. This beehive's center is the ancient Tilma of Our Lady Herself.

Since that trip, the bees have been a part of my life and all the circles I hold to honor our dreams.

PART 4

THE HEALING HIVE

*"The stories that go unnoticed
are the most important ones to tell."*

~ All the Light We Cannot See ~ Anthony Doerr

Our bee sisters met for a couple of years—diverse in age and cultural background. As our love and trust for each other deepened, our nighttime dreams and the awareness they awakened in us expanded. I witnessed our beautiful healing hive of sisters caring for the sick, weary, and dying. We wrote love letters to lonely strangers, cooked soups, and made homemade bread to be delivered to the doorsteps of the less fortunate. We became a hive that really wanted to give back.

When the opportunity to create a book with this group of women arrived, the bees immediately said "yes." This was an opportunity to give back in a big way. The bees informed us this was their plan and to trust in its sweetness.

Finding 24 authors who agreed to contribute a chapter to the book felt daunting, but I kept trusting the right people would show up. I couldn't be more proud of the women who said "yes." Then I told the group, "The bees want us to write about grief—share about our losses."

I could hear the collective, "Oh shit! What did I sign up for?" ripple across the room.

All I could counter was, "I know. But it's the medicine the bees and Great Mother want to help us bring to our community."

In October of 2023, we came together as a group at Penuel Retreat Center in Ashland City. For an entire weekend, we drank in the nectar brought to us by the bees, and we dove deep into the belly of grief and what that looks like to each of us. We shared our stories of loss—the deaths of parents, siblings, lovers, and babies. The loss of marriages, good, bad, and abusive. The loss of body parts and soul parts. The loss of our childhood, our ancestral stories. Loss of jobs, homes, and treasured possessions.

Collectively, we moved the pain of grief through our bodies and out, and as bee sister, Maria, drummed, we let out a mighty collective wail. Twenty-four women beat our fists against our chests, and the ground and screamed out years of repressed anger and despair. We did it the way the grandmothers of our ancient past did, with teeth bared and naked bellies low to the Earth. We pulled grief up through our wombs, our lungs, our hearts, and our throats.

We stood in sacred circle around a roaring fire between the portal places of lake and labyrinth. Beautiful sister, Kristin, delicately strummed the strings of her guitar, as our hearts opened to the holy verse of her song, "Telling the Bees." We fed the flames of the fire our regrets and forged new alliances.

We had written the titles of our stories on paper and held them out towards the crackling embers.

"We call in the ancient grandmothers of this land. We call in our loving ancestors and guardians, angels, nature allies, and elementals. We call in Mary Magdalene, Yeshua, Mother Mary and the bees. Please honor us with your deep wisdom so that we can share it with the dreamers to come. May our grief stories, our prayers, be alchemized by the flames of this fire. May their essence rise up as purifying smoke from the great cauldron of creation, the sacred womb of Pachamama. Rise up into the night sky. May the cosmos gather our stories together into a beautiful constellation of healing light. May each story return to us as a guidepost back to the lost soul parts of ourselves and anyone else who reads our sacred words. May these stories offer healing that expands and crosses over the timelines and dimensions of our ancestors and the generations to come. So bee it so."

What showered back down from the heavens was our raw, sinewy, bones-of-truth ruins as stories blessed by the grandmothers, the bees, and our Great Earth Mother.

We have crafted this hauntingly beautiful collection of stories in service to the millions of women and children who have lost their own way and their voices. We rise together from our raw truths, shouting, "No more!"

During a recent healthy debate with my son about my fears around sharing my personal stories, he spoke up and asked, "Mom, when are you going to stop protecting them? Your silence is enabling these cycles, too."

Whew! Coming from my child, my son, this was a major wake-up call I needed. I needed the push to find the courage to lead this project.

This book is my answer, Son.

The stories in this book are real and visceral and authentic and sometimes unapologetically badass, don't-give-another-single-fuck, pure truth. We are a world grieving a million losses, a world where we're expected to return to our own living only three days max after a devastating loss. A world where we walk around pretending like we're okay. We're not okay. If we don't create fundamental spaciousness for the deep rhythmic pangs of loss, like the mudslides of South America, the pain will find its way out, cutting straight through us and destroying everything in its path.

These brave stories intimately capture the vivid details of core wounding and how these 24 women survived the storms of their lives and are here to share their hopes and healing dreams for a better world.

PART 5

ALUNA BRIDGE

"Do not neglect hospitality, for through it some have unknowingly entertained angels."

~ Hebrews 13:2

Our losses should be honored, and time should be taken to integrate the mental and emotional shifts we experience as grieving humans. If honored as sacred, some of our greatest spiritual lessons are gained from the mystery of death and the more profound journey it can provide. This work heals not only the dying but also our ancestors, future generations, and the very planet and universe we call home. It's all connected.

The dream of Aluna Bridge started back in 2010 after I lost my father to suicide. Not long after his death, I began my own personal spiritual journey, eventually leading me to the "No One Dies Alone" (NODA) program at the hospital where I worked for many years. I began seeing firsthand many from our homeless community come in for care for their terminal diagnosis and have nowhere to go. No family to turn to for support. In 2023 alone, we lost 180 friends on the streets of Nashville due to exposure and illness.

I have also witnessed families struggling with the stress of trying to navigate the process of hospice care for their loved ones while also trying to take time for their own emotional needs and grief tending. This became my mission—my calling—to create a bridge of awareness and love for our community of dying, uniting those in need with acts of kindness. That is the heart of Aluna Bridge.

In 2023, I formally created the nonprofit Aluna Bridge/Aluna Guest House. A large portion of the profits from the sale of this book will support the nonprofit, as well as community nonprofits working to protect our bees and the lands that help sustain their survival.

Why the name Aluna?

During my own spiritual journey, I came across the name "Aluna" from an indigenous pre-Colombian tribe known as the Kogi that live in the Sierra Nevada de Santa Marta mountains in South America. Aluna is the name the Kogi give to the Divine Spirit, the creator of all. The life source, the essence of Spirit, connects all humans with the one Source.

The Kogi see Aluna as the great sea of water that existed before creation. She's the great womb of creation and the place where all returns. According to the Kogi, Aluna is also the great light of the moon, lighting our path and marking our cycles of life, death, and rebirth.

When I researched the name further, I learned that in Africa, the name means "approach." In Hawaii, it means "to descend or loosen." In Portugal, it means "student." I couldn't help but notice how this word globally defines the transition experience. When we embark on or approach any kind of journey, be it spiritual, emotional, or physical, we must approach it like students, allowing ourselves to loosen from what we think we know and descend into the depths of unknowing. By surrendering to the will of the Spirit of Source that courses through us, we're guided towards new beginnings—new life.

Aluna Bridge was created to hold space for those transitioning out of this world and into the next. A space where they're cared for, loved, and supported during those final sacred moments between breaths. Like a lamp post rising from the shadows, Aluna Bridge will be the light helping to support and guide individuals and families through the grief process.

I believe Aluna's spiritual gifts are reciprocal. Those volunteering and supporting the organization also enter as students, understanding those we care for are our greatest teachers.

It's my hope that the love and connection created by Aluna Bridge will expand into our community, impacting families and inspiring all to walk more gently on this Earth, acting as stewards and guardians to all God's creatures, big and small, that require grace, and mercy, or just an extended hand.

In bee shamanism, ancient wisdom holds that our little winged friends are psychopomps, meaning they can travel between worlds. Burial traditions honoring the mystical power of bees and their interconnectedness with the Divine have been observed in almost every ancient culture on every continent. Honey was even used to embalm the pharaohs of Ancient Egypt.

The Merovingian King of France, Childeric, was buried in a garment covered in bees made from gold and garnet. This is believed to have inspired the "Napolean bee," later known as the "fleur-de-lis," and symbolized immortality and the connection to God.

Most European families of old kept a hive of bees on their estates that were cared for by generations. They practiced the daily ritual of "Telling the Bees," which is the tradition of going out and giving a report to the hive. You would tell the bees your worries, goals, and special announcements like weddings, births, and deaths. During death, the hives would be draped in a black veil so that they, too, could mourn the loss of the family member.

There are historical accounts of bees that were so close to a family member who died that they were witnessed as a swarm attending the funeral.

Bee shamanism draws from the teachings of the ancient Greek priestesses, known as the Melissae (Greek for Bee), who were the great prophets of the Oracle of Delphi.

It has been a beautiful, mystical experience witnessing the marriage of these ancient pathways to spiritual healing and freedom evolve and form this incredible sacred model for hospice and grief support: The dreams, the bees, and Mary Magdalene.

PART 6

TRAVELING MERCIES

The weavings of time and souls are wild and mysterious.

I answered the call of the dreams and the bees at the beginning of last year. I was thrilled, feeling so in my power, and ready to really get this book project and the nonprofit up and going. I felt this bigger push and knew the timing was finally right to jump in head first.

The universe; however, stepped in and quickly let me know, "You're actually not ready for this dream just yet. There's more to learn. We know your favorite learning model is to take a hands-on approach, really immersing yourself in the experience, so. . ." Insert drumroll.

In April of 2023, I was diagnosed with renal cell carcinoma. I was only two months into a new job, so my benefits hadn't started. I'm still spinning from the fact that less than six months ago, I had to have around 80% of my right kidney removed. I haven't even had my follow-up imaging appointment yet to confirm whether or not I'm cancer-free.

The universe was like, "You know what? Let's just go ahead and register her for the advanced, escalated program. We need to really push her."

The week right before my nephrectomy, I had to go in for my pre-op labs. My husband was having a routine colonoscopy and needed a driver, so we just scheduled both on the same day. I finished up my labs and got the call from Kenny's doctor that his procedure was over, and I could meet them in the post-op area.

I walked into the room and found Kenny still coming to from the anesthesia. We made funny jokes that eighth-graders tell each other about butts. The doctor entered the room, and I immediately sensed the energy shift. *Oh God. Something is wrong.*

He pulled out photos taken during the procedure and worked as best he could to try and help us understand that what we were looking at was a very aggressive form of cancer. *What is this? Are you kidding me? Is this some kind of cruel joke? Both of us? CANCER?*

Yes. It was true. And it's still true. At this very moment, as I type, I'm sitting next to my dear husband as he receives his seventh chemotherapy treatment.

Our bodies, minds, and souls have been tested, purged, and shredded over the last few months. My mind has frequently reflected on those visions I experienced in the past of Mary Magdalene watching with helpless hands as her beloved suffered on that cross. I have had moments of absolute dark-as-night despair and fear that this beautiful soul might be ripped away from me and our children. Watching him suffer through his treatments and hearing him say, "I really feel like I'm dying," has brought me to my knees, begging for mercy and grace.

My husband's first meeting with his assigned oncologist was three days after my own nephrectomy. My dear sisters, Kristin and Jennifer, stepped in and physically went with him and his parents to his first few doctor's appointments so they wouldn't be alone as they learned the details of what was growing in his body and determined the best course of treatment.

I remember the sinking feeling I felt when he came to my bedside and tried to remain strong as he explained that this was serious. "*The doctor said it's stage 3 or 4.*" I remember feeling the pangs of fear and anxiety pushing up through my body. This was devastating. I needed to cry but was in so much physical pain from my own surgery that I had to work to contain it all within. In that moment, I clearly felt a cracking within my physical heart. It was as though the entire world as I knew it instantly shifted into a new state of uncertainty. Everything felt utterly out of my control.

For most of my life, I felt like I had been the one planning and leading and fixing and managing and controlling and cleaning up so many of the day-to-day happenings for myself and those around me. But this. This shook me to my core. I couldn't fix this. I couldn't fix him. I couldn't even go to his appointments in the beginning with him.

I felt completely helpless. But not hopeless.

I had to really lean into the new territory of allowing others to help me. Help us. My bee sisters swarmed in helping our family in all the ways. So grateful to my sister Leslie for organizing a meal train that fed us for weeks, so that I could focus on my own healing. With every bite, sip, slurp of their healing soups, stews, breads and broths, I could feel the love of my sisters deep in the belly of my soul, teaching me how to trust and receive.

Their love letters and words of encouragement, and the endless nights of prayers and healing energy work they have collectively sent has been what has lifted and carried me through the darkest of days. I am forever grateful.

Over and over again, my bee sisters have asked, "How are you managing all this?"

And, "How are you going to finish this book project?"

My answer has always been, "The book is non-negotiable. I will finish this. We will finish this."

And now we've arrived. We did it! This book is a creation bound in love and utter faith in the healing power of our sacred words, stories, dreams, and Mary and the bees.

Thank you for stepping into the depths with us. We acknowledge and honor your courage.

GRIEF TEA RECIPE

Channeled from the Bees

~ Leah Benjamin

You will need a cup of your favorite steeped tea and one ice cube.

Prepare your cup of hot tea and choose a cozy space to nestle.
It's okay if you're standing up or sitting
in a usual space or a new space;
any space will do.

Bring an ice cube to your cup of tea
and gently slide it into the hot liquid.

Notice there is change.

Maybe there is steam.

Perhaps the ice cube crackles.

The ice is melting, and the hot water is cooling.

There is a space where the ice and hot water meet.

There is a dance there.

The ice is welcomed to merge with the larger pool of liquid.

The hot tea is adjusting and changing with the transforming ice.

When you are ready, begin to sip this medicine into your body
to begin its next ventures and forms.

Blessed Bee.

CHAPTER 1

THE LOST YEARS

Reclaiming the Lost Voices of the Grandmothers

Dasha Allred Bond

*"There is something at work in my soul,
which I do not understand."*

~ Mary Wollstonecraft Shelley

MY STORY

How could you, as a mother, abandon your own babies? My mother was only three! You left them at a movie theater, for God's sake!

But the words caught in the vice of my throat. I swallowed hard—the family secret. Down, down, down the toxic bitterness, pushed down into the darkness of my belly.

Looking into the pale-gray eyes of my dying grandmother, I thought, *If I let this moment pass without asking. . .*

Her eyes seem to say, *Yes. Ask.* But I couldn't.

With a heavy sigh, I cracked open a window. *Just let it go. Allow the truth to die with her.*

"What's your favorite memory?"

"I don't much wanna talk about the past no more." Playfully, she flipped her palms up. "I want to know about my future. Tell me what you see."

Is she kidding? Ninety-two years old and dying. What does she think I'm going to see?

Her forehead furrowed. *She's afraid she won't see them again.*

Her only sister died only a month prior. A few minutes after Aunt Ginny was pronounced dead, she sat up in bed and asked for one more cup of coffee. "Two parts sweet milk and a tablespoon of sugar, please."

Aunt Ginny sipped in the final drop, then peacefully died again. My grandmother joked with the hospice nurse, "I guess they don't have Community brand coffee up in Heaven."

Granny's sweetheart, Morris, died six months before my aunt. Those three "white-haired kids," as we called them, were best friends and lived together for over twenty years. We knew the mourning would kill my grandmother.

"Granny? Aunt Charlotte said she's heard you talk to Aunt Ginny and Morris at night."

She turned away, embarrassed.

"You know I see them too. I don't think you're crazy."

Growing up, I believed my grandmother when she said, "We are the same kind of wild, you and me." It was like we belonged to a mystery school where we spoke the languages of plants, animals, and things unseen—the language of the haunted and lost—the dying, the dead.

My imagination and love of nature can be traced back to many summers spent with my grandmother. She taught me the beauty of wild places: skinny dipping in blue holes, eating blackberries straight off the bush, wild plums off the tree, honey from the honeycomb, and how to calm my heart and my breath so I could talk to the bees.

When I returned from college on weekends, we sat and talked for hours on her front porch, giggling between puffs of clove cigarettes and sips of muscadine wine.

Despite all those light-filled moments, the same question haunted me. *How could this woman have abandoned her children?*

I often wondered if she gave me the care and attention to make up for the time lost and stolen from my mother and her siblings.

I ran my fingertips across the thin skin of her palms. "I see them. They aren't going to leave you. It won't be long now."

"Good. I'm ready to go."

She pointed to a painting of a magnolia bloom floating on water.

"I want you to take that—the magnolia. Your daddy made the frame from one of the fallen pines in our forest. The magnolia was painted by an old friend of mine."

"Did you know the magnolia tree is believed to be one of the oldest trees on the planet? Its species is even older than the bees. Ancient beetles pollinated it."

"Do you remember our special magnolia tree?"

Before I could answer, her breathing changed to soft snorgles.

I watched her sleep and thought of our multifaceted past.

Growing up impoverished, she loved to preach the gospel of gratitude. My great-grandparents were sharecroppers who raised seven kids in a tiny shotgun house, where the gravy was always thinned out and the butter saved for special occasions. Granny would remind us, "We didn't have a pot to piss in."

On one occasion, she scolded me for only wanting to wear Wonder Woman Underroos. "You're spoilt. Child, all my drawers were made from flour sacks. On my wedding night, your pawpaw went to raise up my dress for a peek, only to find my big ass read "Self-Rising!"

She lived in what the Deep South calls "the sticks." In the stillness of night, I often woke to a woman's screams from outside. Granny's whispers found me in the darkness. "That's just old mama panther telling her babies to come down from our roof. Don't be scared. They're our kind of wild." I found safety nestling deep in the warm curve of Granny's back.

My mother tells the story of traveling home alone with my grandmother. Their vehicle choked and died along a three-mile stretch of gravel road. They walked through the black-as-pitch night with only a sliver of moonlight guiding their steps. The sound of a low growl trailed only a few feet into the tree line. And then the screams came. *Panther warning.*

"Just keep walking. Steady steps," my grandmother urged.

The panther followed them the entire way. *Predator or protector?*

"That's the way of our kind of wild. You're safe until you're not. Life can turn on a dime," Granny warned.

Sometimes, her stories grew distant and sad. Putting her hands in mine, she pointed to the little scars, indentions, and misshapen corners of her nails. Her eyes welled up, "Just look at these ugly hands."

I stared down into the cup of her hands as her words spilled out like loose-leaf tea. My tiny fingers worked to hold tight to every syllable. The harder I tried to hold onto her memories and secrets, the harder the force of gravity yanked back. Tiny droplets of her life spilled out everywhere.

The still cupped parts of her stories swirled and rippled into images and words I read like brail. I saw the swollen, bloodied, splintered-raw fingers of her youth. The hard labor worn across her brow. Entire seasons were spent picking cotton under the heavy heat of the Mississippi drought.

I saw the cruel faces of men possessed with insatiable hunger. Raised fists. Tobacco-stained, drooling lips bristled against toothless gums. A tiny baby, too small for this world—oxygen-starved and blue. Then, her hands closed up. Her mind would shift to somewhere I couldn't penetrate.

"Never mind, me," she said, "I've laid those demons to rest."

Sixty years ago, she disappeared from my mother's and her siblings' hopes and dreams. For three years, no calls, no letters, no stories, not a single word.

My Aunt Charlotte, the oldest female, only a child herself, stepped into the role of mother. Without my aunt's strength, love, and utter selflessness, my mother would've been a lost little soul.

Then, one day, my grandfather pulled into the driveway, opened the passenger's side door, and out stepped Granny, behaving like nothing ever happened.

She could be as gentle as mist but as fierce and protective as a mother goose. She loved hard and grieved even harder. She suffered many losses: two husbands and Morris, all three of her sons, a grandson, her parents, and all her siblings. In the end, I suppose she felt abandoned.

I heard her make little comments under her breath, "I'm being punished. Watching all my loved ones suffer and die."

Where did you go?

On October 6th, 2022, her cremated remains were entombed in the Earth along with her secrets. I placed a bouquet of wildflowers atop her grave. Her favorites were plucked from the land she had lived on for almost a century—goldenrod, cabbage rose, pink azalea, and gardenia. I wrapped them with a twig of muscadine vine and tucked in a single magnolia leaf—a portal door. Honey bees buzzed around the colorful blooms, and I found myself talking to them.

Can I share her story? It feels like it's somehow mine to heal.

I was scheduled to lead our Dreaming with Bees circle a few weeks later. The theme was "Working with the Stories of our Ancestors." The night before this circle, I prayed. *Mother Mary and the bees, please help me connect with my Grandmother in the Dreamtime.*

In the dream, I sat with my grandmother below our special magnolia tree. She told me stories about how the Choctaw had lived on that patch of land and the magnolia held sacred medicine.

We found hundreds of arrowheads surrounding the tree over the years, so I had no reason not to believe her stories. "If you have something heavy on your heart, something you feel like you can't even tell the preacher man, not even me, you can tell the tree. Her mighty branches reach into Heaven where Jesus and his mama can take it all away."

Granny placed my hands on the bark of the tree. "My story has always been your story, too. It's right here, written out in this book. The medicine hides in the questions that haunt us."

Light began to emanate from the cracks of the bark, and I found myself spinning through time and space. I watched Granny's life flash before me- heartbreaking, grueling, bittersweet, and also so beautiful.

I felt everything: her pain, her pleading to be set free: *Free from who? What? Where?*

I saw the lifeless baby again. I saw the edge of a blade held taunt against the skin of her wrist. The smell of whiskey-fueled anger. Shards of broken glass, broken promises, over and over again. I saw babies running to hide beneath the cover of darkness. Darkness felt safe. Until it didn't. I saw the raping of body. The raping of mind. The raping of soul. Her own family. Defiling her body. Violent thrusting. Lifeless gray eyes. Ocean's deep gray eyes. Drowning. Choking on cock and cum. Choking on tubing forced down, down, down into the darkness of her belly. Force fed. Restrained. Padded walls. The smell of cold, sterile, colorless concrete floors. The shock of ice baths. No one could hear her screams for help. "We are the same kind of wild," she muttered as her fingers picked at unraveled seams, nails clawed, trying to find the way out! "Look at these ugly hands!" Her cries echoed out from the edges of the dream. Her questions gnawed holes into my awareness. "Where are the blue skies? Where are the green grasses and tall pines where panthers can seek sanctuary with their babies? Where are my babies?"

The next day, I could still feel my grandmother's energy. Her perfume lingered in my hair.

I shared the dream with my bee sisters and asked a new question. "Do you think it's possible my grandmother was institutionalized during the lost years?"

And while no one will ever know if this was my grandmother's truth, that question became like a balm. One by one, the elders in our circle of women broke their silence and began sharing this had happened to them. One sister shared that she called the police to beg for sanctuary away from her abusive husband, but when the police arrived, he accused her of being mentally ill, stating her broken bones and bruises were from self-harm. She was institutionalized against her will, unable to even contact her family for help. I was shocked to learn this was a common occurrence many of our mothers and grandmothers suffered. Sane women committed to institutions to control and silence them.

It felt like an entire puzzle corner locked into place, but the full image of what rested at the center of my grief was still missing. I sat with plant medicines before and knew how effectively they could tear down the walls and constructs of ego. I was comfortable in this space, as it's the Dreamtime itself. I was committed to breaking cycles of ancestral trauma for the sake of my children, so I made plans to sit in ceremony.

I sat chewing the fibrous matter mixed in honey, finally swallowing the beautiful plant medicine. Down, down, down my throat into the darkness of my belly. Down, down, down into the rabbit hole. I came out on the other side to find my grandmother waiting for me. All the grandmothers were waiting. I felt their love and protection. We were back on the land of my childhood, back under the magnolia. Panther stalked protectively around the perimeter of the grandmothers who gathered.

Granny led me to the creek's edge. When I leaned down to peer into the waters, I was surprised to see reflecting back, not my face, but my daughter's beautiful face. I began reliving her childhood trauma through her eyes. I saw and felt her broken heart as she experienced the problematic divorce of her parents. I felt the abandonment she experienced when her father disappeared entirely from her life and her baby brother's life. I saw through her eyes the loss of our home, our family dog, Luci, and her school friends. I saw her fear of living in the small shack, where millions of field mice lined the inside of the thin walls that surrounded us.

I saw her stepping up at such a young age, as best she could, trying to help me mother her little brother while I worked three jobs to try and keep the lights, heat, water, and food on and in their little bellies.

I was so busy trying to survive that I completely overlooked the broken hearts of my children and dismissed any signs they might've been suffering emotionally in silence. Like the generations before me, I moved on like nothing happened. *Everything's okay. We're fine. This is just a temporary setback. I just need to stay strong. Keep pushing through. Keep getting promoted at work. I will get it all back.*

Looking at it through my child's eyes, I realized I also abandoned my own children emotionally. The haunted words of my grandmother echoed across the expanse—*my story is your story.*

The plant medicine continued to push through my bloodstream, push through more doorways of my mind. My daughter's face shifted into my own in the depths of the water. The slideshow of my past set to play. I sat across from my ex-husband, begging him to sign the divorce papers. After our separation, his sex and drug addictions amplified. His mental state was explosive, and at times, I feared for our lives. I was willing to do anything to protect my children. Anything. I even told him I wouldn't ask for any child support or alimony in the divorce.

In the end, he agreed to sign, but under certain conditions, one of which he insisted be added to the paperwork. It said I agreed to pay him a percentage of profits if I finished and published any writing projects I started while married. We were married for 11 years, so this was a lot of written material. One of those projects was a novel based on my childhood spent with my grandmother on the land of our ancestors.

That was 14 years ago, and to this day, I haven't been able to work on the novel. Those stories were soul parts of my childhood I didn't want him to have any access to, so I shelved them, not realizing I was abandoning the pathway my wounded inner child was using to express her voice. I saw this core trauma playing out from one generation to the next.

The grief of it all finally rose up through my body. I thought I'd vomit, but what issued out instead was the guttural screams of what felt like thousands of grieving grandmothers.

An amazing synchronicity occurred within minutes of this experience and the realization that I needed to reclaim my own voice and lost stories. I checked my phone, and a writing professor who pushed me to write the novel left me a text message wishing to reconnect. I hadn't spoken to her in many years, and there she was, showing up as soon as my awareness decided to take back my power.

THE MEDICINE

"The medicine hides in the questions that haunt us." In a seminar I attended, psychoanalyst Dr. James Hollis explained that we're all haunted. Haunted not only by the memories of our deceased loved ones but also by our own traumas, hidden secrets, regrets, and what he called "our unlived stories." He went on to add, "Sometimes we repress stories, and their presence may only be surmised when they leak into our dreams, our bodies, our children, our anesthetizing addictions."

Here's a quick exercise to help connect to the things that may haunt you:

Take time to go into the wilds of nature. Take off your shoes and ground into the Earth. Maybe press your back against a tree. Close your eyes and call in the energy of the bees and Mother Mary. Start with just these two questions and see what stirs your awareness.

What stories of the Grandmothers do you feel in your bones?

Where in your body is your most profound grief hiding?

When questions and memories begin to replay, it's essential to pay attention. Much like the nightmares of dreams, the nagging feelings that pull at our emotions can be our minds broadcasting an SOS to draw attention to cycles that no longer serve our highest good.

Our loved ones who have transitioned beyond the veil show up daily, dropping hints and coded messages—breadcrumbs guiding us back to living a more mindful and loving existence.

Return to the places in the wild that call to you, trusting that a bridge exists between worlds. Visit http://www.dreamingwithbees.com to access a free series of guided meditations to help you explore the healing magic of love and forgiveness more deeply.

Password: Beeyond the Veil

Dasha Allred Bond is a bestselling author, certified Dream Coach, and Shamanic Healer who has studied with Laura Hileman, Freedom Folk & Soul, Gaia Sisterhood, Robert Moss, Sandra Ingerman, Dana Micucci, Ariella Daly, and the late Will Sharon. With her beloved husband, Kenny, and two children, Lilli and Avery, she has pilgrimaged across Southern France and England as well as sacred parts of Mexico and North America, attuning to the energetic ley lines of our lands and the stories carried by the rocks, the rivers, the trees, and the bees. She feels a deep connection to the language of nature and the divine feminine and masculine aspects of herself revealed to her through the dream archetypes found in classic myths and personal stories.

In 2021, she began dreaming with the bees and Our Lady of Guadalupe. Answering their calls, she visited Our Lady's Shrine in Mexico City and the Pyramids of Teotihuacan. This journey catalyzed the rebirth of her true story and more profound work into the mysteries of consciousness, the multi-verse, and the many ways trauma shows up in our minds, bodies, and energy fields.

Dasha is a certified End of Life Doula. Much of her focus is on helping dreamers move through their seasons of grief. In early 2023, Dasha created the nonprofit Aluna Bridge - Hospice Sanctuary for our community members experiencing homelessness. Also, in 2023, Dasha was among 25 bestselling authors who released two books, Shaman Heart: Sacred Rebel and The Life-Changing Power of Self-Love. Her current works include a memoir, Wild Life Whispers: Book of Remembering, and a novel, A Nun's Tale. You can find more details about her Dreaming with Bees circles, healing sessions, written works, and other intuitive offerings at the links below.

http://www.dreamingwithbees.com

http://www.penelopeponders.com

http://www.alunabridge.org

http://www.instagram.com/penelopeponders

CHAPTER 2

COMING HOME TO MYSELF

An Adoptee's Journey from Abandonment to Belonging

Jennifer Harvard, LMT

*"The circles of women around us weave invisible nets of love
that carry us when we're weak
and sing with us when we are strong."*

~ SARK Succulent Wild Woman

MY STORY

"My life would have been so different if it hadn't been for the big mistake. I can't go to my high school reunion and face those people after being embarrassed by my big mistake."

"Mistake." She said it. My biological mother, the one who couldn't remember the month I was born, spoke those words to me a few years ago. Of course, it was something I considered since I was old enough to consider anything. Growing up, the words *adopted* and *abandoned* seemed to go hand in hand, and *why would someone be abandoned unless they were a mistake?*

For as long as I could remember, I wanted to meet my biological family. *Who were my parents? Where did I come from?*

For much of my youth, I felt like I didn't fit in anywhere. I was always on the outside looking in. I wanted close connections, but it was as if an invisible wall separated me from the rest of the world. No one else could see it but me or so I thought. Even at home with my adopted family, I felt I didn't belong. I didn't look like them or act like them and let's face it, they weren't equipped to handle the anger and sadness that came with raising an adopted child. Old-school corporal punishment should've whipped me into shape. Honestly, I suspected they were pissed at getting a defective child with anger issues and took it out on me regularly.

One night in 1993, I woke up from a dream. In this dream, I was a tiny baby just hours old. I felt the nurse pick me up and walk down a long corridor into a dimly lit hospital room. As I passed from the nurse's arms, I felt the warm embrace and held the gaze of two beautiful blue eyes staring back at me.

I was safe. I was home. This feeling was fleeting because I was quickly pulled from these arms. I cried out, tears streaming down my small cheeks, shivering to the bone, blinded by the fluorescent lighting and stark white walls as I was put back into my tiny crib in the nursery. I cried out for a mother who would never hold me again. This is when the darkness began to creep in.

As I grew older, I began to fight back. "You're not my real mom!" I would say, slamming the door behind me. On the other side of the door, inside the safe space of my room, the tears came. I thought I hated my parents, mostly my mom. She was so hard on me. Every day I would get yelled at and punished for things like not turning off a light or not wringing out my washcloth. I thought she didn't love me, so why should I love her? I felt this deeply and longed for the kind of love that accepted me as I was. I was broken, and I belonged nowhere. I ran away from home several times, drove fast, drank a lot, and didn't listen to authority figures. My path of self-destruction had begun. The hole in my heart continued to grow, and I did everything in my power to fill it.

During the summer of 1985, I left my high school job at a local daycare to visit my new boyfriend. Climbing into my car that afternoon, I rolled down my window and cranked up the tunes. Night Ranger was on the Radio. Singing along with the music, wind in my hair, I pulled out onto the two-lane highway. SLAM! There was a loud crash followed by darkness. The next thing I remembered was a voice saying, "How many fingers am I holding up? What's your name?" Darkness came again, followed by excruciating pain. I spent three months healing from all the injuries. This wasn't the first time I had wrecked my car. I totaled three but this time I almost killed myself. I'm not sure I cared if I lived or died.

I married the boyfriend I met the year of the accident. He was older than me and very mature, at least to a seventeen-year-old. I wanted to be out of my parent's house so badly and to be loved and cared for. Husband number one had his own trauma. He was difficult, but I may have been even more difficult. The hole in my heart couldn't be filled. He tried. Maybe they all tried in their own way. Even though the marriage was a train wreck, we had a beautiful daughter. The year I was pregnant with Chelsea was one of the happiest of my life. I finally had someone else to love who'd never leave me, but the bliss didn't last, and my self-destructive behavior continued.

Towards the end of my first marriage, I was sinking deeper and deeper into alcoholism. From the first time I drank, it was clear that I wasn't a normal drinker. I was 14 years old and had a sleepover.

"Let's raid my parents' liquor cabinet! Drink up!"

MTV is blaring in the background. I'm dancing with the TV antenna as a microphone. *I feel dizzy.* Everything goes black. It's morning now. *My head is killing me, and why in the hell am I on the den floor?*

"Touch your hair," my mother says as she stares down at me from her chair. It's caked in vomit. *Oh God, what's that smell? I'm going to puke.* My friends are enjoying a nice breakfast in the other room. *Bacon. Yuck.*

By the end of this marriage, I couldn't control my drinking. *Where's my car? Did I drive myself home? My head is spinning, and I can't remember what happened at the bar last night.* One particularly bad binge landed me in a treatment facility. Here, I began to be curious about who I was, what I wanted out of life, and what my spiritual leanings were. I prayed when I was hungover or when I did something that I felt guilty about, but who was I praying to? Support was highly suggested, so after I left treatment, I began attending 12-Step recovery meetings. In those rooms where so many people felt hope, I felt squashed. I just allowed myself to be released from the self-inflicted bondage of my parents' religion, Christianity. At every meeting, I heard, "We are a spiritual, not a religious program," yet, they closed with The Lord's Prayer. "Our Father who art in heaven. . ." You can't get more Christian than that! After years of addiction, abuse, and mental health struggles, I knew the devil that threatened to send me to Hell wasn't real. I was familiar with Hell because I'd been there. Hell isn't a place. It's a state of mind.

I left husband number one after I got out of treatment. We weren't growing at the same pace. I started going to Yoga classes and joined a Buddhist community. I worked in a health food store, so I became interested in alternative health practices and new spiritual paths. I was happy for a time, but as always, it didn't last. I fell in love with someone young and immature who couldn't support me in the way I needed support. After we split, I relapsed. Enter husband number two. I finally met my match. He was a worse alcoholic than I was, and our life together was extremely dysfunctional. My daughter Mia came out of this marriage, and she was such a light in my life. I got sober again, this time for many years, but I felt trapped within the confines of another failed marriage with two daughters to take care of.

Miraculously, amid all the chaos, I finished massage school. Helping others brought me so much joy. I suppose that somewhere deep within me, there was always a tiny spark. I wanted to give up many times, but I didn't. There was a divine plan for me. I just couldn't see it. Years of alcohol abuse blocked my path to Spirit, but I got glimpses during the times I was sober.

In June of 2005, I said yes to a date with a man I met when I was 20. I knew from the first time I saw David I'd never be the same. David was an addict, too. Like the others, we had that in common. We drank together, and then we got sober together—sort of. We married in 2006, and my last child was born. We named our sweet boy Kai.

I got sober in 2011. This time, there was no joy and no freedom. I filled the gaping hole inside me with alcohol, drugs, men, food, you name it, and it only grew in size. I couldn't run from myself any longer. I was sober, and I was in Hell. I remember my first panic attack. I couldn't sleep. David, who wasn't sober yet, didn't come home one night. The next night came, and I didn't sleep again, and then a third night. *I'm going crazy.* Heat rises over my face, my hands get clammy, and I begin to shake uncontrollably. *I feel dizzy and thirsty. I can't think.* My heart races, and I feel like I'm going to pass out. *Will it ever end?* This out-of-control feeling became the norm. I started seeing a psychiatrist and was diagnosed with panic and anxiety disorder. All sense of normalcy dissolved from my life. I was stuck in a place where there was nowhere to hide. The gaping hole within me became the Grand Canyon, and I couldn't climb out. Day after day, I tried to release myself from the bondage of mental illness. I took to hiking three miles a day. I lost 30 lbs. I felt as if I was disappearing. Actually, I *was* disappearing.

Amid the chaos and trauma that came with living with an alcoholic, my father was diagnosed with bladder cancer. He was always proud of me, and I thought that if he died, there'd be no one left to truly love and support me.

During this period, I relied on the support of a women's circle. The women became my sisters, and although I still suffered, I had a soft place to land. They supported me and held me up when I barely had a leg to stand on.

Those painful days of anxiety and panic turned into months. Somewhere deep within, I found strength. I was held up by others until I could eventually walk again. I began using the tools I was taught through Buddhist practices and nature-based spirituality. I was miserable. Suffering is a great catalyst for change, and boy, was I suffering!

In my women's group, we created vows to usher in the beginning of spring. I was in the midst of the most miserable year of my life, and my vow was simply, "Let go." I wanted to let go of my desire to control situations that I couldn't, such as my alcoholic husband and my dying father. I even wanted to let go of the idea that I had to get rid of anxiety to live my life.

One day in May, while taking a hike, I wrote down my vow and placed it in my favorite tree. I had been visiting this tree since I got out of alcohol treatment in 1992. She knew me. I told her my secrets. I hugged her and left her presents from time to time. I walked around to the back of the tree, stuck the paper deep within a crevice, and continued on the path.

In July, my husband and I decided to go for a hike at the same location. I was ruminating about my father's cancer, and as I exited the car, my husband said, "You need to let it go." We arrived at the entrance of the trail, about two miles from my tree, and walked up the wooden steps that led to the path. David was a few feet ahead of me when something under my shoe caught my eye. I bent down to pick up a piece of paper that was neatly folded in half. I opened it up to read the words "Let go" in my handwriting. My husband said, "If that isn't a message from the Divine, then I don't know what is."

I met my biological mother about a decade after the dream I had when I was a newborn in the hospital. It turns out the dream was actually a memory. She *did* hold me for a few minutes. Since meeting her, she has disappeared from my life again and again. This used to hurt, but today, I know it's her issue, not mine. I am not damaged. Recently, she sent me a friend request, and I didn't accept. "Let go." Thank you Divine Mother for teaching me how to do it with love.

After that day, I slowly got better. I continued my hikes, finding messages from nature everywhere. Each day, I found at least one heart stone. My collection is massive now. The women's circle I was in dissolved, but I felt inspired. My husband got sober that year, and my anxiety *finally* let up. I felt more grounded and held by Spirit than I ever had. I knew that women's circles were important so I came up with a plan. I used my own experience as a bodyworker and spiritual seeker to create a retreat for women based on the idea that every woman has divine gifts to share with the world. I began to find women in my community who were drummers, herbalists, artists, and yoginis, and asked them to teach at my Retreat. In September of 2016, the first Wise Women Retreat was born. I believe I made $400 on that retreat, but it was worth it. I studied breathwork, Ayurveda, Shamanic journeying, and more, and began hosting new moon circles once a month to keep the circle of women going strong. Since 2013, I have stayed true to my path, using my background in the body, mind, spirit connection, as well as my lessons from grief and despair. Every moment of suffering had a purpose. In 2017, I changed the name of my business to Gaia Sisterhood to reflect the work I do in the World. This Sisterhood allows women to experience a safe, sacred space to connect with other like-minded women. Today, we gather to honor and celebrate each turn in the Celtic Wheel of the Year as well as the cycles of the moon. It's through this that I honor The Great Mother as well as my Celtic heritage. This is my life's work, and I'd never have found it without moving through the grief of being abandoned. For that, I'm grateful.

> *"A circle of women may just be the most powerful force known to humanity. If you have one, embrace it. If you need one, seek it. If you find one, for the love of all that is good and holy, dive in. Hold on. Love it up. Get naked. Let them see you. Let them hold you. Let your reluctant tears fall. Let yourself rise fierce and love gentle. You will be changed. The very fabric of your being will be altered by this, if you allow it.*
> *Please, please allow it."*
>
> ~ Jeanette LeBlanc

THE MEDICINE

Much of what I do in Circle is to create rituals and ceremonies for healing. Here is a short Self-Love Ritual.

You'll need essential oils such as rose and lavender. Dried Rose Petals are nice as well.

You'll also need a candle and some soft music. Carve out at least an hour where you can be completely alone.

Draw a warm bath and bring your candle and music into the bathroom. Add 10 drops of lavender oil and 7 drops of Rose oil. Sprinkle roses into the water. As it runs, face the bathroom mirror. Slowly and mindfully disrobe and take in what you see. Your beautiful body has possibly birthed children, worked hard, been through illness or abuse, and yet here you are, perfect in your unique way. Gaze into your own eyes and say, "I love you unconditionally." Take a drop of rose oil and anoint your head continuing the words, " I love you unconditionally." Anoint your face, by placing both palms over your eyes, and continue moving down to your shoulders, your breasts, your belly, your hips, your legs, all the way down to your feet stopping at each body part to say, "I love you unconditionally." Once you are done anointing yourself, turn on the music and soak in the bath taking the powerful human you are. Dry off, make a cup of hot tea, and spend some time journaling about your experience. It can be hard the first time you do this, but it gets easier.

To join my local community, or to attend retreats in Tennessee and internationally subscribe to: https://Gaiasisterhood.org

Jennifer Harvard is a women's circle facilitator, licensed massage therapist, Reiki practitioner, breathwork coach, and aromatherapist. Her background in bodywork and spirituality spans almost 30 years. She has received thousands of hours worth of training in massage, Ayurveda, Reiki, breathwork, aromatherapy, cacao ceremony, shamanic healing, and more. Since 2013, Jennifer has led countless women's retreats both locally in the state of Tennessee and internationally. She is the founder of The Wise Women Full Moon Retreat as well as The Goddess Craft Market, which honors women in the healing and visual arts.

Her business, Gaia Sisterhood, honors and celebrates every woman by celebrating each turn in the Celtic Wheel of the Year.

Connect with Jennifer:

Instagram: https://www.instagram.com/Gaia.sisterhood
https://www.instagram.com/Goddess_craftmarket
Facebook: https://www.facebook.com/Gaia_Sisterhood

Chapter 3

WATER IN THE DESERT

Grounding Meditation for the Loss of a Loved One

Angelica Dunsavage

"A flower blooming in the desert proves to the world that adversity, no matter how great, can be overcome."

~ Matshona Dhiwayo

MY STORY

A phone call. It's funny how we rely on these little rituals throughout the day, like stepping stones guiding us along the path of our lives. We take them for granted, thinking they will always be there. Worse yet, we are sometimes annoyed when they come, seeing them as a disruption to our constant activity. I felt similarly, until one morning, when the phone call never came. I tried calling over and over, hearing ring after ring.

Why on earth would she be sleeping this late? Why is no one answering their phones? Are they all at an appointment I forgot they had?

Then, I got a call from the one person I didn't expect…

Dad? Shouldn't he be at work by now? Oh no, what happened?

"Hey Dad, what's going on? No one has been answering their phones."

"Pal, Mom's gone," he said.

"What do you mean, gone? I just texted her last night! I called her before my interview…"

"We tried to bring her back…we worked on her for an hour…she's gone. We're still trying to figure everything out, but I'll call you later, ok?," he said. *Nothing is ok! What? How do I?*

I sunk to the floor of my apartment, in the little corner between my kitchen and my bedroom. Though I can see light from the Arizona morning sun streaking through the window, it feels like the color leached from the world. It's the reverse Wizard of Oz. *There's no place like home.*

The loss of you hit me like a tidal wave, unmooring me from the "before" and sweeping me into an "after" that I never thought possible. I am knocked off my feet, drowning in a sea of words left unsaid, places left unvisited. *I went to sleep having a mom. I woke up without one. Gone. Mom's gone.* Time has no meaning in this ocean, an endless assault of waves leaving me helpless and exhausted—it's the worst possible loneliness. I let the waters of grief sweep over me and swim down into its depths. "There are moments when you're in so deep, it feels easier to just swim down"… *I know what that feels like now, Lin Manuel. You're right. It's quiet uptown. Empty. Silent.* Thought after thought crashes into my brain.

Why didn't she listen to me? I told her she should take better care of herself. She promised.

Why didn't she call for help? Did she have her phone on her?

I'm 27. She had me when she was 27. At 27, she became a mom. At 27, I lost mine.

Why?

I don't know how much time passes, but a thought enters my head:

I'm alone, like she was. There's no one coming to get me off this floor. I'm not her. Everyone said I was always the strong one. I need to get things done.

I take the first step into this unknown *after*. I get up off the floor and do what I've always done—get to work. I write a to-do list, send emails, book flights, and make phone calls. I arrange my life into its respective cubicles as if my mother's death can be organized by the Marie Kondo method. I had no idea in that moment what the cost of putting an ocean of grief into a bottle like a model ship would be. The same thought kept circling: *no one is coming to get me. I have to get myself up.*

In the following days and weeks, my role in my family shifted from 'taken care of' to caretaker. As the only child of an only child, when the middleman—or woman in this case—is gone, suddenly everything falls to you. The funeral passes, and I'm forced to be the strong one as everyone else crumbles around me. I get asked by family and friends if I'm moving back home.

"Well, what's so important out there?" *Uhh, my life? Everything I've been working for?* "Well, who's going to help your grandparents?" *I don't know. I'm 27. I barely take care of myself. I never thought of this.* All this pressure and guilt is topped with a healthy dose of "well, I know this is difficult, but it's all a part of God's plan." *Oh really? Well, I'd like to talk about this plan because it sucks, bro.* Slowly, I feel the bottled ocean in my chest start to darken, the waters turning black and cold with swirling thoughts of resentment.

You left me all of this. This wasn't supposed to be my job, and you put this on me.

"Have you ever been to Sedona?" my friend asks. We're sitting at brunch, and I'm making a valiant effort to get through my omelet and mimosa without actively breaking down. It's been about two months, and I'm still not able to get through a day without crying or screaming.

"No," I say. "Why?"

"Well," he says, "I think you need a break." *You don't say.* "It's really pretty up there, and they say the energy has been known to be healing." *Of all the hippie nonsense.* "They also have good food and lots of wineries, so worst case scenario, you get away for the weekend, have some wine, and go shopping." *You had me at wineries.*

"Sounds like an okay idea," I say. "Why not?" *Beats staying in my apartment by myself and staring at that spot on the floor.*

I go home, book an Airbnb, and start doing some research. *Energy vortex. . .what the hell is an energy vortex? Raising vibrations and spiritual enlightenment. . .I'd like some enlightenment as to why whoever's up there took my mom away. Riddle me that, vortex! Sounds like Sedona hasn't moved on from Woodstock. Oh, look, a cool shopping center with a wine store! I can't pronounce that name to save my life, but it looks nice. Well, I have something on my list to do, and maybe I can get some ideas once I get there.*

If you've never driven to Sedona, the view sneaks up on you. My phone navigation told me I was getting closer and closer, and looking at the surroundings, it all looked the same. But then you crest one ridge, and another world opens before you. The red rock formations stand out in stark contrast to a landscape of clay and olive green paired with a dazzling blue sky. *I don't know about magical, but there is something about this place. This is the most beautiful thing I've ever seen. Who knows what this weekend will bring, but you can't fault them for the view.*

I spend my first day following the plan: shopping, eating, and drinking wine. As I go from place to place, I begin to notice something: *why does everybody seem so chill here? Like, obviously, the people on vacation seem chill, but even the locals seem oddly happy. I have never been surrounded by this many truly content people.* Slowly, subtly, their energy starts to affect mine. The tightly held knots in my shoulders begin to loosen, and this blunt east-coaster finds herself conversing with random strangers! For the first time in months, I feel myself beginning to breathe again. Across from the shopping center is a large turquoise building with a giant mural. *Now that's a hippie store if ever I saw one.* And I find myself crossing the street as if my feet are being pulled toward this shop by an energy outside of my own. The incense-scented shop is a labyrinth of jewelry, books, crystals, and items I have never seen before. It's exactly as I expected it to be—yet strangely comforting in its chaos. I see a kind-looking older woman who appears to be working there.

"Excuse me," I say, "I'm visiting the area, and I've heard a lot about these energy vortexes. Is there a guidebook or something you might have that shows where the spots are?"

Her smile creates slight wrinkles around her mouth and eyes. She says, "The vortex energy is all around us. There are over 100 different ones, but yes, we have a book on the most popular ones and their properties. Come with me."

She guides me through the maze of shelves and pulls out a skinny book. While handing it to me, she says, "Here you go…is there anything else I can help you with?" Her eyes stare into my soul, and I can feel she knows what I'm about to ask even before I do. My eyes start to tear up, and I say, "I don't know about any of this stuff…but I just lost my mom, and it's been really hard…is there anything you recommend for grief?"

My voice starts to crack by the end, and I'm pulled into a hug by this woman I met five minutes ago, yet she seems to know exactly what my soul needs. "I'm so sorry, sweetheart. I lost someone important to me, too, and it can really tear you up. Let's see what we can do," she says. I follow her blindly, sniffling my tears as she takes me to the crystal section.

"Carnelian for grounding, rose quartz for love. Carry these on you until you begin to make peace with it." I nod, and while a week ago I would've never set foot in this store, let alone listen to someone tell me some rocks will help with grief, I believe her. She took out a gray/black stone bracelet and slipped it on my wrist. "Lastly, smoky quartz for absorbing darkness. There's a darkness in your energy—it's understandable, given what you've been through, but you can't let it win. You're meant for light." *She sees my ocean—somebody sees me.*

There is a land of sky and sun. Of deep rocks and canyons. Of light that goes on forever. I arrived there when my soul needed healing, not truly knowing what I was searching for —comfort? a fresh start? a way out of the grief I had trapped inside me. I didn't believe in the Spirit of place at that time or the power of nature to heal wounds. All I know is when I climbed that path on Airport Mesa vista and sat on the rocks looking at a limitless horizon, I knew a part of me would be okay, and another part would never be the same. As I make my way home, I turn on the radio, and Brown Eyed Girl, my mom's song, starts playing. Without thinking, I knew that it was her, telling me she was still there and she was in a good place.

"Hi, Mom. I miss you too."

Three years later, another phone call. A doctor's appointment.

"So what's been going on?" she asks.

"Something's not right. I have no energy. Just going to the grocery store makes me need a 2-hour nap. I never used to be like this – I could run back-to-back rehearsals and then go to kickboxing. Just the thought of that now is exhausting. I'm in constant pain. My hair's coming out. I'm gaining weight no matter what or how much I eat. I'm just so tired. I've seen other doctors, and they don't believe me. They say I don't present all the classic symptoms, and it's just stress or Covid weight. That I just need to work harder. If you knew me, you'd know how hard I work. I used to think that everything could be accomplished by just working harder—this can't. I know what this is because I grew up with it. My mom…"

I don't mention the moodiness, how it feels like I could cry or scream on a dime, or how I lay on the couch and mindlessly scroll on my phone for things I don't need, craving that little dopamine hit to get me through another day. It's like looking into a mirror and seeing the person you tried so hard not to be. I'm doing the same things I used to judge her for doing. Sorry for being a jerk, Mom. Turns out we're more alike than I realized. I wish you were here to help me navigate this.

And then finally, even before the series of tests and treatments, the sentence I had been waiting a year to hear…

"I believe you," she said. "Let's start from a diagnosis and work on treatment. Do you have any questions?"

I feel doubt and fear crushing my chest in a vice grip. I know what I want to ask, but speaking it out loud feels like a verdict that can never be reversed. *Don't you think it's better to know? What about your husband or your friends—you don't want them to experience the phone call you did.* I take a deep breath and whisper: "Will I die young like my mom?"

"Well, we can never anticipate things that far in advance. But from what you've told me, your mom's treatment did not account for the interconnectedness of symptoms we now know to be true. I believe that if your mom had gotten the treatment you're getting from this age, she'd likely be around today. I'd like to think she'd be happy you're getting the help she couldn't."

I start sobbing in my chair under the fluorescent lights. The stopper in that bottle I held on to for three years pops out, releasing the ocean I poured into it that day in my apartment. I cried for her. I cried for me. I cried for everyone in doctors' offices, waiting for someone to believe them. I cried for all the times I pushed myself past my breaking point, working harder and harder for achievements and recognitions that mean nothing if they cost everything. The way out of this cycle comes through asking someone else for help. *I thought I could do this all alone, but this is too much for me.* I realized in that moment that the path I wanted wasn't one of hustle. It wasn't one of hardness or pretending that everything was under control while a storm raged inside me. That moment on the red rocks, where everything seemed so small, and the horizon seemed endless, flashes in my mind, and a message: *You've been surviving. It's time to live.*

Beyond the veil of grief there is hope. Beyond the veil, there is life and a knowing of yourself that cannot be achieved without dismantling what came before. There is a clarity in loss—finding what your soul needs and, with time, the strength to chase it. It's been three years since that moment in the doctor's office. Three more years since my mother's passing, and I still miss her every day, but in many ways, I feel more connected to her now than I ever have. She was a much stronger person than I gave her credit for. I can see her in myself without flinching. I'm not that knowledgeable on numerology, but it's not hard to ignore the life-death-rebirth connection that's happened in these sets of three and how these transitions have influenced my personal goals and creativity. I've embraced energetic healing modalities, grounding in nature, and meditation – you know, all that hippie nonsense I was so quick to dismiss! I've done some soul-searching and have made changes in my career and lifestyle to prioritize peace and balance over productivity. Have you ever taken an honest look at yourself and decided you didn't like where your life is going? Believe me, that was a struggle. But I'm back in the land of sky and sun, planning to visit those red rocks as often as I can because that's where I found my water in the desert.

THE MEDICINE

When the ocean of grief threatens to sweep you away, grounding and body-focused meditation can help to bring you back to the present moment. Neuroscience has proven that body awareness practices can reduce symptoms of stress and anxiety. The practice below combines grounding meditation with body awareness.

Begin by taking a seat with both feet on the ground. Try this practice outside with your bare feet on the Earth (if possible).

Once seated, begin by closing your eyes or focusing on a neutral spot on the ground. Bring your awareness inward by taking three deep breaths. Breathe in for four counts, hold at the top for four counts, and release for four. After these initial breaths, let your breathing return to its regular pace.

Take some time to check in with how your body is doing right now. Are there areas of tightness or fatigue? There is nothing you need to change. Simply observe.

Bring your awareness to your feet, noticing the connection between your feet and the ground. Feel Mother Earth supporting you, and imagine your feet rooting down into the Earth's energy.

Shifting upwards from your feet through your legs and hips, begin to bring awareness to your spine. Take a breath in, and slowly visualize your spine as a snake, growing and lengthening up from your hips through your neck, into your skull, and out the crown of your head. Repeat this process as you like to gain even more length.

Go back to the bottom of the spine and lengthen again, pausing at the shoulders. Extend through the shoulders as your shoulder blades drop down and away from your ears. Lift the shoulders up toward the ears once again and squeeze, holding there. Now, release back down. Allow your shoulders to melt down your back.

Return to your breathing. Notice any additional sources of tension that arose while you were releasing your shoulders. Release any tension between your eyes. Release your jaw. There is nothing you need to hold onto.

As you begin your next breath, check in again with your body. Does anything feel physically different than it did at the beginning of the practice? How do you feel emotionally?

Allow a few final breaths before opening your eyes and turning your awareness outward. Take a minute to express gratitude to Mother Earth for supporting you during this practice, and when you are comfortable, open your eyes.

Dr. Angelica Dunsavage [she/they] is a music professor, conductor, composer, and professional singer. She has taught vocal music in the public school system, at the university level, and in community ensembles. Angelica has a master's and doctorate in choral conducting and a bachelor's in music education. She is active in professional music organizations as a researcher and presenter.

Outside of music, Angelica advocates for holistic health and mindfulness, especially for teachers and those in caretaker roles. She is a certified Reiki practitioner and operates a studio from her home. Angelica combines Reiki with other modalities such as crystal healing, Alexander Technique, and body mapping. She is an avid reader of historical fiction and fantasy, a participant at Renaissance fairs, and believes that everyone can embrace their inner pirate. She is a proud Leo and Ravenclaw. Angelica resides with her husband and two dogs, Riley and Eliza.

www.angelicadunsavage.com

CHAPTER 4

THE VOICE MAGNETIC

Alchemize Wounds into Wisdom

Maria Brannon, Vocal Embodiment Guide, Sound Healing Practitioner

"Your voice carries frequencies as unique as your fingerprints. It holds the key to remembering your inherent wholeness."

MY STORY

I left my body and gave away my voice for over 20 years. Even as a professional vocalist, I lost joy in singing. On my journey of reclamation, I ended a 7-year "starter" marriage, built and burned two businesses, healed childhood trauma, dissolved stage fright, and learned how to deeply work with the medicine of my voice to sing myself home.

"I think I'm having a heart attack; we have to go to the ER now," I say as calmly as possible, startling my sleeping husband awake. My heart is pounding out of my chest; *this is it; I'm dying right here and now. I was trying to breathe and calm myself. I'm only 21; I've barely gotten started with my life.*

A 2 am visit to the ER in New York City is surreal. A colorful and eclectic mix of people are strewn around the waiting room in various states of distress and discomfort. I sign in on a clipboard, and we wait in a small, dimly lit, curtained room that smells of disinfectant, with only the illusion of privacy. Soon, nurses hurried around me, took my blood pressure, and checked my heart. A young doctor slides through the curtain door and asks me if I've "had any major changes recently." He's telling me my heart "looks good." *How can it look good? I can't breathe and feel like a giant bass drum is pounding in a ribcage five sizes too small. What does he know?!* I quietly reply, "Not really, but I got married a few months ago."

He looks at me like he hit the jackpot, then tells me I'm "just having an anxiety attack." *Oh, cool, just an anxiety attack, which I've never had in my entire life; great, thanks, Doc.* He gives me a prescription for Valium and sends us on our way.

Relieved to find out I wasn't facing my immediate demise, I wondered now what? My body was obviously crying for help. *I got myself into this, and I'd better figure it out.*

My body knew long before I could admit it—I'd chosen a path that looked great on paper but was a straitjacket for my heart and soul. The truth was, I'd left my body long ago to fend for itself, so when it needed my attention, it had to shout!

Looking back now with hard-earned wisdom, I believe my soul had a contract to experience this self-inflicted challenge to spark my awakening, catalyze my spiritual growth, and reclaim my voice. It did *not* feel that way at the time.

In my mind, divorce wasn't an option. My six-year-old self still remembered the earth-shattering feeling of my parents' divorce. I was determined not to be another casualty of the D *word*. Plus, friends and family had all been dumbfounded when, at age 20, I declared that I was getting married to a foreign man 10 years older than myself. I was stubborn, and of course, when you're 20, you're certain you know everything—I had to prove them wrong.

Cue the start of dramatic dream visitations. They recurred in groups of similar themes, with the top three being predatory wild animals stalking me, powerful storms coming for me, and ancestral or familial situations.

No matter the scenario, I always escaped or woke up just in time to avoid harm. Whenever I awakened from these intense adventures, I never felt scared; I was just highly alert, which was interesting. In waking life, if animals were hunting me, storms were chasing me, or bees were flying into my ear while hanging out with family, I'd run for my life in fear! I got curious about my recurring dreams and what they were trying to tell me; maybe they knew something I didn't. *Maybe there was so much more.*

I visited the massive four-story Barnes & Noble at Union Square immediately. I wanted to be in the buzz of energy only available at this behemoth.

Bizarre, I was living in an NYU dorm on Union Square with my classmates only two years before. That's when I was still completely dedicated to my training as a "triple threat" (singer, dancer, actor) and was in an intense musical theater program called CAP 21 that was part of Tisch School of the Arts—a mouthful, I know.

Suddenly, I was in my old neighborhood with a very different purpose, looking for a book on dreams, spinning in disbelief that I was locked into a marriage at 21. For the first time in my life, I couldn't find much joy in singing or anything else for that matter; I felt so far away from myself. *How had I abdicated my voice so completely? Had I ever felt ownership in the first place?*

Luckily, my soulmate city was still there for me, and the bookstore welcomed me through its magical portal where I could disappear for hours at a time. The perfect book would pop out at me just when I needed it or right before I needed it. A lot of NYC felt that way for me. The constant seas of people offered a certain amount of freedom to be exactly whoever I was at any given moment, and unlimited mystical synchronicity was possible around every corner.

Can we take a detour for a minute? I need you to understand how much I freakin' loved NYC.

It was love at first sight when we met in its grittiest 1980s graffiti era when I was five years old, brought along by mom and my older sister for a weekend intensive with our dance teacher's studio. I was surrounded by teenage dancers in their leotards, leg warmers, and parachute pants in Times Square, and I learned the Time Step (classic tap dance combination) for the first time. *I feel so at home here in this magical place; I've never felt this electric before.*

From then on, New York was tattooed on my heart, and I knew I had to live there.

The second time I fell deeper in love with NYC, my parents and my very sweet hometown boyfriend flew with me from Little Rock to help me move into my first dorm at NYU, on 10th and Broadway. It was a grungy old building with what we'll agree to loosely call *character*. Old brown carpet, radiators that blasted hot enough to think you'd landed in Hell, and windows you had to crank open for some semblance of city fresh air. *I don't care that it's tiny and old; I can't wait to get settled!*

On that day of reignited passion for my new city, I watched my loved ones pile into the gaudy limousine that was cheaper to use than a taxi and waved goodbye as they faded out of sight. Simultaneously, a full-body feeling of ecstasy started to take over. *Am I floating? Is the sidewalk made of the prettiest sparkling diamond prisms I've ever seen? I can't stop smiling, and people probably think I'm crazy, and who cares anyway?!* I'm practically skipping; maybe I was actually skipping around the block, around my new neighborhood. *My new neighborhood. Whoa. I'm here, living my dream right now. Holy shit. This is really happening.* It still gives me a surge of excitement and blissful, expansive joy to feel into that first afternoon on my own.

Years later, stepping into the Barnes & Noble portal, motivated by my body's cries for help, I asked myself, *how do I get back to that state of joy? Where has my voice gone? I loved singing and dancing my whole life.* Now, I'm completely paralyzed by perfectionism and fears. Uninspired by my work and passion, I was caught in an endless spiral of the comparison game and self-doubt.

I wandered through the sections on self-help and psychology until I found the section on dreams. Something unique winked from the shelf among the multitude of dream dictionaries and lackluster titles. *Conscious Dreaming: A Spiritual Path for Everyday Life* by Robert Moss instantly resonated with me, especially as I saw that he incorporated shamanic practices in his process with an emphasis on tapping into your own wisdom. A second hugely impactful book, *Anatomy of the Spirit: The Seven Stages of Power and Healing* by Caroline Myss, called for me to take it home, too.

I'm grateful these books found me; they were vital in helping me recognize the ley lines of wisdom that connected my body and spirit.

My dreams guided me with golden breadcrumbs, and my body was the legend of my soul map.

The universe quickly confirmed I was on the right path. Soon after I started devouring the guidance within those pages, I found a weekend workshop with Robert Moss offered nearby and a live lecture at a local church featuring Caroline Myss.

In the workshop with Moss, I started to learn about navigating the dream realms and loved the practice of shamanic journeying to re-enter dreams with the rhythmic pulse of trance-inducing drumming. I connected with other like-minded soul explorers, and our intimate dream group met in Murray Hill for several years because of that weekend. I was learning to trust my voice again, to build self-confidence, and to strengthen my inner guidance system.

A pivotal moment came when a familiar recurring dream visited:

I'm standing alone outside; my eyes struggle to adjust to the inky darkness. Before me, a large pond is encircled by a shadowy forest. I cautiously make my way to a small bench by the water; a large tree stands to my right. Hesitantly, I sit down. I know I am here for a purpose. I sense the black panther that's been stalking me for so long, but I tell myself to be brave. It's behind me, and I let it come close. I pull my hair to the side and offer my neck to wait for the bite. There is no pain or fear.

Instantly, we're transported into the cosmos and land on the surface of a tiny asteroid or planet. Perched among a million stars twinkling against the velvety black sky, I ask with confusion, "So everybody dies?" I look left at my guide, and he has shape-shifted into a tall, thin African man with tiny travel collector spoons stuck into his wild hair, and he gleefully exclaims, "No, child! Everybody lives!"

Relief washes over me, and I feel so much joy and gratitude to know that we are not just these temporary bodies; we live on; everyone lives on. Oh! The only possible "death" is not remembering my own light, my true and everlasting Spirit. Sleepwalking through life is about forgetting who we really are. I'm here to remember my infinite light and to help others remember theirs!

My perception of my life was altered in that flash of awakening. As Moss states in *Conscious Dreaming*, "The role of the animal messenger in the dreams of modern city-dwellers is often to recall us to our wild side and the natural path of our energy." I knew I had some seriously scary things to face, and now I *knew* I could be brave.

It only took 20 more years of bumping up against all kinds of challenges to get to the embodiment of freedom and self-love I now carry.

My love affair with Nashville was a slow burn, but once the flame lit in 2009, there was no question that I was in the right place. There's a lot I could add here about the trials and tribulations of pursuing dreams as a singer/songwriter, front-woman of a band, traveling solo multiple times across the USA to play small venues and grow as an artist, and growing deeply in love with my dear husband I've been blissfully married to for over a decade now, but that's for another book.

In 2019, I started an intensive two-year shamanic practitioner training program that included a process called Guided Energy Medicine. At the women's circles, I attended around that same time, we often used the frame drum as a resonator for our voices, which felt so natural and liberating to me. *Yes, our voices are our medicine.* I was hearing this from the circles and simultaneously from my shamanic mentors across the country; we *are the medicine we've been waiting for.* This was not a new concept, but it was a potent message I needed then.

Another influence I resonated with near that time was an experience of a sound bath by Sara Auster. The walls came down around my idea of what music had to be and freed me to imagine how this new-to-me outlet of creativity might be perfect for my healing. *Could I work with sound in a new way that was simply for me?*

With my frame drum and a used set of crystal singing bowls, I started to explore reclaiming my voice as a gateway of personal healing and direct connection to the divine. This was the first time I could remember since childhood when I felt free to express my wholeness without outside (or inner) judgment. It felt like possibility, expansive, and joyful. It was that high-frequency electric feeling I had with my beloved NYC.

I sometimes drummed myself into theta brain state and would hang out there for deeply healing, intuitively guided inner child sessions. I would invite any version of myself that needed to be heard or felt to come forward in my mind, and then we would talk, cry, shout, and sound together until it felt like something had shifted.

While I held this space for myself, I also offered various sessions to friends, local healers, and family to get real-world experience in holding that space for others. Sound healing, shamanic practices, and the Guided Energy Medicine process I'd been learning started to merge and intersect in beautifully unexpected ways. I was reclaiming and freeing my voice in a sacred relationship to the powerful mystery it held within while helping others do the same.

THE MEDICINE

Building self-trust is a huge part of connecting to the power of your voice.

Learning to get still, deeply listen, pay attention, and then act on my nightly dream wisdom was crucial to building my self-trust muscle. Self-trust creates a strong foundation from which the voice can launch, whether that's speaking from an authentic place, singing with freedom, or any other way you choose to express yourself and *be* in this world.

Find something that anchors you into your spiritual center. The options are endless; prayer, meditation, dreamwork, singing, and journaling are some of my favorite ways to go inward. Find something you can practice that anchors you to your body's inner knowing (earthly heart) while simultaneously connecting you to your soul's wisdom (divine sacred heart). This is the powerful place we become a bridge between Heaven and Earth.

As a vocal embodiment guide and sound healing practitioner, the first thing I want to do with any beautiful souls I work with is help them feel safe in their bodies and give them some tools to do that. I spent such a huge part of my life disembodied while unknowingly living in a state of flight or fight and freeze or fawn.

Suppose our highly sensitive nervous systems are functioning in a state of dysregulation. In that case, no amount of intellectual work we do will successfully help us alchemize the pains of our past into rich wells of wisdom that fuel our soul's growth.

Our minds compartmentalize and help us to forget and forgive, but as trauma researcher and expert Bessel van der Kolk, M.D.'s book states, *The Body Keeps the Score*, and traumas can get stuck in our cellular memories.

Thankfully, I've learned that no matter how long that lock has been closed on our painful past, our voices carry a unique frequency that is perfectly tuned to help us turn the key to realigning to our well-being. We are the medicine; we just need to remember.

Do you know how to hum? Great!

Let's tune up your heart and calm down your body.

Get comfortable and take a few deep belly breaths with this pattern:

- Inhale slowly for four counts.
- Hold for four counts.
- Exhale slowly for eight counts.

Continue Breathing:

- Place one hand on your heart, and one on your belly.
- Or one hand lightly on the back of your neck, the other with palm placed lightly over your forehead.
- Acknowledge your body and give it some attention in this gentle way. You're already soothing your nervous system.

In this calm state, imagine the droning buzz of bees, the hum of the Divine—bring to mind someone, something, or somewhere that gives you joy and connects you with pure love or ecstasy.

Let that feeling expand in your heart, and when you inhale all that beautiful emotion, let the hum or the buzz of your voice carry it through the hive network of your nervous system. Send that delicious, golden, gooey sound to the darkest, tightest places you notice and let it filter in, gently opening those spaces to more lightness and love. Let the sweet vibrations smooth any rough edges of your inner landscape.

You're using your unique voice to realign to your wellness and true light while physically calming and toning your vagus nerve, resulting in nervous system regulation.

Do this as often as you can; the vagus nerve loves to be toned. Frequent daily practice will help your body become more and more resilient to the effects of stress. Stress is unavoidable; how we react to it is up to us (and our nervous system).

Find a guided version of this experience along with other love offerings at:

https://iridescentknowing.com/dreamingwithbees

Maria Brannon, founder of Iridescent Knowing™ and The Voice Magnetic™, a private practice facilitating 1:1 Shamanic Sound Alchemy™ sessions, group sound bath experiences and retreats, 1:1 SoulNote Vocal Embodiment Sessions™, dream work, stone medicine, and more.

She's dedicated to holding a safe and loving space for others to remember their authentic selves, access their inner wisdom, and deeply connect to the power of their voice.

People have said that while working with Maria, they've experienced:

- "Brain tingles"
- Full body chills and soul remembering
- Messages from Spirit that bring clarity
- Deep rest and stress relief
- Shamanic journeys filled with helpful insights
- Reconnection with fragmented parts of Self
- Relief from physical pain
- Clarity for the next step on their path

Some friends call her an energy alchemist, but she also answers to Rainbow M. When she's not spreading her sonic love waves, she's usually cuddled with one of their two Siberian Forest cats and a good book or on an adventure with her husband, Beau.

Maria is a graduate of NYU's Tisch School of the Arts Musical Theater Program and a seasoned performer. She's also a certified vocal resonance facilitator, dream guide, guided energy medicine and stone medicine practitioner, and Gene Keys guide.

Connect with Maria:

https://iridescentknowing.com

Instagram @iridescentknowing

https://thevoicemagnetic.com

Instagram @thevoicemagnetic

CHAPTER 5

BREAKING FREE FROM EXPECTATIONS

The Power of Finally Being Who You Are

Christina Marta Beebe

"It's simple," they say, "and you too have come into the world to do this, to go easy, to be filled with light, and to shine."

~ Mary Oliver

MY STORY

THE NOTHING

The sting

Heavy

Falling

Endless falling

Through darkness

Nothing to hold onto

Panic

Lost in silence

Alone

Black pit of despair

Deep bleeding rip

In my heart

My soul aches

Sharp waves swell up to sting

Overwhelming darkness

Threatening to devour

My heart and soul

Threatening to overpower me

Wipe me out

Then dissipate

Gray

Color has slipped away

Into numb gray

Bled away

Gone

"I expected more of you as a mom," my husband told me after he helped me pack my life into my little silver Toyota Yaris.

His words severed my soul.

"Fuck you!" I wanted to tell him. I poured every inkling of my being into excelling as a mother and wife. I followed all the rules and instructions and studied hard, only to fail. Nothing was good enough. I was too much, too intense, yet never enough.

"I did the best I could," I told him as my heart sank deep into the dark blob. I held back the enormous wave of grief, threatening to flood my soul in sorrow, as I hugged him and then placed myself in the driver's seat.

Don't cry. Hold it together just a little longer, I coached myself as I reversed down the familiar driveway, then forward through what would never again be my street.

I did everything by the book. I was a virgin until our wedding night. I kept the house clean and orderly. I breastfed Hugo until after his second birthday, as instructed. I was constantly researching and applying age appropriate activities since the day he was born. I fed him only healthy foods and water, in addition to my breast milk, and made his baby food from fresh fruits and veggies. Even while he was in my womb, I never drank any caffeine or alcohol. I took the best prenatal vitamins I could find, ate healthy, exercised every day, and did my best to keep calm so he would feel safe and secure in my womb. I read and sang to him often and played soothing music for him. I was part of every mom's group and did my best to give him a healthy balance of peer social interactions and alone time.

As for my husband, I gave sex to him on a regular basis, even when I didn't want to. I kept the finances in order, the fridge and pantry filled, and the house cleaned and organized. I made sure not to have any male friends so he could feel confident and secure in my faithfulness to him. I planned our date nights and fostered an open and warm environment for him to feel safe and welcome to share his thoughts and feelings with me freely.

I did all the things. I followed all the rules and instructions, yet it didn't matter. Our marriage ended in divorce.

Yes, it's true I'm a lesbian. But that wasn't supposed to matter. The church taught me to marry a male best friend, regardless of sexual orientation. That's what I did. Being sexually attracted to women as a woman was a sin. I didn't want to go to Hell, so I secured my place in Heaven by marrying my male best friend.

Eleven years into our marriage, it all fell apart.

"I feel like you're not sexually attracted to me like I am to you," he told me one night.

I felt naked under a spotlight.

"It's not just you. I've never been sexually attracted to men. I know, intellectually, you are sexually attractive. I'm just not sexually attracted to men at all, only to women. But you're my best friend. Always, I love you in my heart so much."

The silence felt like shards of glass raining down inside me, cutting my heart and gut.

"I knew something was missing! How could I be so stupid? I married a lesbian!" he finally responded.

I went through many types of therapy to try and switch me over to the straight side. We went to a couples therapist, who told us, "I'm surprised you made it eleven years together," and strongly suggested we divorce to save our friendship. I went to an EMDR trauma therapist, who often fell asleep during the sessions, and a sex therapist, to whom I was sexually attracted. The sex therapist had Bible scriptures written all over her office walls while telling me something about my clitoris. I don't remember anything else she said. I just remember the word clitoris coming out of her mouth while feeling hot and sweaty, listening to her, trying not to let my clitoris palpitate, and feeling judged by all the scriptures closing in on me.

All the therapy only made me bitter and angry toward Jon's penis. I tried desperately to keep our marriage together, as it shattered in my hands, cutting me open, raw and bleeding.

It was a long 13-hour drive from Tennessee to Texas. Why Texas? I would rescue my new online lesbian friend from her abusive girlfriend, and we'd live happily ever after together. That was the plan. But that's not what happened.

"You're fucking up your life!" my psychologist yelled at me through the phone. I had just told her I wouldn't make it to the session because I was going to Texas to start my new life.

"I have nowhere else to go," I told her.

"You're going to lose everything!" she yelled back at me.

"Yeah, I know. I already did. I don't know what else to do."

"He's not going to let you see your son. You just lost your son and your house. That house is half yours." she continued.

"Yeah, I know," the cold black glob started to rise from my gut into my heart. I couldn't hold it back. "I gotta go," I told her and hung up to try to focus on the road.

All the deep, dark, heavy grief seized my gut, my heart, twisting, squeezing. I let it out in a screaming cry, all the pain, all the years, all my failings, all the losses, all the dark, bottomless grief, blurring my eyes, trying to focus on the road. I lost everything. There was nothing I could do. I did everything I could. I felt like I was falling, powerless, nothing to hold onto, cold, dark, bottomless falling.

I'll drive myself off this bridge and end everything, end myself, end this misery.

No! Just try this new life. Stephanie needs you. Just get there and rescue her. Just focus on rescuing her. She needs you.

My mind raced through all the heavy grief endings I'd endured, the huge, black, sticky glob of grief that threatened to destroy me with every loss. It started the day I was born when my mom wouldn't pick me up when I cried. My uncle told me I would cry and cry, but my mom would just sit there, unconcerned, until finally, my Oma (my mom's mom) came to my rescue. My Oma became my safe place. She became my world. But the damage was already done. The message set in stone, "If you cry for help, no one will come."

My mom was always emotionally distant from me, no matter how hard I tried to be close to her. She would tell me she loved me, but I never felt it. She yelled and snapped when I tried to be close to her. I felt her as prickly.

When I was nine, she randomly left us and left me, the eldest of three, to take up all her responsibilities. The bitterness started the day she left and continued until the day she died.

In 2017, she developed drug-induced schizophrenia, locked herself in her bedroom for ten days, starving herself to bare bones, and died on the tenth day. My little half-brothers were living with her and tried to convince her to leave her room. But she only yelled at them through the closed door. They called the rest of us siblings for help. We didn't know what to do, and we all lived in other states, hundreds and thousands of miles away.

When I got the call that she was dead, I felt relieved we didn't have to deal with her craziness anymore. But I also felt a part of me died with her. It was the hope that died, the hope that one day we'd be emotionally close and have a nurturing mother-and-daughter relationship. That hope died with her. That was December 11, 2017.

Three months later, my Oma, who was my world, developed dementia, forgot who I was, then died on March 11, 2018. A big part of my identity died with her.

If I'm not Oma's girl, who am I? I felt the inquiry deep in my soul.

I was always Oma's girl since the day I was born. Everyone knew this. I was still Jon's wife at that point and actively engaged in my son's life.

Oh, the pain, swelling up another monster wave of black, a bottomless pit of despair, threatening to devour me as I took loss inventory on my drive to Texas.

I'm not Jon's wife anymore, and my baby stayed there with him. I lost everything. I lost everything! Who am I? What is my life now? I lost everything.

After 13 hours of personal grief history analysis, I drove onto my new driveway in Texas, into my new life.

"I'm going to be Stephanie's wife," I told myself out loud. "I'm going to rescue her, and we'll start our life together."

I've always prided myself on being solution-oriented. I'm not like my mom. I'll find a solution. I will rely on myself. I will find a way forward. I will not give up.

I got settled into the Texas house alone. The plan was for Stephanie to sneak out of her house while her alcoholic girlfriend was passed out on the floor. But she couldn't do it. She was afraid because her girlfriend found out about me and called me repeatedly, threatening to destroy me.

I was completely alone, with no plan, in a huge four-bedroom house. At first, I was hard-set on death. I had a fork in my hand as I lay on the cold, hard front bedroom floor close to the electrical socket.

Just do it. Just end it all. Just stick it in, and it'll all be over. Just stick it in.

I dropped the fork as my deepest insides twisted. Massive waves of thundering black forced their way through me in gut-wrenching emotional convulsions. Choking on my snot, barely able to breathe, I hoped to choke to death on my own inner slime, hoping to pass through the death portal.

No! Pull yourself together! Hugo! You have to stay alive for Hugo!

"I don't want you! I want Dad!" The memory of Hugo's little three-year-old voice slashed through my heart. He had yelled that to me toward the end of my marriage. It was after Jon told me (regarding Hugo), "He's not hard! You're hard!"

Those three quotes echoed through me over and over again:

I had expected more of you as a mom.

He's not hard! You're hard!

I don't want you! I want Dad!

I poured out my life to them. They were my life. Yet, I was never *enough*, and I was *too much*.

"Oh, the pain! Death! Death! Please, take me! I have nothing left!" I cried out, willing my end. *I can't do this anymore. I can't do this life.*

"Fuck!" I yelled out. I pulled myself up, and wrote out a plan of action. I made the most of my nine months in Texas. It was the first time in my life that I lived alone. At first, I only felt a constant sinking, bottomless pit of despair threatening to take me out. I dragged myself through each day, like Atrau and his horse in *The NeverEnding Story*, dragging themselves through the sinking mud of depression.

But then, I joined a couple of dating apps and met some amazing women. I had lots of lesbian sex for the first time in my life, and I understood why people like sex. I started walking around the house naked, singing and dancing freely. There was no one to tell me I couldn't. I had freedom! I was free! But I also missed my son, and Texas was too far from him. Whether he wanted me or not didn't matter anymore. I wanted him.

After nine months away from him, I U-hauled myself and my new life back to Tennessee. I realized I was never really alone.

In 2019, when my marriage with Jon was starting to fall apart, and I was seeking all sorts of therapy, I followed the breadcrumbs to the woman who saved my life. She wasn't one of those therapists. She was different. She breathed life into me. I imagine it's how little Claudia felt in *Interview with the Vampire* when she had nothing and was about to die but was brought back to life (to a new and vibrant life). I'm not saying

I transformed into a bloodsucking vampire. I use that analogy because, in that scene, Claudia thought she would die beside her dead mother in a moment when she had no hope. Then, her life was transformed into something completely different. Her eyes became bright, and her hair restored to bouncy curls. My hope was restored, and my life completely changed. This gracious and deeply loving woman saved my life and stayed with me through it all, lovingly holding me energetically, even when I couldn't feel her.

When I was in Texas, we continued sessions via Zoom. She has taught me how to live, how to breathe, how to meditate, how to listen and trust my inner voice. She is love, and her love sustains me. I'm no longer Jon's wife nor Oma's girl. I am my own. I belong to myself. I am free.

HOME

Unfolding song

Blossoming forth

In a story of my own

Freedom

Letting go

Freedom

Come and go

Flowing

I am my own

I'm learning the beauty of being alone. I lost my marriage but found myself. I'm never really alone. Everything breathes. I'm learning to break free from the claustrophobic constructs of culture and the preconceived notions that no longer serve me in my journey to freedom and fulfillment.

I create my world. I make my path. I'm learning to be creative in the story I tell myself. I can change the meaning of anything.

I make love and light my focus rather than "following the rules." When one door closes, another will open somewhere else. I look for the open door. I listen to my dreams, the bees, the ancient ones and spirit guides, the goddesses, the angels, and my higher self. They show me what I need to know when I need to know it, and they comfort me. I trust them. I consult my tarot and oracle cards for guidance. I feel the spirit world speak to me through them.

I tell myself, "Don't be Atrau's horse." I view my life as a movie. I'm watching my own movie, and I call the shots. I don't want the main character to die in the quicksand of grief. There's hope. Do the next little step. Rest when you need to. But always get up again and try something new.

I share my story with safe people. And when life starts to feel gray and stale, and the shadow of grief starts to creep in, I try something new. The boy in *The NeverEnding Story* needed to give the princess a new name. He didn't realize how vital his role was. My role is important, too. And so is yours.

With each significant loss, I write a page in my grief book with a poem to honor that loss. Emotions are just energy. Grief hurts. But it will pass. Breathe. Always remember to breathe deeply, slowly, and intentionally. Look for the new door. It's there waiting for you to step through to the next adventure.

HER NAME

Her name

Dances in my heart

On soft pink clouds

She sees me

Bright green tiger eyes

Anything is possible

When I hear her name

Time stands still

And everything she is

Joins her name

In my heart

Blossoming forth

In the warm sunshine

Reflecting on the river

Of her love

I'm held forever

In her strong embrace

Where I'm completely known

Where she and I are one

Wild and free

Love rasa

THE MEDICINE

The most effective medicine in my life has been, not being told what to do, but creating the space and quiet to find it myself, especially in nature. I encourage you to do the same. Walk among the trees, breathe deeply, and listen.

Hugging a tree has been known to help raise a person's vibrations and bring a comforting calm. Hug a tree and notice how your heart feels. Breathe in your true nature as part of the whole. You and nature are one. How does that resonate with you? Write down your experience in a journal.

Christina Marta Beebe resides in Middle Tennessee. She is a Tantric Bhakti yogini, Reiki master, published author, writer, proofreader, poet, life coach, artist, artisan, mother to one, sister to many, and lover of nature, especially trees. Her most recently published book is one of poetry, entitled *Wild & Free*. She grew up in sunny Southern California, where she spent most of her free time relaxing at the beach, adventuring in Disneyland, and hiking the hills.

She loves wandering in the forest, spontaneous adventures, witchy sisterhood gatherings, and Kirtan. She holds a bachelor's degree in psychology from California State University, Fullerton. She has worked as a church counselor at Saddleback Church and a psychiatric technician at Middle Tennessee Mental Health Institute. Christina has recently begun her journey learning about, and engaging in, the wonderful world of plant medicine.

Connect:

Email: xtinabeebe@gmail.com

Facebook: https://www.facebook.com/christina.beebe.336

Website: https://www.healingintentionsreikiroom.weebly.com

Amazon Author Page:
https://www.amazon.com/author/christina-marta-beebe-108

BEE COCOON RECIPE

Channeled from the Bees

~ Leah Benjamin

You will need mashed potatoes, hummus, baba ganoush,
dip, or any food that is both soft enough to sculpt
and firm enough to hold form.

In addition, any other bite-sized piece of food will do.

On your plate, choose a bite-sized piece of food
and separate it slightly,

leaving a bit of room around it.

Take your mashed potatoes or hummus
and begin to form gently and tenderly,

a cocoon around the bit of food you chose.

This cocoon is a holy surrounding for the sacred morsel inside of it.

Thank the bees for keeping the buzzing and hum

of the outside world going

while whatever happens inside the cocoon takes place.

The bees will continue their cycles

along with many other life forms on different time cycles.

They will do this for as long as the cocoon needs
to hold the sacred morsel.

You may choose to ingest the cocoon food

and let it carry through the nourishment of your body.

Or, you may set it outside for the spirits.

Blessed Bee.

CHAPTER 6

ADULT FRIENDSHIPS

Find Your Soul Besties with A Simple Body-Centered Practice

Elizabeth DeVaughn, LPC-MHSP

"The body never lies."

~ Meggan Watterson, Mary Magdalene Revealed

MY STORY

Female friendships have always been harder for me than romantic ones. That's still a hard thing for me to say, and I'm bowing down to the miracle that is Brené Brown for helping us all to be a little more vulnerable and brave.

I've had my fair share of wacky misadventures in dating, but female friendships have just had a certain singe-factor. I didn't play video games as a kid, but the girlfriend thing felt like the one area where I couldn't get the gold coin to advance to the next level.

Throughout my life, I've dreamed of the kind of friendships that preteen movies are made of—endless belly laughing, confiding, inside jokes, sister-cations, walkie-talkies, midnight witchy ceremonies on a lake, all the things. Most of all, I wanted depth: soul-level depth, trust, realness, and connection.

Even though I developed great friendships from childhood through young adulthood, as I entered graduate school to become a therapist, I longed for more depth and longevity. I had developed the deepest conscious love and trust with my beloved—a wonderful man I've been married to for twelve years, and I wanted that same level of depth and nourishment with female friends.

In the midst of grad school, I started my own therapy. Among 800 other patterns, my brilliant and annoying therapist helped me break through, relationship patterns were one of them. I began seeing what had been holding me back from the friendships I longed for.

Having grown up in a house of addiction, enmeshment (lack of boundaries), and trauma, I learned to hang on to attachment figures by doing a strained, off-kilter dance of performance, perfection, and staying concealed.

Growing up, real emotions and concerns were kept hidden (leading to cycles of resentment and explosions later). I have brutal memories of my anger and other emotions being laughed at and dismissed. I learned to keep my real self just out of view, which, while keeping me unscathed as a kid, left most of my adult friendships lacking the depth I was so hungry for.

Halfway through grad school, the skies cleared, and it appeared that my hard work in therapy was about to pay off. As if out of a misty portal from a whimsical land of sunshine and cool girls, two women I admired in my school cohort suddenly started talking to me—a lot. Just as I resigned to be happy with a great marriage and lots of cats, it seemed like the tides were about to turn.

These two women and I quickly struck up a friendship, so quickly that they were soon eager to introduce me to their other two friends.

Can this be fucking real? These two goddesses atop the ivy-covered mountain not only want to be friends with me, but it's a group thing now.

With the witchy lake ceremonies so close that I could smell the pine and palo santo, I was all fucking in.

And off to the races we were. No sooner had I met the other two friends than they declared their unwavering love for me, and I was too swept away in belly laughs and expensive restaurant dates to question it.

The *I love yous* were passed around like joints, and it felt like I reached the pinnacle of girlfriend achievement. Hand me my award; I had solved the great girlfriend puzzle.

We were a thing. Our group text became a daily check-in. We connected and shared deeply, and we were there for each other when life was fucking life. It was paradise for a while.

Even with my historical struggles with female friendships, I knew deep inside that I was good with relationships. Thanks to the work with my annoyingly spot-on therapist and the deep safety and love I was building with my now husband, Garrett, I trusted myself enough to know that I was skilled with relationships.

I also knew that relationship pattern healing comes in waves. My challenge was to show up more fully, speak my truth, and name my emotions and needs as authentically as possible. I also had to trust that true friendships would strengthen with this practice, and weak ones would fall away.

What a perfect friend group in which to practice these new skills.

Around the same time I decided to make an effort to show up more fully, I started having panic attacks—bad ones, as in hospitalization. I had never in my life experienced anything more terrifying. The most unsettling thing was that they seemed to come out of nowhere.

To this day, I believe the panic attacks were mainly a result of a lifetime of accumulated stress. I also don't deny the interesting timing and that they were telling me something I didn't have the capacity to admit at the time—that maybe I didn't feel as safe in this seemingly miraculous friend group as I thought I did.

The girls and I took a trip to the mountains one winter. Not far into the drive, I had a panic attack. We immediately pulled off the interstate and into a restaurant parking lot, where I called Garrett. Under that much stress, I had no filter; at that moment, I was a five-year-old child, scared at a sleepover and crying to come home.

My hurried words poured out faster than my brain could keep up with. I told Garrett I wanted to go home and didn't want to go with them. Ever the caring partner, he told me he would support whatever I wanted to do and offered to help. I decided that my worries were unfounded, and I chose to press on.

Knowing that panic attacks were a thing for me in that season, the group was nurturing and kind. We stopped for a bite, allowed time for me to gather myself, and continued with what turned out to be quite a fun road trip.

During the rest of the trip, I begrudgingly noticed an unsettled feeling inside: the same unsettled feeling I had in childhood when the grownups held back resentments. It was hard to shake, especially because I couldn't think of anything that had gone wrong.

After the trip, I started approaching the women one by one to ask if everything was okay, sensing that something was off. One of them said to me,

Actually, I have been having some problems.

Great! Finally, an honest response. Thankfully, with all the work my therapist and I had done, I could move past my ego and listen to feedback that could help me show up and be a better friend.

She and I had a great conversation, and I learned some things about myself that I could do better. I was celebrating a fruitful, hard conversation among girlfriends. With my stomach now settled and relaxed and an effortless, bright smile back on my face, I summoned the courage to make a final request:

"Will you let me know if anything bothers you in the future so we can work through it without letting resentment build?"

"Definitely."

Sweet. No more childhood trauma replay for this girl.

Time went on, and despite a great conversation, the unsettled feeling returned quickly, and it was now showing up whenever I was with them. Each time I would pull into one of their driveways, I found myself clutching my necklace of crystals and praying for courage. Courage for what? I couldn't tell you. Being with them started feeling like a disorienting fog mixed with shards of glass, and I couldn't explain why.

I was so confused because, to my knowledge, any rough spots had been ironed out. I approached a couple of them to see if everything was okay, and the only answer I received was,

"No girl, all good!"

"Okey dokey."

My panic attacks continued, and I started running late to our gatherings. Today, I'm aware that running late is a coping strategy.

The familiar feelings of fog, shards of glass, and confusion, mixed with belly laughs and connection, started feeling like an upside-down tornado gaining speed by the second.

On the arrival of one of our most highly anticipated friend dates yet, I had another panic attack. I had also just had all four wisdom teeth pulled, and I decided that it'd be best for me to stay home. I sent a text in our group chat to let them know that, on top of the panic attack, I was still feeling goopy from surgery and that I would need to stay home. Based on the group vibe I was feeling, I felt like a bad child, looking up at mom and dad, confessing my horribly wrong decision to stay home.

I received no response. None. Not that night, and not the next day. Not at all.

Along with more confusion and hurt, this scenario so deeply triggered old attachment wounds that I started experiencing suicidal ideations. This was bad.

I took a few days to talk with my therapist and spend time with Garrett. I started noticing how differently I felt in my body with them compared to how I felt with the group.

As I spent time inward and with people I felt truly safe with, a new emotion emerged: anger.

My deep inner wisdom—along with my self-advocating, pissed-off lioness— started to activate, like a long-dormant, cobwebbed switch that had just been flipped.

No. Absolutely not. This is bullshit. It is never wrong to take care of yourself. I am not too much. I am worthy of friends who will talk to me before resentment builds. I will not co-create my childhood. No.

As an emerging relationship specialist and almost-therapist, I needed to do everything I could to repair the relationships. I was open to the possibility that there was something I wasn't seeing. I reached out to the group to see if we could talk. They agreed, and we set a date.

As the date grew closer, my chest grew tighter, my stomach more nauseous, and my throat felt like it was closing. I did not feel safe with these women. Shit.

It was the morning of our scheduled in-person talk. My whole body was damn-near shaking its head, "No." Not safe. The group dynamic was too much for my nervous system.

My fingers trembled with anxiety, and my stomach twisted in knots as I typed the word *cancel*. Barf. I can't do this.

At the same time, I heard my wise, inner lioness:

I don't think it would feel this scary with safe friends. I think safe friends would be concerned and would want to work it out, even if they feel angry at first.

So, with all the courage that Brené Brown had taught me thus far, I sent a group text letting them know that I didn't feel safe with the group and would reach out to them individually.

In my texts, I expressed that I was unsure where the strained energy was coming from but wanted to do anything I could to repair it. I expressed that I felt safer with one-on-one conversations and asked if they would be up for talking.

Out of four women, I received only one response. For my mental health, I deleted it the next day after I froze like a block of ice and stared at it wide-eyed for what seemed like days.

I remember that the word "dramatic" was used more than once, and the message was that she would not have a conversation with me individually, although she was willing to carry on as usual in the group.

As grief-stricken as I was, the work with my therapist was about to pay off. Because fuck no, did I agree with a friendship that left no room for real-ass conversations? No.

As quickly as the friend group appeared out of the misty portal, it fizzled out even quicker after that day. One of the women and I attempted to continue, and while I was grateful for her willingness to have real conversations, too much damage had been done on my end. I needed a clean slate.

The couple of months after the friend breakup were the hardest. These women had become attachment figures. Thanks to social media, which I quickly blocked, I knew that the group was carrying on together, which triggered my worst fear,

Geeezus. Despite doing literally everything I could think of, I still can't have deep closeness in friendships. Husband and cats it is.

I felt dysfunctional like the girlfriend gene was missing from my DNA. I felt lonely. But I also had nuggets of inner wisdom and trust, assuring me that not only did I do great work to co-create conscious friendships but that I also had to practice trusting that there were women out there who could reciprocate.

Thanks to some great therapist friends and colleagues, my husband, and my annoying therapist, I started trusting my inner wisdom more and more. I moved through a mountain of grief and rage. I trusted my natural skills, and the safe people around me mirrored back a truer reflection of myself. I continued practicing being as authentic as I could. I slowed my inner pace way down, and I started feeling what true safety felt like with people outside of Garrett.

I spent a ton of time in nature, where, from the void that formerly housed the stomach-churning self-questioning and anxiety I felt with the group, I started to grow a quiet, still, deep inner sense of trust and groundedness. It was the real me. I will never forget that feeling. I heard my own voice, and I trusted it.

I felt my roots grow deeper into the earth's, and I felt nature giving me big, squishy hugs, hearing,

Spend a lot of time here; you're in the right place.

So I did, and I was.

I had to have an attachment experience that helped me face my fears, and I had to trust myself and my body through it.

And you'll never guess what came out of that initiation. You guessed it, smarty-pants. Friends. Mother-fucking amazing ones. Friends that, to this day, leave me feeling inspired, bright, lifted, seen, loved, cared for, safe, cheeks exhausted from laughter, and always wanting more. I attracted friends who are capable of reciprocating and who want what I do: depth and realness.

I now know what it feels like to have a hard conversation with a safe girlfriend, and to come out the other side stronger and closer. That's what I dreamed of.

I even got my fucking witchy ceremony on a lake.

It took years of grief and anger for me to appreciate the lesson, which, for me, was to not label the group as bad, wrong, or monsters (although it's okay to be angry with harmful behaviors). They weren't a match for me. Looking back, my body was communicating that to me all along, before the first panic attack.

The initiation for me was to trust myself and my body's signals, above all else. And to know I was worthy of friends who were a match.

I had to go into my depths and back to trust that the body, indeed, never lies.

THE MEDICINE

Brave, dear reader: I hope that my story can help you trust yourself more deeply than ever before. I would love to share a simple yet powerful practice that can help you. Pour yourself a cuppa tea, get cozy, and meet me at the metaphorical lake for a witchy (body-centered) ceremony.

This experience helped me see the power of somatic work, which means "dealing with the body." Ten years after this experience, and as a seasoned psychotherapist, I've learned that body-centered practices are the most potent for healing outdated relationships and trauma patterns. The goal is to increase your ability to tune into your body's "safety" signals and its "danger" signals.

Trauma skews our connection with and perception of our bodily signals. This becomes tricky because bodily signals are key in determining who's safe for us and who isn't.

To start, create a quiet, calm place for yourself, and do anything you can to ensure you won't be disturbed. Grab your cozy beverage, journal, and anything else to help yourself feel at peace.

Think of a time when you felt happy, light, inspired, expansive, cared for, loved, or safe. And dear one, if you can't think of a time when you felt like this, don't worry. Pull up a memory from a movie or book where one of the characters felt this way.

Once you have a memory, bask in it. Make it sensory. What do you see, feel, smell, hear, taste?

Now, notice if you feel any physical sensation linked to the memory. Does your stomach feel open, your chest less tight, and your legs heavy in a good way? Is there a smile naturally spreading over your face? Are you smoothly swaying, as if your body's saying, "yesss?" Do you feel light yet grounded? How about warm or chilled?

If body signals are hard to recognize, don't worry. Do you see any colors? Do you feel any emotions? Do other memories pop up that signal happiness? What thoughts do you notice? Sometimes, noticing signals in the body is hard at first so we can tune into other signs.

Write down any physical sensations you notice and other signs mentioned above, as these are your sacred indicators that will help you discern what's aligned with the truest you.

The more you tune in with these signals, the more attuned you'll be to the right people for you. And I hope you know you're worthy of that.

Elizabeth DeVaughn, LPC-MHSP, is a clinical psychotherapist, Somatic Experiencing® student, and has been a specialist in relationships, codependency, and complex trauma for over a decade; she specifically helps clients heal the root cause of outdated, trauma-based relationship patterns. Clients find Elizabeth as they outgrow traditional talk therapy and search for a healing path that leads to tangible, long-term results.

Elizabeth owned and operated her private clinical practice in Nashville for over nine years, and she now helps women and couples all over the world heal the root causes of outdated relationship patterns through specially tailored, somatic, and slightly witchy courses, memberships, and retreats.

Elizabeth is an outspoken activist for animal rights and disability rights, as she and her husband live as an interabled couple. Her favorite things include hiking, crafting, dancing, anything witchy or to do with cats, girlfriend time, and early morning coffee on the porch with her artistic, hilarious husband of fourteen years.

If you find the above practice helpful, know it's an important first step toward healing outdated relationship patterns on the deepest level.

If you'd like to take the next powerful step, Elizabeth warmly invites you to download her free *Hard Convo Cheat Sheet* straight from her website.

Please also follow along with her Instagram page for the latest relationship and trauma pattern healing content.

Connect with Elizabeth:
Website: https://www.elizabethdevaughn.com
Instagram: https://www.instagram.com/relationship_pattern_therapist

CHAPTER 7

GRIEF AND GRATITUDE

How Plant Medicine Helped Me Heal

Kim Louise Eden

"Grief can be the garden of compassion. If you keep your heart open through everything, your pain can become your greatest ally in your life's search for love and wisdom."

~ Rumi

MY STORY

I stepped out of the shower into the milky white steam of my bathroom and approached my vanity. I slid my hand across the damp, glossy surface of my bathroom mirror to reveal the blurry reflection of a person I no longer recognized. I tapped my finger on the glass.

Am I dreaming?

I question tapping a few more times.

Which side of the mirror am I on?

My mind swirls, confused if I'm in the real world, the world of daytime dreams, as I call it, or the nighttime dream world, or one of the countless dimensions in between.

They all get blurred sometimes.

I check to see if I can breathe.

Deep breath in, deep breath out.

Okay, I'm in the daytime dream.

I don't breathe in the nighttime dream world. Sometimes, that's the only way I know where I am. I get dressed and feel the familiar cold, numbing feeling slip into my thoughts. My old dark companion leads me to the darkest place of hopelessness and abandons me. No rational thought can exist here. I want to escape, but there is no light to see. The darkness steals my will to even try. It's been with me for a few days now. No, months. It's something I thought I left in my past, but then I suddenly found myself wrapped in its vice-like embrace. I've done so much work around this, yet I fall off the cliff of my highest high; I thought I'd reached an optimum spiritual awakening just to plummet face-first into the deepest valley.

I remember the day when I looked at my mentors at the end of our ministerial training, and I proudly announced, "I think I'm ready to dive into my sexuality and those wounds."

Their eyes widened as they looked at me with concern.

"I got this," I said. "I'm in such a great place."

I now understand where the concern was. When I said I'd let that door open, it flew open, splintering into a million pieces. Exploding out of that space was a long-forgotten, unrecognizable part of myself. It flew forward with the white-hot rage of a demon clawing its way from Hell. She was fucking pissed.

She used to be a beautiful young woman who believed in fairytale love.

In the summer of 2005, I started my new job in the surgical department of a large research facility. My new boss took me on a tour of the labyrinth of bland white hallways with gray steel doors evenly spaced. Outside each door was a black sign with white letters that let you know what each room was intended for.

"This is radiology, and across the way is cardiology," my new boss chirped in her pleasant singsong voice. "And down that way is the cath…" Her voice trailed off in my mind and became background noise.

One of the gray doors opened, and a tall, handsome, olive-skinned man stepped out. Our eyes met, and I melted instantly.

"Oh, Kim, meet John. John, this is Kim, our new surgical technician," my boss said.

Neither of us said anything. We just stared at each other.

"Oookay," she said awkwardly, continuing down the hallway, her heels clunking on the tile floor.

"This is one of the operating rooms." Her voice trailed off in my head again. I looked back. John was still in the hallway, watching us walk away. Our eyes met again before I turned and followed my boss for the rest of my tour.

What the heck was that? My mind quipped.

I felt like I knew him and instantly started to fall for him. I quickly found out he felt the same.

We were inseparable. We couldn't stand to be apart. He was like a junky, desperate for his next fix. I was happy to be his drug of choice.

I quickly found he was not alone in his mind. It was like there were two of him—the sweet, loving, romantic partner and the other dark demon that scared me. I could see the change in his eyes when it took over. It was a part of him that sent chills down my spine.

Ultimately, it was this darkness that forced me to end the relationship.

"You need help," I told him.

"I know."

"I need help, too," I said gently, touching his face. "You go and get better for you, and I'll go get better for me. Once we are in a better place, we'll get back together," I say hopefully.

"Promise?" he asked.

"Promise," I reply, kissing his cheek.

We both sought help for our issues. Me for my depression and him for his bipolar disorder.

We still saw each other daily at work and discussed our progress.

He proudly reported his doctor put him on lithium, and he's feeling much better and having fewer episodes. Things seemed to be moving in the right direction.

Work had an after-hours gathering at the local dive bar. It wasn't my thing, but one of my co-workers wouldn't take no for an answer. Secretly, I was hoping to see John there.

When I arrived, John was already intoxicated and tipsy. He was talking to another female co-worker. He quickly stepped away from her when he saw me walk in. Jealousy filled me. She was his ex. He tried to talk to me, but I waved him off.

"You're nothing but a whore," I hear his voice across the room. He was talking to his ex. He hurled a few more drunken insults at her. It was not him. It was his dark demon.

I didn't care for the woman on the receiving end of his abuse, but she also didn't deserve that kind of treatment either.

"John, stop!" I demanded. I was the only one with the power to command his demon. "You're drunk. Let me take you home," I offered.

He agreed, and I took him on the quick ten-minute drive to his house.

He paused before exiting the car.

"Will you come in and look at Bubbles?" he asked. Bubbles was the dog that we got when we were together.

"She has a runny nose and isn't eating well," he continued.

"Sure," I said, putting the car in park.

We headed into the back of the house where the dogs were kept.

"She looks fine," I said, facing him. But it wasn't him. It was his demon. I saw no hint of him, just darkness.

He grabbed me, and we argued. He tossed me face down on the bed and pulled my pants down. I froze. I had been in this place before. I didn't fight; I just stared at the wall, waiting for it to end. He stopped and scooted away from me, sitting with his back against the far wall.

"What did I do?" he repeated over and over as the gravity of his actions hit him.

I pull my pants up but still lay on the bed, afraid to move.

"You will never talk to me again," he sobbed.

"Nope," I managed to say. I was numb. I was still processing and in shock.

He slid his hand behind the open bedroom door and pulled a rifle from its hiding spot.

He put it in his mouth, and his hands slid down to the trigger.

"John! No!"

I clambered up from the bed. I could only think about what would stop him. *He won't shoot me*, I thought. I planned to put my head on top of his.

"Stop, please don't," I pleaded as I ran to him.

My face was two inches from his.

"BANG!"

He pulled the trigger. An inhuman scream erupted from my throat.

He didn't die immediately. He screamed a loud, gargled, animal-like scream. He choked on his blood with every breath. I tried to find a way to stop the bleeding, but it wasn't possible. He died on the way to the hospital.

I had to suppress a part of myself during that time. Allowing myself to feel anything wasn't possible. The young, beautiful woman who believed in fairytale love was gone. She shattered, broken into a million pieces. I pushed this broken and beat-up part of myself into a dark cell and locked her away.

After some time, I let her out. She needed to grieve and be grieved, be loved, to be witnessed and supported. I honored her, sat with her, and let her rage. Once the anger was done, it gave space for the murky darkness of depression to seep in.

What's the point? I screamed internally.

Allowing myself to feel would be death. I wanted to end this pain.

I texted my husband, "What's the combination to the gun safe?" He gave it to me, no questions asked. I dialed the number, opened the door, and pulled out my revolver.

My fingers danced lightly over the metallic surface. The bumpy grip fits my hand perfectly. I turned it and stared down the dark tunnel of the barrel. The little honeycomb chambers nestled the bullets snuggly in their places. A quiet calm came over me.

Is this how he felt? I thought.

I held it to my head. It was cold against my temple. That was all I felt.

I don't want to make a mess for my family to clean up.

Should I just go out in the woods?

I took a deep breath and sighed.

Let's give it a minute, and if I still feel like this tomorrow, I can always do it tomorrow.

My inside joke with myself: How procrastination saved my life.

The depression didn't ease up. I couldn't move, think, or feel anything but hopelessness.

I heard a faint whisper pleading with me.

You need community.

I signed up for some online classes and attended a retreat. I told them bits and pieces of my story but held back how close I was to not being here. I had a trip planned to Bolivia. I held onto the hope I would find answers with Grandmother Ayahuasca.

In December of 2023, I found myself in Rurrenabaque, Bolivia. It was a balmy ninety degrees. Any kind of movement left me sweaty and gross. I was on a shaman *dieta*, which meant no deodorant or pleasures of the five senses.

After my afternoon shower, I walked to the sink and looked into a small eight-by-ten mirror nailed to the wall. The other side of the mirror was liquid. This world flowed differently. There was no daytime dream, nighttime dream, or worlds in between. This place simply was. It was alive and digesting all the things brought to it. It was its own magic.

The jungle called to me. I felt like I had returned home. It felt so familiar. Everything hummed with the divine vibration of the Source. I was surrounded by a million bees buzzing in their sweet harmony.

I made my leap and dove deep into my purpose with Mother Ayahuasca as my guide. She flowed into my being and showed me the truth of existence—we are fractals of light in the prism of all things. It's a nameless thing; it just simply is as I am.

I dove into my grief and found myself face-to-face with all the traumas of my past. Ayahuasca showed me how holding these traumas builds a prison that clouds my perspective of reality and restricts my spiritual movement, like a bird in a cage.

I purged my pain, stories, and grief, one by one, freeing me from the constrictions of my trauma story. After each ceremony, I held a burial for the things I purged the night before. I gave space to grieve and feel. The jungle happily received and digested it, transforming it into something beautiful.

I wandered the jungle alone, seeing the world in a new light, free from bars and restrictions. I am simply in a moment of gratitude to simply be.

THE MEDICINE

During my journey with Ayahuasca, a process came to me on how to transform thoughts that did not serve me.

It's called the Rainbow Breath.

- Find a comfortable space where you'll be undisturbed for a few minutes.
- Take three deep breaths in your nose and out of your mouth to help settle yourself.
- As the intrusive thoughts come into focus, take a long, deep breath.
- As you take this breath, visualize it turning into a rainbow.
- Let this rainbow swirl around your body and envelop the thoughts not serving you.
- Breathe out the rainbow for the trees, grass, and other plant beings to digest and transmute.
- You may need to repeat it a few times if it's a particularly sticky thought.

I have found I'll yawn or even burp on certain occasions. This is good. It's a type of purge that helps to remove what is no longer serving you.

One other valuable teaching Aya gave me was this:

When we give our thoughts emotion, we give them control.

Kim Eden is an Intuitive Empath, PSYCH-K® Practitioner, Reiki master, NLP practitioner, holistic herbalist, hypnosis practitioner, life coach, and ordained minister. These are just labels. The reality is she is an energetic being having a human experience and simply is. She feels it's her purpose in life to be the vessel that light shines through—to offer hope to the hopeless.

Kim grew up on a rural desert farm in southern Arizona. She spent most of her childhood lost in her imagination. The open desert was her playground; her best friends were her horses, dogs, goats, and cats that called the farm home.

Growing up, she was always the oddball and outcast. She saw the world differently, even at a young age. She could see the energy that flowed into everything. She realized she was called to help and could hold space for others. Kim does not believe one modality will heal everything.

This belief has led Kim to learn different modalities. For over 25 years, she has been working on her spiritual development. She has attended courses at Arthur Findlay College to study mediumship and psychic development. She has numerous certifications and additional training in holistic modalities, energy psychology, and energy work. She has traveled to learn with shamans, maestros, and healers throughout North and South America.

She credits Stephanie Urbina Jones and Jeremy Pajer, at Freedom Folk and Soul, for giving her a solid foundation.

She is grateful to Miguel Kavlin, at Sach Runa in Bolivia, for his retreat, which allowed her the space for healing.

Connect with Kim:

Website: https://www.peacefulpath.net/

Email: Kimeden@Peacefulpath.net

Facebook: https://www.facebook.com/peacefulpathinnerillumination

YouTube: https://www.youtube.com/@peacefulpath1866

CHAPTER 8

THE GIFTS YOU WERE BORN WITH

Exploring Purpose Through Dream Traveling

Jan Hatcher

"All that we see or seem is but a dream within a dream."

~ Edgar Allan Poe

MY STORY

Standing near the wreckage, watching the reporters gather to announce the demise of this famous actress, I knew she was dead, but she was still in one piece. Just like the infamous Babushka woman pictured in JFK's assassination photos, I, too, was an unidentified witness. I stood there knowing the facts of the scene as my adolescent physical body lay asleep in my bed.

We fill our days with a chosen task, then retreat every evening only to get up and choose again what this body in this time at this specific place will perform. Is this all we do daily, or is there another dimension we experience while our physical body rests? I know the latter to be true.

Some of us have one magical day after another, yet many do not, as they have not yet woken to realize the choice is actually theirs to make.

Many are still acting out the thought processes of a parent, teacher, or mentor and not living out their own ideas and beliefs. To me, 'to be awake' means the decision to truly see the reality of our current time and our role within it. Prophets have spoken and written of these times, and to not recognize the chilling truths of climate change, war, and the lack of empathy toward humankind is ignorant.

The people I'm referring to as *awake* are people sensitive to these changes and reaching out to learn and heal all they can about their individual spirits and bring to the forefront their genius or gifts that they may have been told to ignore, or, in my case, told were evil. I'm a seeker of my truth and grieve the loss of 58 years of not realizing my gifts, one of them being a *dream traveler*.

> *"All human beings are also dream beings. Dreaming ties all mankind together."*
>
> ~ Jack Kerouac

Mom walked on two years ago this past June. She was certainly ready, often wondering out loud what the purpose was once the body no longer responded to the needs of the individual or the mind no longer capable of making choices and learning new things.

I admired how she created a safe home for her children to be raised, how she believed in natural healing, and her love of family, music, and beauty. It wasn't her fault that she was ignorant of the many gifts a human mind was capable of, like dream traveling. Yet for her generation, whatever was of the unknown, the unseen, and not in the Bible, was considered evil.

I suppose the time between now and the day of this event that changed my life has blurred some details. The date is easy to find, seeing it was a famous actress who died that morning, June 29, 1967.

I was twelve, when a maiden begins her moon cycle, an incredibly sensitive time in a female's life. Since it was summer, we all had different directions to go that morning. As I came into the kitchen for breakfast, everyone else was busy making cereal and toast while listening to the radio announcer with alarming news of the night before. He told his audience that Jayne Mansfield was killed in a car accident in New Orleans. He went on to say that she had been decapitated, at which point I said she had not. This didn't ruffle any feathers; everyone just kept on rushing around, getting ready to partake in whatever plans they had made for the day. Maybe I said it more than once, repeating, "I was there, and she died, but she didn't lose her head."

No one really paid any attention to me, which was the usual response to this third-born. However, this morning was different. My mom heard what I said and promptly took me to another room. She told me I must never do whatever I did to acquire that knowledge. Then she said that whatever I did was evil. I told her in my dream, I was there at the scene and saw the woman was killed, but she didn't lose her head as the announcer said. I was arguing the truth of the event, and she was judging how I acquired this information, but I didn't understand.

In hindsight, I thought dreaming like this was normal for everyone. Why would you question something you knew? I didn't have the knowledge of what happened, or how it happened, or why I was able to tell my family she didn't lose her head.

I wasn't given any time to think about it; I just knew I was there at the accident and witnessed the truth of the reported account. My mind wasn't mature enough to question my mother's decision that I ignore what happened, to eliminate the possibility of traveling while sleeping, or what it may have meant. It never dawned on me that there may possibly be varieties of ways to continue living while the body slept or other realms parallel to ours, like the kind we see in sci-fi movies. These ideas of parallel realms are out there teasing our minds with immense probabilities as scientists are constantly discovering new truths about the expanse of our brains, spirits, and souls.

If I could've ventured out into the study of what that all meant at twelve years of age, I wonder what my life would've looked like. But the truth is that it was too soon, and the landscape was still too primitive and distrustful of the unseen. The only way to acknowledge the unknown was to call it 'religion' and assign rules and limitations as guided by centuries of multiple interpretations from various religions. Religious leaders still battle today for the minds of the unawakened and reinterpret the ancient texts to fit whatever the current times dictate to manipulate the masses.

Soon after my dream traveling disclosure, I was told it was time to get baptized. I had to publicly tell the world I believed in only Jesus when I didn't. I didn't know what I believed, but I was sure there wasn't only one way to be in kinship with the unknown, to be in harmony with the spirits, and to hear from my higher self throughout my day. My findings were that all tribes had names for the same unseen energy of the collective mind, and it didn't matter what you called your higher power. In other cultures, a *seer* or *sage* was given the task of assisting the tribe members with their gifts. Still, those in denial of the unseen worlds instead separated those with a special gift and labeled them, imprisoned them, or medicated them to a state of compliance. I was simply told what I did was *evil*, and I was to never speak of it again.

Life is a process, and evidently, my gift was not for me to learn just yet; therefore, it was unconsciously tucked away and filed as a great loss, a part of my soul that detached, laid down, and waited for me to find it again. That was fifty-eight years ago, and much has happened since then that I don't regret. Nor would I want any do-overs, but part of the grief of losing that part of me makes me sometimes wonder who I would be if I developed that gift sooner. As in all grief, my *what-if* thoughts come in waves of depression and sadness, and then I'd go back into reinventing who I'll choose to be next, not knowing that part of my soul that separated from me as a child is *still* missing.

It wasn't until much later in my life that Mom confessed to being able to speak in tongues, which was okay because it was something people did in the Bible and, therefore, *not* evil as she perceived my dream traveling to be. But it told me she had a special connection to the collective mind and to her higher self. It made me think that was how I chose her to be my mom. Yes, I believe we choose our parents and then spend an extraordinary amount of time figuring out why.

From that point on, so much of my life was not of a harmonized flow with my higher self. I tried to fit in even though I knew I was different. The level of high, intense energy and thoughts addressing the volatile times I experienced in my youth, away from the confines of my family's religion, was extremely difficult to manage. There was a lot of searching for who my tribe really was. The nation was still at war, which I fought against. I fought for equal rights for women. Then, of course, that subconscious theme that my natural state of being was *evil* may have caused havoc in my waking life.

I tackled life as though I was totally fearless and certainly thought of myself as badass, but deep inside beat the heart of the dream traveler, and I, therefore, searched for her, to be reconnected with that part of myself, my true self, my happy self not knowing she was actually missing. My deep search began with my sobriety.

When you know you have reached the bottom, you either get sober or you die. I was a mom; I chose sobriety. I chose to get away from the numbing devices people find themselves pursuing to forget—to forget all the past choices that developed a well-rounded, wild, crazy life story, but it did nothing for the relationships in my world. I didn't know why I lived in so many states, swinging from job to job or trying so hard to find my purpose. Mom was thoroughly convinced her purpose was to raise Christian women, be a good wife, and work hard so she and Dad could live comfortably. At least, that's what I saw and believed she felt her purpose was. I didn't know what mine was. I guess I figured it would just appear, and I'd know. Still, in every job, every relationship, every attempt at recognizing my purpose, I saw hypocrisy, lack of integrity, deceit, no honor, no love. Every corner I turned was like a huge wall, keeping me from finding that purpose, that alleged contract we make before coming to Earth. I suppose it could've been my missing soul part that created this wall in order to protect that little girl from being hurt again. Or was it from years of ignoring the loss of her that built that wall? Of course, it was me building all that negativity, that callus on my spirit, and only I could knock it down.

Again, my children being my motivation, I started studying. Books fell off shelves on my path. Healers, shamans, and sages showed up at the most curious of times and gave me a little nudge. I started finding groups of women searching for their truths and purpose and joined in with them. One group was a phone call I led with women around the country, and we'd exchange two things with each other once a week. We each shared something that changed for us that week and a gratitude. Sharing these two weekly events was like stepping stones that encouraged and lifted each of us strangers to a better place of self-love.

Then, there were times I'd fall away because the inevitable shadow came into the process and caused doubt and opened a way for that unjustified wave of fear to slide onto my path.

I believe love is one attribute that makes a person whole. I also believe that love can be found in many ways, such as nature, art, food, a gathering of friends, moving streams, a walk in the woods, or ocean waves on a shore—anything bringing a calm, gentle warmth to my soul. I believe love can also entice the spirit to invoke the gifts one carries in their heart. Ideally, love with a partner is the natural way to invoke the gifts of the heart, but this partnership often does not come to fruition.

"She remembered who she was and the game changed."

~ Lalah Delia

It has only been through a guided journey that I've even come close to regaining that gift of dream traveling. Group healings, drums, sound baths, visually guided sessions, classes in shamanism, Shirodhara, and many books on dreaming are only a few of the tools I've tried and used to dream travel again. Still, it's not the natural self-induced travel I did when I was 12 when my heart was innocent and connected easily to my higher self. When children use the gifts our brains are capable of, the ones that society now encourages them to ignore, life could easily move within a conscious state of bliss and do miraculous things. It's their gifts and natural abilities to connect to the energies of love we should be learning.

Women and their gifts have often been feared. My studies as long ago as junior high were stories based on the abuses women have had to endure. The abilities of a woman to produce another human being should be revered and precious in the eyes of all, and not to forget it's her body, and she has complete sovereignty not only over her body but also any abilities she has been gifted. It's the same as the wisdom of the elders that should be revered, and they, too, must be given respect and not be treated as nonessential. I guess that's why I appreciate the ways of the native cultures; they respect all living things, and all living things have something precious to offer the tribe.

THE MEDICINE

To use the dreamworld where random visuals and storylines are actually serving a purpose which helps our subconscious work out all the mysteries of the waking world, you have to first be able to remember what you are dreaming.

I have been recording my dreams for years, and I notice patterns, messages, unique items, spirit animals, family members living and passed, short scenarios, and more. Sometimes my dreams repeat, often with different faces, but the storyline is the same. The more I record my dreams, the less crazy they seem. I'm now to the point where my dreams are similar to a mini-movie and enhance my waking world.

Tips: Have a pen and notebook next to your bed, and upon waking, immediately write down a title of the dream and assign a feeling to the dream. Example: Walking the dog, feeling angry. Then you will be able to remember more of your dream. Another trick is to take vitamin B before bed. There are also certain stones to set next to your bed or under the pillow.

Herbs will enhance dreaming as well.

External: Anise's licorice-like fragrance can keep nightmares away. Mugwort enhances prophetic dreams. Sage leaves bring more peacefulness and healing. Burdock is effective at keeping negativity, anger, and sadness away. Mullein can help you to ward off nightmares.

Internal: Valerian root for more vivid dreams. Best method: tea or tincture. Ginko Biloba increases brain function, making dreams more vivid. Best method: capsule or tincture. Peppermint enhances lucid and vivid dreaming. Best method: tea or tincture.

We all dream several times a night; therefore, why not start paying attention to your other life, your life beyond the waking world? When you're first paying attention to your dreams, there are similar themes: Something is chasing you, you lose your purse or car, getting lost in a huge building and can't find the exit, big cats chasing you, and your legs won't work, you try to scream, and nothing comes out, to name just a few. As you practice, first remembering your dreams and then recording them, you'll notice those themes change. They'll begin to make more sense. The goal is to use your dreaming to improve your awake life.

There are dream coaches, classes, and books available that teach us how to record and interpret our dreams as well as how to prompt our dreams in order to create the life we wish to live, as well as healing for humankind and our world. I believe all that's necessary is the conviction to search for your gifts, and the Universe will provide. Be open. Be aware. Be grateful.

MEMORY OF A SAGE

A street vendor in Missoula, Montana handed me a child's toy as I was looking at her handmade earrings. She placed the toy into my hand and told me I should keep it, for it belonged to a part of me that was missing. She named that part of me Happy and hoped I would get her back, for she is trying to return home.

Jan Hatcher is a lifelong explorer and compassionate practitioner of natural, effective healing modalities that have benefitted herself and others. Upon receiving her Bachelor of Science in Exercise Science at 44 years of age, Jan conducted innovative aqua therapies as a personal trainer for medical exercise at Vanderbilt Medical Center. Jan went on to work in corporate wellness, developing customized health programs through companies' human resource departments across seven states. Jan has served as a life coach and medical exercise trainer and is certified in QiGong, Reiki, ThetaHealing, and End-of-Life Specialist. Jan's passions are the study of natural healing modalities, fiber artistry, traveling, Native beliefs, music, hiking, reading, and empowering mothers of newborns.

Jan Hatcher P O Box 143 Thompsons Station, TN 37179-9998

CHAPTER 9

AUTHENTIC SELF-MOTIVATION FOR BUSINESS LEADERS

A Shamanic Ceremony to Unwind Your Relentless Achiever

Jill "GiGi" Austin, MBA

"Who looks outside, dreams; who looks inside, awakes."

~ Carl Jung

MY STORY

For three decades in corporate America, I sent my *warrior yang* into battle, leaving my softer *yin* behind. My relentless achiever ruled my existence, winning a life of success with little joy.

Striving to belong with the *big boys* at the executive leadership table, I motivated myself with harsh words and critical thoughts. I didn't know I had a choice.

A dream woke me to the truth.

"Will you return to me soon?" I ask my warrior soulmate, willing it to be so in my dream. He pauses at the door, poised to leave for battle, and turns to look into my eyes. Instantly, my heart knows he may never return.

Alone in my grief, I sink down on my knees, and my heart floods with tears. *I've lost him already.* A chasm opens inside, and its inky dark begins to overtake me as a diffused light appears in the room. I lift my eyes to see three beings illuminated by the gentle glow.

"You are in the middle of the Prophesy of the Warrior and the Rose," declares the first being.

"When the *warrior* can stop and hear the *song of the rose*, he will transform into the guardian, fiercely loyal to the needs of those he protects and serves," adds another being.

"Rose will unfold into a safe space and freely share her creative, intuitive, and nurturing gifts," says the last being.

*I'm the rose, I woke up thinking. Oh, **and** the warrior.*

Climbing the ranks in hierarchical and male-dominated work structures, I buried or disguised all the qualities I deemed *too soft* to safely reveal and still succeed. The more I suppressed my gentle *rose* nature, the more armored and driven my *warrior* became.

Something vital was missing from my outwardly successful life of high achievement—big title, big responsibilities, big money, big house, big vacations—and big void.

In meditation, I asked for help from a guide. A figure in a beautiful white gauzy dress glided forward and spoke as she held out her hands.

True empowerment comes from inner alignment. You need to marry yourself.

Marry myself? What do you mean?

Picture the ancient symbol for Yin-Yang—a circle with a dark swirl and light swirl intertwined. You're seeing the divine dance between the divine feminine, the yin, and the divine masculine, the yang. The Divine marriage in motion.

Your energies are meant to support and complement each other in a sacred partnership.

Thank you for your gift of knowledge. What is your name?

I am Beulah. I am the goddess of marriage and protection.

What'll it take to get my yin and yang to play together nicely, let alone be ready for marriage? Let's try counseling and see what happens.

"We're here intending to work things out between you in preparation for marriage. Are you both willing to try?" Both parties reluctantly nod their assent. "Good. Yin, you start. What do you want to say to Yang?"

Yin surges to her feet, and with hands on her hips, she shouts, "You never listen to me when I tell you to take a break! All that stress burns us out and makes us sick. When I try to rest and take care, you call me lazy and warn me if I don't get up and press through it, I may never feel like working again."

"Hold on a second! You're not being fair," rebutted Yang. "I had to join the 'yang gang' to reach the top. If I hadn't pushed, competed, strived to be the best, and worked the hardest and longest hours, I'd never have made it to the leadership table. I had to outman the men to make it."

"Congratulations. Your relentless drive for accomplishment won us a life of achievement at the cost of joy, fun, friends, relationships, tenderness, and beauty," Yin declared as she burst into tears and slid down into her seat.

"And another thing," Yin sobbed, "You ignore me. You've hijacked my gifts of intuition and creativity, cloaked them with data and cleverness, and used them to fuel your success, taking all the credit. You believe you've done it all by yourself, but I'm still here, and I'm lonely."

"There's your complaining voice again. No wonder I'd rather work than spend time with you."

"Can we take a pause here? Let's take a deep breath. This is hard. It's understandable you feel this way. You are not alone in these feelings. The same internal discord you're experiencing is playing out in the world around you. If a yin-yang imbalance isn't addressed internally, you project it externally on others, especially those closest to you. Sound familiar?"

Yin and Yang glanced at each other and looked away. "That's what happened this morning when I wanted to relax instead of rushing off to exercise class," observed Yin. "You called me an undisciplined mess!"

"I was right!" exclaimed Yang. "We need regular exercise, or the next thing you know, we'll never go to class again, and our bodies will suffer."

"Since *you* didn't listen to my needs, I turned to hubby and asked him to walk with me instead of going to class. I knew it was too cold to go and assumed he'd turn me down," confessed my Yin.

"How'd that work out for you?" scoffed Yang.

"Hubby refused. But I see now it was *his* internal *yin* articulating his needs, and *his* internal *yang* honoring them, unlike *your* disrespectful response," Yin said pointedly.

"What I see is *you* were looking for someone to blame for your laziness! I was doing my job," defended Yang. "How else will I keep us moving if I don't push and prod?"

"It's not just me we're talking about," shot back Yin. "The team suffered from your over-achiever drive. You had to *make* yourself talk to them every morning. You wanted to skip small talk because it was a waste of time."

"Give me a break! Every minute I spent chatting was another minute I had to stay late to get work done. Besides, I hid it well."

"Don't kid yourself! Your 3 a.m. action-item emails greeted them first thing. They were on to you, believe me. The team wondered if you cared about them personally or if they were just a means to get stuff done."

"What was I supposed to do!?" Yang exclaimed, throwing up his hands.

"Time out! This is big! Let's take another breath. Recognizing the pattern goes a long way to changing it. We'll talk about other ways to motivate yourself in a moment. First, I'm going to ask you to indulge me."

"What do you want us to do?" sighed Yin.

"Stand up, please."

"What silly-ass thing is this?" grumbled Yang, rising to his feet in slow motion.

Yin shot Yang a look of impatience. "Stop being dismissive before you even know what we're doing."

"On the count of three, we're going to turn to our left counterclockwise in three complete circles."

"Oh, for the love of…"

"Would you shut up and just do it!" broke in Yin."

"One, two, three, turn once. Turn again. Turn the last time. Nicely done. Now, please take a seat."

"Why'd we do that?" asked Yang.

"Let me ask you this first. Where are you both at?"

"The breath I've been holding for a long time has released," replied Yin.

Yang tilted his head to the side with a quizzical expression and admitted, "My blood pressure has come down a few notches."

"Thanks for those observations. We'll explore motivation alternatives by starting with chemistry."

"I hated chemistry," groaned Yin.

"Chemically speaking, you were stuck in a dopamine loop."

"I thought dopamine was a good thing, egging us on to get 'er done," observed Yang.

"Yes, and you've heard the expression 'Too much of a good thing?' If we keep driving hard to achieve without cooling our system down, the body produces more dopamine than our brain can handle. Yet, we yearn for the reward, pushing for more, feeling like we can't get enough."

"You make it sound like I'm an addict," Yang said, narrowing his eyes.

"In a sense, you are. Does the term 'workaholic' ring a bell? Relentless?"

"Nailed it!" exclaimed Yin.

"I don't like the workaholic label, but what's wrong with never giving up?" questioned Yang.

"It's not wrong. It's just not helpful, chemically speaking. When dopamine production is in over-drive, we can't access our brain's logic, strategy, and problem-solving function to help us discern what is worth spending our energy on. To know when enough is enough or when to pick our battles."

"Are you saying when I'm 'jacked-up,' I can't think clearly?" Yang asked.

"Exactly. And when experiencing stress, we all get chemically jacked-up, to alert us to potential harm. Stress can come from an outside threat like facing a bear or an *overbearing* boss."

{Groan}

"Or stress can come from the *bear* inside being tyrannical or self-critical. Your body can't tell the difference between the outside and inside bears."

"Ugh!" grunted Yang. "Bears? Really?"

"You mentioned the idea of cooling our system down, interrupted Yin. "Is that why we did the three turns?"

"Yes. Step one is noticing the stressful pattern and shifting the energy by unwinding it and neutralizing the charge. Next comes self-compassion, which soothes the savage beast—or bear, in this case. Self-compassion produces oxytocin, the love chemical."

"Are you kidding! Self-compassion? Love chemical?" said Yang with a head shake.

"Self-compassion is not for the faint of heart. You'll be happy to hear it has two sides—one tender, one fierce."

"I vote for the fierce one."

"We'll get there. When in over-drive, the way into our strong, fierce side is our tender side. Remember, we need oxytocin to calm our system to access thoughtful and logical action. Picture comforting a good friend who is stressed out or struggling. Would you call them names or make fun of them for being upset?"

"They wouldn't be a close friend for long," observed Yin. "I'd say, 'That sounds hard,' 'You are not alone,' and 'I'm here for you.'"

"How about you, Yang?"

"I'd ask how I can help and tell them, 'I've got your back, buddy. You've got this.'"

"Now exchange seats with your friend and tend to each other with the same comfort, kindness, and support."

Taking Yang's hand, Yin said compassionately, "It's hard when you think you can't let up or you'll lose your edge. You're not alone. Plenty of leaders feel the same. But it's exhausting."

"What are you asking of me?"

"To stop draining all our energy on work and reprioritize what we do spend it on. More juice for family, community, and yes, exercise, too, please."

"You're not asking me to stop getting things done?" Yang asked, relieved.

"I'm asking you to do things *differently*. To guard our power and wield it wisely, aligned with what we most value."

"Yang, are you willing to listen to Yin's needs and channel your determination into protecting and guarding your energetic resources? To inspire and motivate with fierce self-compassion, standing for what matters most?"

"I am."

"Yin, are you willing to be grateful for all Yang provides? And to soothe the strife and struggle with tender self-compassion and kindness."

"I am."

"Excellent! Let's end with takeaways and next steps."

"I love knowing how to intervene 'chemically' on the over-drive cycle," observed Yin. "It feels blame-free."

Yang said, "I like knowing how to access the fierce side through the tender side, thanks to Yin. Notice. Unwind. Soothe. Support. Act thoughtfully *and* fiercely."

Yin beamed with delight. "I love feeling like a couple again. How about you?"

Yang nodded. "It feels good to be on the same team. Energizing and empowering."

"Now we know how to break out of over-drive when we find ourselves there. But what do we do about the past?" questioned Yin.

"Agreed. I'm ready to become a *recovering* 'yang-ster.' Don't I need to make amends?'"

"You've hit on 'next.' Amends help us resist slipping into relentless habits or patterns. We'll attend a shamanic ceremony to clear the past by claiming harmful actions, forgiving, and offering gratitude. Amends will flow into your marriage ceremony. How does that sound?"

Yin and Yang nodded and smiled.

Yang, the *warrior*, heard the *song of the rose*—Yin's soothing self-compassion—and transformed from a relentless achiever into a fierce guardian.

That dear Reader, is how the prophecy came true.

THE MEDICINE
A Shamanic Ceremony

Rest comfortably where you are safe and undisturbed.

- Breathe.
- Listen to the drumbeat.
- Follow it within to the deepest place of heart you know.
- Notice an opening to a passageway.
- Before you enter, an ally shows up.
- Allow your ally to guide you through the passageway.
- Emerge into a beautiful meadow space.

Step into your Yang.

- It's time to be cleaned and healed.
- Go back in time to a moment or situation where you, Yang, caused hurt, harm, or pain to Yin. Where you may have reacted with (or from) aggression, callousness, obsession, overachievement, acted without regard for the consequences, disrespect, or ignored her and went it alone.
- Breathe.
- Accept that it happened. No Judgment. No resistance.

- Breathe.
- Feel the pain that was caused and imagine the consequences.
- Accept that it happened. No Judgment.
- Recreate the moment or situation and imagine you responded proactively and notice how you feel.
- Bathe yourself in forgiveness. Forgive. Let go of the old that has bound you to the dark moment and bring in the Light.
- Promise yourself you will notice when the invitation to be reactive arises and commit to pause and respond proactively.

From this place of lightness, forgive yourself for anything you did or imagined you did to cause hurt, harm, or pain to Yin.

Bring in the light. Say, "I forgive myself and release the energy of the past."

Move to a moment where you came shining through for Yin. Perhaps you stood up for her, achieved something important or brought focus. Feel that moment. Bathe it in gratitude. Say, "I am so grateful for my ability to manifest, focus, organize, and assert."

(Pause: add other qualities.)

Thank Yang. Ask him to wait by the altar.

Step into Yin.

- It's time to be cleaned and healed.
- Go back in time to a moment or situation where you caused hurt, harm, or pain to Yang. Where you may have reacted in irritability, resentfulness, martyrdom, smothering, withdrawing, or become very critical.
- Breathe.
- Accept that it happened. No judgment. No resistance.
- Breathe.
- Feel the pain that was caused and imagine the consequences.
- Accept that it happened. No judgment.

- Recreate the moment or situation and imagine you responded proactively and notice how you feel.
- Bathe yourself in forgiveness. Forgive. Let go of the old that has bound you to the dark moment and bring in the light.
- Promise yourself you will notice when the invitation to be reactive arises when you get triggered, and commit to pause and respond proactively.

From this place of lightness, forgive yourself for anything you did or imagined you did to cause hurt, harm, to pain to Yang.

Bring in the light. Say, "I forgive myself and release the energy of the past."

Move to a moment where you came shining through for Yang. Perhaps nurtured, brought a wide lens view or intuition. Feel that moment. Bathe it in gratitude. Say, "I'm so grateful for my ability to create, intuit, have perspective and compassion."

(Pause: add other qualities.)

Join Yang at the altar.

THE WEDDING

Face each other and join hands.

We now reunite our divine energies with these sacred vows.

I, Yang, say to Yin:

I honor you. I respect you.

I cherish your qualities of creativity, perspective, compassion, and intuition.

(Pause: add other qualities.)

I support you in your power, purpose, and passions.

I promise to bring my full Yang self to our marriage, our sacred union.

I will delight in you, and I ask you to delight in me.

I, Yin, say to Yang:

I honor you. I respect you.

I cherish your qualities of manifesting, focus, organization, and assertiveness.

(Pause: add other qualities.)

I support you in your power, purpose, and passions.

I promise to bring my full Yin self to our marriage, our sacred union.

I will delight in you and ask you to delight in me.

Together, say:

With these vows, we open a refreshed relationship container.

We trust in the light and invite in the unknown.

We ask for a relationship container filled with vitality, love, fulfillment, joy, and bliss,

Or something even better,

Beyond our *wildest dreams.*

We promise to notice our triggers and moments of reactivity,

And commit to pause and communicate with each other and work it through, that we may restore our divine dance.

Fully embrace. Dance around the meadow.

It's time to return.

- Bring Yin and Yang fully into your being. Picture them clasping hands together in front of your heart. This will remind you to dance.
- Your ally returns to show you the way.
- Travel from the meadow into the passageway.
- Pause at the exit. Face your ally.
- Your ally has a message or wedding gift for you.
- Listen to the message. Understand the gift's purpose.
- Place the gift somewhere safe.
- Thank your ally.

- Return to your body.
- Awaken.

Download the ceremony audio here:

https://www.recoveringyangster.com/

ACKNOWLEDGMENTS

Much gratitude for the teachings from the Power Path School of Shamanism on Yin/Yang, The Kabbalah Center for the forgiveness ritual, the Center for Mindful Self-Compassion for the chemistry lesson, and my friend Michelle Miller for three turns to the left.

Jill "GiGi" Austin, MBA, CEO, and founder of GrowthFlows, coaches business leaders to find their authentic leadership style and self-management approach. After three decades of relentless achievement in corporate America, Jill refers to herself as the original *recovering Yangster*. She combines her Yang *and* Yin qualities with her leadership experience and business acumen to help others unwind their relentless achiever and recover their joy.

Nationally known as a trendsetter in her industry and field, Jill served as Chief Marketing Officer and Assistant Vice Chancellor of Strategic Marketing at Vanderbilt University Medical Center. She was responsible for brand identity, market positioning and presence, marketing strategies, and growth for Vanderbilt and its affiliated network. Jill also chaired the Association of American Medical Colleges' General Institutional Advancement Council.

Having trained in various energy-shifting practices, Jill is an advanced shamanic practitioner and a certified Feng Shui consultant. Additionally, she has completed formal studies in astrology, the Kabbalah, mindful self-compassion, Google's Search Inside Yourself, tarot, Strength-Finder, chakras, the divine feminine, sound healing, and VortexHealing®.

A classical musician, Jill loves to sing and has been a life-long participant in various settings, from school and church choirs to Nashville Symphony Chorus and circle song groups.

She currently serves as Board Chair of Vox Grata Women's Choir and is an alumni member of Leadership Nashville, Leadership Middle Tennessee, and the Healthcare Executive Forum.

Jill is married to her soulmate, Tracy. She has five adult daughters and sons, including spouses, and is "GiGi" to three grandkids.

TRX is Jill's favorite exercise. Her Yin *and* Yang agree.

Connect with Jill:

Email: info@GrowthFlows.com

LinkedIn: https://www.linkedin.com/in/jill-austin-8492882/

CHAPTER 10

THE FATHER WOUND

Manifesting the Love That's Missing

Emilie Collins, RN, AS, BSN, MSN

"Forgiveness is not always easy. At times, it feels more painful than the wound we suffered, to forgive the one that inflicted it. And yet, there is no peace without forgiveness."

~ Marianne Williamson

MY STORY

You can survive without a father. I identified someone who loved, nourished, and cherished me. He became my surrogate father.

I placed Dad in an imaginary box with a lid and set him aside. Up went a heart wall so my heart would not break. Unexpectedly, sadness, anger, and weeping would leap out. The grief lasted years. The ache in my heart was always close—just under the surface.

Dad demonstrated kindness, generosity, and integrity. He had a strong faith and was ethical. I learned so many things from him. He taught me to put a worm on a fishhook, to love music, and to play the saxophone. To teach me to dance, I stood on his shoes. He held my hands. We danced. He was my hero and protector.

The United States was actively engaged in WWII. My ancestry traces back to Scandinavia. Our country and family farms invaded. The young men of this Viking lineage signed up for service, including my dad and his two brothers.

Dad, the middle son, remained stateside. The Army sent his two brothers into combat zones. The oldest returned home. The youngest died overseas.

Their mother died young. Dad was five. My spinster auntie helped raise the boys, filling the mother role. For years, she grieved the death of her sister and the young man buried in France.

Longevity is a gift. It allows one to see the big picture and outcome. Deployment and grief are common themes for military families. Strength of character and courage is advantageous.

Sept 1945. The war is over. Dad returns to South Dakota. I'm a toddler.

March 1958. Family meeting.

"Girls, I've something to tell you. Mom and I are having a challenging time providing for you girls."

"Dad, what does that mean?" I asked him.

"I'm getting a new job. We will be moving."

"What? I thought you liked your job. I'm confused."

"The Air Force has a better job for me," he replied. "We're going on an adventure to Arizona."

Dad presented moving as an adventure, and I liked adventures. We left on a cold, blustery winter day. I was in seventh grade.

April 1958. Family meeting.

"I've news. I'm going on an adventure."

"Dad, can I come too?" I asked, expecting a positive reply.

"Not this time. The place is far away. Only soldiers go."

"That doesn't seem fair," I told him as my heart sank.

Dad deployed for six months to a remote island site. My first time without him, and I felt his absence.

I love you, Dad. There's a hole in my heart without you. Hurry back home.

Mom worked diligently, keeping us busy and adventure-focused. I played saxophone in the school marching band, learned to swim, and discovered scorpions in my shoes. That summer, we went to California. We visited Disneyland and other fun places. I saw my cousins and played in the ocean for the first time.

When Dad's assignment ended and he returned to us, all was well.

My heart is singing and healing.

August 1958. Family meeting.

"Girls, we're all going on an adventure."

"Dad, all of us?" I asked, knowing that sometimes we weren't included.

"Yes. We're moving to Florida. My new job is there."

"Dad, are they going to send you away after we get there?" I inquired. My heart waited for his response, hoping he would stay.

"I don't think they will." I felt relief, if only for a moment, in his somewhat positive reply.

September 1958 to June 1961. I had my father's love and attention. I had friends and amazing adventures. We visited state tourist destinations.

We lived on the ocean side of Merrit Island. From the beach, I looked skyward. I saw astronaut Allen Shepard launched into space. My high school band went to New York City to march in the Macy's Thanksgiving Day parade.

"Dad, the sea turtles are laying eggs. Can I watch?" I asked him.

"Be quiet. No flashlight," he replied.

"Dad, I love you, " I told him as my heart filled with warmth in his attentive presence.

"Dad, I need your help. My bike tires need air."

"I'll get the pump."

June 1961. Family meeting.

"Adventure time again."

"Dad, where are we going?" I asked.

"Only soldiers go to Alaska. It's too cold for you. I'll be gone eighteen months."

"Nooooo. Not again, Dad. That's forever."

Mom packed. We returned to South Dakota. I would be a senior in high school. Clicks and friendships had formed. I was the odd duck out.

This is not fun.

Playing saxophone in the band made my life bearable.

My godfather, who lived a mile away, stepped up as a surrogate father.

As a child, when Dad deployed, I sang the hymn *In the Garden* written by Austin Miles (1913). I found comfort and peace with the heavenly Father.

May 1962. I graduated from high school. Dad remains in Alaska.

I'm missing you, Dad. The hole in my heart is getting bigger.

September 1962. I entered a South Dakota diploma nursing program. The junior college was two hundred miles away. Everything I took to school fit in a tiny brown suitcase. I had no way to come home.

Dad, I'm missing you. I'll study and make you proud.

January 1963 to May 1966. Dad is in South Carolina. My sister is happy, jumping and singing, "Daddy's home." She was his shadow.

June 1963. I completed my first nursing school year. On my two-week break, I rode a Greyhound bus for three days each way to visit my family. It's been two long years without Dad.

"Hi, Dad. I've really missed you. I'm sad without you. I need hugs," I told him the moment I finally saw him again.

"I missed you too, sweet girl. Come here and get all the hugs you need," he replied. "How's school?"

"I love it. It's fun. Chemistry is hard, but I get it."

"Good for you."

My sad heart is feeling a little better. Yea! I've got four days with Dad.

School was expensive. My godfather loaned me money for tuition. I worked part-time after class.

I miss you, Dad, but I'm busy studying. I need good grades. I want to be a smart nurse.

September 1964. "The Army needs You" banners were everywhere. The Vietnam war was raging. Nurses were essential. Recruiters came offering an incentive for two years' service following graduation. I'm an Army PFC in my senior year.

August 1965. Nursing graduation day was Mom's birthday. I'm now a Second Lieutenant. Dad remained in South Carolina.

I phoned Dad.

"Dad, I'm furious. This makes two graduations and my commissioning you have missed. Why didn't you come? You've no deployment card this time. I miss you. I needed hugs from you."

"You wouldn't understand."

"Might be surprised. Try me." I received no explanation.

November 1965. Officially an RN, I leave for basic training. I learned the technical battlefield skills needed for the injuries we'd encounter. We practiced under mock gunfire and mortar conditions.

Wow, what an eye-opener. I wonder if I've made the right choice joining the Army. Too late now. Punt and get on with your job, girl. Going to make Dad proud even if I die. I want Vietnam.

January 1966. My assignment is an East Coast Army hospital. After touring the hospital, the chief nursing officer said, "You'll be here. This is our obstetrical unit. Come meet your head nurse."

Shit. This was my worst subject, and I didn't like obstetrics. You must be kidding. I want to take care of the sick and injured soldiers. Going to be a long two years.

April 1966. This grief hole in my heart deepened.

Four days with dad in almost five years is not enough.

Dad and I are both on the East Coast. He was a ten-hour drive away. I request four days off. I drove to see my dad, mom, and sister.

"Dad, I need a ton of hugs. I really miss you."

"You look spiffy in your uniform. How long can you stay?"

"Thanks. Two days. I have a four-day pass."

My heart is singing. I love you, Dad. I've missed your laughter and funny jokes. I miss hearing your saxophone playing. I miss your wisdom and lessons. I miss you and all our adventures. You are my hero.

May 1966. My sister graduated from high school. Dad was there. Almost immediately, he deployed to Asia.

More sadness again.

Mom moved to Missouri near her sister. My sister is engaged.

September 1966. My sister is married, while I'm engaged and planning my wedding. I want my dad's blessing on the marriage.

Ah shhhhhit. He will not come any time. Not again. This isn't fair. You missed your youngest daughter's wedding. I'm angry now and incredibly sad. This hole in my heart is getting bigger.

February 1967. On my wedding day, I was holding my godfather's arm. A bittersweet day, and I loved him dearly. Dad remained overseas.

Dad, an occasional short letter is not enough!

October 1967. I'm honorably discharged. I've learned to love obstetrical nursing. With deployed husbands, I witnessed grief surface in the military spouse giving birth.

December 1967. It's my parent's 25th anniversary. Mom called. She was giggly.

"Your dad is arriving today. I pick him up in an hour."

A week later, mom called. She was sobbing uncontrollably.

"What has happened? Who died?"

"Your dad is filing for divorce."

Nooooo! I'm gut-punched and disemboweled. My heart explodes into a million pieces. My life force is exsanguine. I receive an emotional death blow. Dad, don't do this to us. We need our family together again. Please rethink this.

We were a happy, loving family. Letters gave no indication anything had changed and did not prepare us for this emotional bomb.

December 1968. The divorce is final on my parent's 26th anniversary. Dad left five days later, returning to the same base in Asia.

Much later, we learned he had a mistress during his first deployment. He married her ten days after the divorce. She was 26 years younger and close to my age. He was 56.

Dad, you have pissed me off royally. I'm brokenhearted and terribly angry. You old fart, why couldn't you keep your zipper up? So much for the lessons I got about being good.

I'm feeling abandoned, resentful, grief, anger, and devalued.

November 5, 1972. Dad was visiting South Dakota. My sister and I arrive. Dad finally meets his first grandchild, now almost four.

Dad and my sister's husband were in Asia together. We are playing cards. My sister's husband speaks.

"Sir. Don't you have something to tell the family?"

"There's a new baby born last month," Dad replied.

At sixty, he has a three-week-old newborn, an eleven-month-old, a twenty-month-old, and an adopted four-year-old.

What in the world were you thinking? Oh, you weren't thinking with your brain but your crotch. So much for my children getting grandfather time. This hurts big time mega pain.

November 15, 1972. Back to Asia.

My heart is aching. I need you, too, and so does my sister. Are we just throw-away daughters?

August 1974. Dad served 20 years in the Air Force. At 62, he returned to South Dakota with four small children.

Fuck, fuck, fuck. Dad, three of your children are the same ages as your three grandchildren. How am I going to heal this great sadness and anger?

I visited. Dad and family moved into my childhood home.

I'm sobbing on the inside and clinging to my sister. This feels so wrong. I haven't forgiven you. Still hurts, yet grateful you are home. Auntie is 90 and needs you.

April 1975. Dad visited my home only once.

I thought you were coming alone. Shit. Guess the "old stud muffin" didn't have the energy to travel.

December 1975. Christmas was with Dad. My sister and extended family gathered. Auntie was living. My godfather came.

I need all this support. My last Christmas with you was fourteen years ago. I'm sensing this injured daughter's heart might someday heal. This heavy grief and anger feels a tad lighter.

November 1976. I visited Dad.

Sister, hold onto me. Your support will make my visit easier.

Auntie, Dad, and his first two daughters with the three grandchildren posed for a four-generation picture.

January 1997. My family moved to Tennessee near my husband's parents. I'd be 1200 miles from Dad. The boys adored their paternal grandparents. So many fun adventures together. My father-in-law became my surrogate father.

My visits to Dad became infrequent. I tried repairing our relationship.

I'm struggling with this more than you, sister. You live closer with more opportunities for healing.

June 1997. Dreamed a beautiful, buzzy, amazing plan.

August 1997. The setting was perfect. It was the family church constructed by my great-grandparent's family. Dad was wearing a tuxedo. Pastor was at the altar. My husband and witnesses were ready. I just celebrated my 30th anniversary.

"Dad, walk down front with me. I want to talk with Pastor," I suggested.

"Sure," he replied. I grabbed Dad's arm. I'm wearing a pearl-embellished white dress.

"Who gives the woman away?" the pastor asked.

"What?" Dad replied.

"I'm renewing my wedding vows. I want your blessing on my marriage," I explained.

"Oh! Okay."

"Who gives the woman in marriage?" The pastor asked again.

"I do," Dad replied.

My husband gave me a new ring. Precious family members were present but oblivious. Wedding cake was available shortly after that. I received a present from my sister, just like a real wedding. The bees were buzzing.

I'm laughing and smiling inside. My heart is singing. I've received the blessing and a heart transplant. Now I can truly heal my grief-anger and forgive in time. Dad, I got you good! No way was this a half-sister getting the blessing first.

My heart wall came down. I removed Dad from the box.

Dad, stunned, was speechless. Pictures show the depth of his emotional experience. His selfish actions showed on his face – pain, grief, or something else.

It still hurts, Dad!

The planned wedding began. Dad is 85.

After 1997. My infrequent visits were less stressful. It's easier to say, "Hi, Dad." My oldest son played golf with Dad one year and remembers. My youngest has no conscious memory of Dad.

December 2002. Dad celebrated his 90th birthday with all six daughters.

April 2003. Dad received a full military funeral with taps. I saluted him. Three Air Force jets flew formation over the cemetery. One peeled off, indicating a lost comrade.

I'm going to miss you, Dad. I'll love you forever. I finally forgave you. It was challenging work.

January 2024. Grief welled up authoring the story.

My sister writes, "Dad and I were buddies. It's a given that there will be separations in military families. For me, having Dad gone months at a time was very distressing. So much so that when I married a service man, I didn't want children until he was out. I didn't want our kids to suffer the emptiness like I had."

THE MEDICINE

Dreaming began in early childhood. I remember having pictures in my head of me as a nurse. I'd put Band-Aids on everything. Today, we'd call this a vision board. Some dreams manifested quickly, and others took years.

1. Create a dream vision board. Cut out pictures and place them on the poster board.
2. Place the poster where you can see it frequently.
3. Feel gratitude for the Universe providing.

Love is stronger than anger and grief. Forgiveness heals the grieving heart, stops suffering, and prevents illness and disease. Speak (or sing) forgiveness with a grateful heart. The body chemistry changes with gratitude. The body relaxes and calms, and forgiveness can follow.

1. Obtain a journal and use it daily.
2. List what you are grateful for daily: people, places, animals, and others.
3. Review the list often. Send blessings.
4. Notice the emotional-physical improvements in your body.

Needs Assessment.

1. Observe the people, animals, and places in your life.
2. Ask: What do I need to feel loved, nurtured, worthy, and safe? Be specific.
3. Ask questions until the right answers arrive – who, what, where, when, why, and how. Trust and believe in the way.
4. Ask: Is this for my greatest and highest good?
5. Set boundaries. Run from toxic people, places, jobs, and things.
6. Step out in action. Change direction as needed. Use uplifting supportive networks. Be ready to receive.
7. Ask for help.
8. Nurture yourself often.

Heart connection with Source moves in a figure eight pattern.

1. Select a quiet, safe place.
2. Close your eyes, place the right hand over your heart and your left hand on the bottom of your breastbone.
3. Breathing with four counts for each step: In, hold, out, hold. Do this ten times.
4. Return focus to the heart. Breathe normally from now on.
5. Move your intention down into the heart of Gaia and connect. Stay awhile in her love.
6. Return focus to your heart and feel the love.
7. Move intention up to the heart of God, Source, Creator, Great Central Sun, or your word and connect to his heart. Stay a while in this magnificent love.
8. Allow this love to flow back and forth from Gaia — Source through your heart for a while.
9. Return to time and space.

Emilie Collins. She earned a diploma in nursing, an Associate Science degree plus a BSN and MSN degree in nursing. Her area of expertise was obstetrics and pediatrics. Her passion was helping new moms, babies, and children in the hospital and community. She has worked in LDRP mother-baby units and a NICU unit serving on the neonatal transport team. As an IBCLC nurse lactation consultant, she ran an Egnell breast pump rental depot. And she was a clinical nursing instructor.

She was a La Leche League leader, maintained a breast milk bank, and served as a nurse lactation liaison to physicians.

Grieving families of newborns to the elderly benefited from her parish nursing, Stephen Ministry, and Resolve Thru Sharing Bereavement training, education, and skills.

She is a Jin Shin Jyutsu practitioner and Usui, Holy Fire III, and Karuna Reiki Master practitioner, and obtained certifications in Healing Touch and Healing Touch Spiritual Ministry, Quantum Touch I and II, and Medical Intuition.

While traveling in her ancestral Scandinavian country, she remembered being a Viking warrior and uncovered the origin of the deep generational grief. During WWII, the family had an enemy campsite on their farm property, where the women were raped.

Emilie seeks solace in nature, walking among the trees. She brings vital grandmother energy, lived experience, and wisdom to everyone she serves. She loves dark chocolate, flower gardening, reading, and lives in middle Tennessee with her husband of 57 years.

The bees affectionately call her wisdom keeper and Grandmother Hummingbird. She is nurse-warrior-veteran-educator-healer. And she is daughter-sister-wife-mother-grandmother-friend. Of the FATES, she is oldest-crone-elder.

Contact with Emilie

Email: gmhummingbird2024@gmail.com

BEE ADORNMENT RECIPE

Channeled from the Bees

- Leah Benjamin

You will need any food that you would like to sauce,

and any dressing, drizzle, or topping you choose.

This can be sweet or savory.

Your food can be in a larger vessel or just a portion on your plate.

We are drawn to adornments for many purposes. For beauty,
For protection,

To carry or attract an energy.

Your sauce is going to be an adornment for your food.

What would you like an adornment to mean today?

Would you like it to add flavor and pleasure?

Would you like to just enjoy its color?

Would you like for it to represent a sacred balm to soothe?

Would you like it as a gesture that adding something

to what is here makes a new composition?

Would you like protection?

Drizzle your sauce or dressing over your food,

thanking it for its alliance.

Blessed Bee.

CHAPTER 11

WHAT'S YOUR VOICE STORY?

A Path to Loving and Freeing Your True Voice

Leslie Garbis

"There is an ocean of sound within you. Anything that causes you to shrink or contract, whether mental, emotional, or physical, will constrict this natural state of expansion. Observe and then release whatever it may be. Judgment is not needed. Instead, open and expand."

~ Leslie Garbis, from her 'Singing is Healing' oracle deck.

MY STORY

Writing this chapter has been triggering for me. I find myself questioning whether or not I'm magical enough or deep enough to stand alongside these other amazing authors. This voice is not to be trusted. These are lies told by the *Evil Little Fucks* (ELFS for short) in my head. What can I say other than I am here because we tend to teach what we need to learn. Since I've spent my entire adult life singing and teaching singing as my profession, hearing that I've been disconnected from my voice in many ways for much of my life may come as quite a surprise.

Does your voice have a story? I'll share some of the ups and downs of my relationship with my voice. I hope to inspire you to locate your true voice, love it, listen to it, let go of what doesn't serve it, and then launch it. Imagine feeling so connected to your voice that you can't keep from singing and sounding freely.

My primal DNA was activated, begging me to growl. Barely human sounds resonated from the lowest part of my root and womb. They felt foreign and familiar, like the call of a thousand warrior womb women preparing for battle. The wild woman wooden birthing staff my husband foraged, then crafted, called to me with ancient knowing. There was pure listening and connection here as I was guided to use it to stand, sway, and undulate while making guttural sounds and moans. Great Mother reached out to me through this earthy wood element, helping to stabilize and support me. "Ooooooooohhhhh. Ooohh. Mmmmmmm. Uhh. Uuuuuuuuuhhhhh." Jaw loose. Open. Roars and cries. Resonant hums and buzzes vibrated my being. Fully grounded and liberated sounds. Moving through the sensations. The trust of self and voice. Powerful. Birthing Leslie was a complete and total badass who was incredibly tuned in, taking her cues from inner knowing and tapping into profound wisdom. Knowing her place in the ways of the maiden-turned-mother, she knew she could do hard things. She listened deeply and didn't doubt. The power of her voice was unquestionable and evident.

Hell yeah, right? Well, allow me to share more of my laboring story that can start to hint at my wounds. My husband, doula, midwife, and best friend were present for the home birth. At one point, Kelly and Judith left to get a late lunch. When my contractions started to pick up, my midwife Cara called them back to the big event. The heavy wooden door clicked and swung open, and I became the hostess of the party without missing a beat. With my naked, engorged body draped over the birthing ball, I turned my smiling face to my friends, "Did you find something open so you could eat? I hope you had enough time. We love The Rambling House. Did you go there?" Exasperated, my midwife reminded me to "Get back to breathing. Use your voice for birthing, not talking. Stay focused and open. Tune in, not out. Anything else halts the progress and can keep baby from coming." Whoops. Major disconnect. My habit of distracting from my own needs and overdoing for others made a reflexive, involuntary, glaring appearance, even in the midst of pushing a baby out of my vagina! I was back on track. I could do hard things. Next, I was apologizing and trying to comfort my husband during labor. With my head looking back over my shoulder, "Oh Honey, I'm so sorry! I know I keep farting right in your face." With shallow inhales, while catching my emptying bowels in wads of toilet paper, he replied, "Roses, Baby. Smells like roses." Not joking, but from his heart, so I would relax and not feel shame. Deep listening. Pure connection. I jumped back on track. "Uuuuuuhhhhhh. This fucking sucks! Ooooohhhhhh!" Evan was birthed into the warm waters of the birthing tub, from one watery womb to another. My voice helped get him here.

Ready for some contrast? After an empowering birth I'm extremely proud of, something fascinating occurred. Almost as soon as the afterbirth was out, we were cleaned up, and Evan had found the breast, I went from birthing warrior goddess to lost in motherhood victim, feeling like I needed rescuing. It's as if the deep knowing and connection to the voice of my sacred self made their exit with the placenta. It felt almost immediate. Over the next days, months, and years, I have thought so many times, *What about me? Who's here to help me?*

I was priming the pump for my abandonment wounds to come and mix it up with the overwhelm of new motherhood. I feel so much grief and judgment around how quickly I lost myself after such a powerful and intentional pregnancy and birth. I regret that I didn't find balance, time, money, or motivation to take better care of myself and my post-birth body, mind, and spirit. I feel this as a massive loss 15 years later.

I was mostly left on my own after just a couple of weeks postpartum to try to heal my poor beat-up body, nurse non-stop, and learn how to take care of a beautiful wee baby boy. His well-being took precedence of course, as it should be. But what about me? I got lost in the sheer cellular-level service of motherhood and poured everything into it and into him. I can't count how many times and in how many ways I have used the responsibility of motherhood, and especially the Attachment Parenting style of motherhood I willingly chose, as an excuse to not take care of myself and to deeply disconnect from my wise inner voice and my very being. I realize this wasn't and isn't an uncommon theme for many mothers. I also didn't have family or community around to help. In fact, one of my best friends actually left my life without a word during my pregnancy. In my darkest and most lonely moments, I deeply resonated with the "it takes a village" sentiment. Van was a present and loving husband and father, but he had to be gone a decent amount. I had some great friends, but most were quite far away or busy.

Days went by in a milky haze. Time seems to creep when you're at home caring for a newborn through his toddler years. Breastfeeding on demand was consuming. I stayed home with Evan while my husband went to work every day for our family of three. I felt alone, sad, and lost. I tried to find a new community, but I found it hard to connect in the massive sprawl that is South Florida. I felt like a damsel in distress trapped in her lonely tower and, quite frankly, also trapped in her mind.

From our high-rise condo's balcony, I saw the blue waters of the bay, heard the rumble of boat motors as they cruised by, and sometimes even spotted the gray shape of a dolphin. With the Atlantic Ocean across the street, the salty smells and the calls of seagulls beckoned as soon as you stepped outside. Sounds like heaven, right? To say I did not take enough advantage of the beach or the pool is an understatement and a very telling one. I was isolated and dealing with depression. Even so, I was extremely high functioning for our potent little guy with his blonde ringlets, big eyes, and chunky square feet I was obsessed with. I was head over heels in love with our little Greek God. Yet, it was commonplace for me to count the minutes until my husband was home.

Evan and I did a lot of singing, using plastic kitchen items as percussion. Thanks to our weekly Music Together class, we had loads of fun songs and ideas. *I never sing anymore, other than with Evan. Ever. Not even in the shower. People I went to graduate school with are singing on Broadway now. When was the last time I was on the stage or even went to an audition? I should be doing more. I should be using my skills. I should put myself out there. I'm getting left behind. I'm just a mom. I feel so lost and trapped. Where did I go? I can't hear me anymore.*

After music time, it was 'booba milk' time and then nap time, usually for both of us. If I were lucky, he'd go down easily and sleep for at least two hours. *Van should be home by around 5 pm. I can do this. The day is almost over.* The blessed scrape of the key at the door brought tears to my eyes and a massive exhale of relief. After dinner, "Why don't you go down for a swim or go out on the balcony and read a book? I've got cleanup covered." My emotional overwhelm was so huge that I felt frozen, so I did nothing. All I could see was how I couldn't do anything for myself. The discomfort became comfortable. I just couldn't see that I had a choice, nor did I feel like I was worthy or capable. My disconnect was my daily reality.

"Leslie, I saw you birth our son with a kind of strength that amazed me. Don't forget who you are." *If I could only remember. I guess I'll just go to sleep. I'm exhausted and don't want to complain too much to my sweet husband, who just lost his job and is trying not to freak out. I feel like all I could offer is, "I just don't know what to do. I feel so stuck and like I have no life outside of mothering. One day feels infinite, like a year! Van, I am bursting into tears right in front of our sweet boy. There is a fucking chorus of 'I Can't' in my head. I'm lonely, I feel desperate, I need help, and I don't know what to do. I can't seem to take any action or speak to what I need."*

I was ignoring my true guidance (my inner voice) and the voice of God. I couldn't hear. All the other voices in my head (the ones that harm) were too loud. I was incredibly disconnected. It's with certainty that I now know my soul's voice felt abandoned by me. I'd later write a song that speaks to this state:

"I dig down deep and find my soul asleep. Will I wake up, will I wake up? Will I wake up? I wanna wake up…"

Motherhood is an honor and a deep, sacred service. Nevertheless, I allowed myself to be overwhelmed and silenced by the enormity of it. Since I was a pro at prioritizing being a mom, it became effortless to ignore myself and stay out of balance. I found plenty of excuses for not reconnecting to myself when I'd allowed the most important role I played to swallow the whole of me.

I threw my hat in the ring for a teaching gig when Evan started kindergarten. Having taught voice at multiple universities and conservatories pre-Evan, I was on the fence about returning to teaching. However, an adjunct position was available at an esteemed music school at a local university, so I dusted off my repertoire and vocal cords and went for it. I got the gig. I was back in the saddle and had 24 voice students in my studio.

Fluorescent lighting and an upright piano greeted me in my voice studio. Each day could feel like an assembly line moving through, with me in charge. One student walked out as the next student walked in.

It seemed like a portal to a land where I was in the business of helping people connect to their voices and sound their best. Physical tensions and habits were released, limiting beliefs were questioned, and postures were positively adjusted. I loved it when my students grew in their vocal and musical skills. The metamorphoses were astounding. Chins jutting out in the "I'm emoting and trying" position shifted into long necks and open sounds. Lower jaws gripping tightly with control shifted into floppy, free-swinging hinges that assisted vocal freedom. Compare and despair syndromes from trying to sound like Adele evolved into understanding their own unique voice, learning to love it, own it, and work with it. Many students came in not even understanding how to breathe for singing. I felt like a ninja with how quickly I could help them lay this important foundation. I recall one such student in particular, who, in a very short time, was singing a soprano Italian aria with a gloriously supported sound.

Wow, she sounds fantastic. I used to love to sing this song. It was a great audition piece for me. Why am I not singing? What about me? Other than some kickass vocal modeling for my students, I am not even making time to sing. To really sing. What is my deal? Do I even like to sing anymore? Oof. Ego shoots. Ego scores. The 500-pound weight of shame descends onto my chest. I feel like an imposter.

Have you ever heard someone sing, and it just didn't touch you? Even if they had a beautiful voice? In my opinion, one of the reasons is because they're not truly connected to the words they're singing. After all, singers are storytellers. Bringing the words to life in a song takes making them personal to you. Assigning your own unique meaning to them is necessary to share your message from a heartfelt place. Express, don't impress. I taught what my many years of professional singing had not managed to do for me. I remember being disembodied for many auditions and performances in my twenties and thirties. Floating outside of myself like a satellite, looking down on my body while singing, is the opposite of being an embodied, connected singer. Deep grief, regret, and even embarrassment are tightening my chest as I write this. How many wasted opportunities! I now know that getting the fuck out of your head and into your heart is the key.

Going back to teaching voice was deep medicine for me. When it came to being fully embodied and singing from the heart, I taught what I knew to be true. Even though my students were flourishing, and I taught from a deep place of wisdom, heart, and intuition, I was not yet fully walking it. The shame I feel admitting this is palpable.

Codependency has been present in my marriage and in other relationships. It kept me from me. I painfully lost myself in some of my closest female friendships and buried my voice at the same time. There were at least three women I considered sisters and thought would be lifetime friends. I repeated my pattern of over-giving, which, at the time, I wore as a badge of honor. I felt I was deeply and unselfishly showing up for my friends, and it became a big part of my identity. Secrets such as abortions, abuse, and adultery were listened to by my loyal ears and held by my loyal heart. The feeling of being indispensable was something I became accustomed to. After all, I was that friend. Need a ride to the abortion clinic? I got you. Need to offload your guilt about cheating on your husband? I got you. Need to share about your abusive boyfriend, but then you go back to him anyway? I got you. Need homemade chicken soup hand-delivered to you when you or your loved ones are sick? I got you. However, the irony is that I was not and am not indispensable or irreplaceable. Each of these besties of mine, including my maid of honor from my wedding, dumped me with no rhyme or reason as far as I could tell. No altercation or argument of any kind. No heads-up and no explanation. Just ghosted.

What is wrong with me that people keep leaving? Why do they keep doing this to me? I feel so broken and unloved.

It was years before my inner voice of truth asked, *how am I contributing to this repeated experience? What is my part in all of it, and what am I meant to learn?* My fear of being left by loved ones created more of the same in my life.

These days I have a more deeply integrated relationship with my voice and the use of my voice.

"Hmmmmm. Ohhhmmmmm." Audible moans vibrate my chest and buzz my lips. I'm aware, but have no control. These involuntary throat activations have been bubbling up nightly for weeks now. I wonder at the timing, as my chapter deadline is in sight. It's as if I'm in a threshold or doorway into voicing or sounding from my depths. There's no visual with these moans, only a sense of a shift and of a primal remembrance from the womb of creation. I'm paying attention. Inviting. Honoring. Knowing I'm connected to my voice and ready to help others connect to theirs.

THE MEDICINE

Step 1: Invite Reconnection.

With an air of reverence, carve out some intentional time free of distractions. Grab a journal and a pen. Tune into your own voice story with an open heart and mind.

Now, with love, curiosity, and non-judgment answer:

How do you feel about your voice? Both your inner voice and your voice in the world? Think of your speaking voice and your singing voice when answering.

If asked and personified, how would it feel treated by you?

What memories, thoughts, emotions, and physical habits constrict your voice? What does that feel like in your body?

What memories, thoughts, emotions, and physical habits expand your voice? What does that feel like in your body?

Please visit https://www.singingishealing.com/songlibrary to find a grounding breath meditation, as well as a mantra/affirmation that resonates with you. Something you wish to cultivate or something you wish to release might guide you in your choice.

Leslie Garbis, a respected vocal teacher with more than 25 years of experience working with singers and voice professionals, has sung professionally both on the stage and in the studio. She holds two degrees in vocal performance.

Her teaching credits include the University of Miami, New World School of the Arts, Barry University, AMDA (New York City), and Belmont University School of Music in Nashville, where she lives.

Her Singing is Healing business is her current focus, where she is free to use all of her holistic methods and tools (one of which is Pilates, being certified since 2006) with all types of clients, helping them to love and liberate their voices.

Leslie enjoys writing simple chants and mantras for healing and sharing in song circles, workshops and retreats. Her duo, "Enchant Yourself" released their first EP, **THE HEALING WATERS EXPERIENCE**, out on all streaming platforms.

Creating, collaborating, and facilitating workshops, retreats, and song circles in the Nashville area and beyond keeps her busy. Connecting people to each other and a deeper knowing and expansion of themselves through voice, music, and community offerings is her passion.

She lives in Nashville with her husband, son, and chickens, where she is a part-time homeschool Mom and a novice gardener and herbalist.

Connect with Leslie:

Website: https://www.Singingishealing.com
Instagram: https://www.instagram.com/singingishealing
Music: https://open.spotify.com/track/3V9lskxcL8XSuLKap40GJg

CHAPTER 12

EPIPHANIES OF A MOTHERLESS MOTHER

My Journey Through the Wound

Wendy House, Certified Reiki Practitioner

"The heart of a mother is a deep abyss at the bottom of which you will always find forgiveness."

~ Honore De Balzac

MY STORY

It was a typical hot and muggy August day in Nashville, the humidity so thick you could cut it with a butter knife when I walked into the hospital where Daddy had brought you earlier. You had not been feeling very good and were getting short of breath after a fainting spell while on vacation at the beach, so the doctor thought it best to admit you. I had so much going on my mind was buzzing with an extremely long to-do list when I arrived at the hospital. I really couldn't stay long and needed to get going. After all, my over-scheduled life was calling, and I could return later for a longer visit when I had more time. But I didn't realize you'd be leaving us so soon. Nor did I know that later, when I walked into the critical care unit to check why the procedure was taking so long,

I'd unwillingly and unexpectedly bear witness to your departure from this Earth. But I believe your Spirit and the Divine called me in. You knew you were leaving, there would be work to do, and you chose me to witness this sacred journey. During the consultation before the surgery, the doctor made it seem like it was a fairly quick and simple procedure to clear the blood clots from your lungs causing the shortness of breath, with no need for worry and little concern of risk. But the harsh reality was that this simple procedure took you from us unexpectedly on that sticky and hot August day.

The picture of your intensive care room as I walked in to check on you, filled with frenzied hospital staff working desperately to resuscitate you, is forever etched into my mind, like a horribly disturbing dream that jolts one from their peaceful slumber. A haunting nightmare you just can't shake. At first, my brain couldn't comprehend what was happening. It was as if I were watching it unfold on a movie screen, frame by frame, in slow motion. And then, I knew. I knew you wouldn't be going back home. Not today. Not ever. The confused and uncomfortable look on the nurse's face, when I came to check on you, was all I needed for confirmation, but because the circumstances were still unfolding, I had to return to the waiting area with everyone else. What were only about 20 minutes felt like a lifetime before they gathered our weary and worried family from the critical care waiting room. By then, we had been camped out for hours when the doctor finally came in to make it official. They had done all they could do. The horrible dream was true. You were indeed gone.

This can't be happening -I am dreaming this. This is not real! Wake up Wendy! Wake the fuck up now! Why are they saying this? Daddy! Oh my God my sweet father. Does he even understand what is happening? Can someone please help us understand what is happening? Please, God let me wake up!

They led us back to your room, where only machines were keeping your heart pumping now, with another forcing the air into your lungs. The beep, beep, beep of the monitors that filled the sterile and quiet room was suddenly overridden by the gut-wrenching sobs of me, my sisters, and Daddy—your sweetheart since high school. Hot tears filled with anguish and sorrow poured from our eyes like an overflowing river. Your once beautiful and vibrant face was almost unrecognizable due to swelling from the impact of the trauma you endured during the multiple attempted resuscitations. It was excruciating and sickening to see you this way, but we had to hug you one last time. To hold your soft hands. To kiss your warm cheek and to tell you how much we loved you and how wonderful of a mother you were. We did not want this to be how it ended. None of us were ready. You were ripped away before any of us could even understand the enormity of the situation, and within what felt like only a matter of moments, we were forced to say goodbye. With painful disbelief, confusion, and heartbreak, we tearfully and reluctantly let you go.

I recently started my mothering journey when you left your Earthly body on that muggy August day, with your sweet grandson and granddaughter being barely five and two. And we just moved into our new house to start an exciting new chapter. Why did you leave us when I had so much to share when my grown-up adult life was just starting? *I needed you now more than ever, Mama. Why is this happening? Who will I go to with my mothering insecurities and doubt?* You raised six children and were a very dedicated homemaker. You provided for us all so well, doing all the motherly duties without complaint. And when our troubled sister Lisa was incapable of being a good mother due to her addictions, you lovingly and selflessly raised her daughters, too, after your own were already grown. You were called to be a mother; that's what you did. It's who you were. And it was what society at the time expected from you. You were our glue, the matriarch. And you loved your family more than life. We were, in fact, your entire world. I never even stopped to consider if you ever actually wanted anything else.

The days ahead were a hazy, blur-filled roller-coaster of confusion and unrelenting heartache. As I was rightfully, though unexpectedly, pulled down by the heavy weight of immense grief and mourning from this loss, it didn't take long for deep regret and guilt to take up residence in my raw and broken heart. I'd be starting a new business in May, and because of this, I could only drop by quickly on that previous Mother's Day before your untimely departure. And, like always, I forgot your card because I simply had too much on my plate. During our visit, I felt the unspoken sadness my self-centeredness caused. If I only knew then that it would be our last special day together, I would've made absolutely certain to carve out more time for you. To linger as long as I could in your company.

Hindsight.

It is indeed a bitch.

Where was that fucking card? I needed to give it to you! I needed you to know how sorry I was for not taking more time for you. Then, while digging through some junk-filled drawers and searching for family photos, I found it the day before your burial. So I sat down, with uncontrollable tears filling my eyes, and poured my broken heart out, filled with guilt, onto the card, then lovingly tucked it next to you in your casket when I arrived at the funeral home later that day. But I had so much more to say to you, Mama. So very many things were left unsaid. Stories untold. Questions not asked, and hurts unhealed. All of it is now forever lost to a thief called *death*.

The shock and despair of losing you so unexpectedly cracked me wide open and left a gaping hole where your love once lived. The days, months, and the first few years after left me discombobulated, confused, and uncertain. As my own mothering journey continued to unfold, so did the pain. And along with it came old childhood wounds, deep sadness, anger, and regret. My eyes were reluctantly forced open, and the veil of denial was lifted as I was faced with this harsh reality. Navigating the waters of motherhood completely on my own left me feeling a bit like an orphan with no one to turn to for guidance, with both Grandmother and Granny passing years before you. It also sent me down a path of intense healing work and reflection, a path of mothering my daughter and son in ways you were unable to mother me. My priorities were laying a foundation of trust, support, transparency, openness, and healing. Losing you unexpectedly brought up so much that I hadn't worked through in our own mother/daughter relationship, and the lack of closure and suffering it caused gave me a newfound commitment to do so many things differently during my walk through motherhood. While you selflessly provided all the motherly things like packing lunches, washing and ironing our clothes, and preparing meals, there were many days you had nothing left to give emotionally. And at times, dare I say it, I even felt like a burden, unseen and unheard. By the time I came around, being the fifth child, you were probably exhausted and pouring from an almost empty cup. You had already been through a lot of heartaches with my older sisters—teenage pregnancy, abortion, addictions, and intense rebellion would be heavy as hell for a mother to navigate, much less carry. Plus, you didn't receive a lot of the emotional support you needed from your mother due to her on-and-off bouts with depression and her grief from losing a child. Giving birth to my children opened me to a deeper understanding of the pains of motherhood you must have endured, some quietly and privately, and others never even spoken of. Raising a total of eight children must have brought you so many gifts, as well as your own grief, difficulty, and challenges.

As I was moving through my deep healing work after your death, one day, it hit me like a ton of bricks—a simple but clear epiphany. Even though you made mistakes, I realized you loved and mothered me the best way you knew how, that you drew from your mother's well, and she from hers. Decades and lifetimes of hurt, pain, and sorrow, passed down unknowingly through unhealed cycles and patterns, landed unexpectedly in my lap. How in the hell was I supposed to alchemize the suffering and incorporate it into my mothering journey without you here to work through all the chaos? I'll tell you how. I did it through forgiveness and grace, by painfully peeling back layer after layer of forgotten hurts and looking at them through the fresh eyes of a mother. I did it through trial and error—through love, appreciation, and understanding. And, through radical acceptance and embracing all the imperfections motherhood brings—through allowing any cycles of dysfunction and pain to end with me. To see, honor, and learn from you, my mother, your mother and her mother, and the mothers who came before them. To see through eyes of forgiveness and a willingness to understand their journey and how it shaped them as mothers. And to heal it all for my children so they don't have to carry those wounds forward. Thank you, Mama, for loving me the best way you knew how. For throwing me into the fires of redemption so I could alchemize this sorrow, rise from the ashes, and dream with the bees. May all the hurts of the past be transmuted into golden honey and served up as a magical elixir to heal our mother wounds of the heart, for myself, my children, and the collective.

My beloved Mama, I honor you with understanding, humility, and deep gratitude.

I pray I'm making you proud.

THE MEDICINE
Healing the Mother Wound
A Ceremony of Understanding, Transmutation and Forgiveness

Gather a pen or pencil, four small sheets of paper, three small candles or tea lights, a fire-safe dish or container, and a photo of yourself with your mother. Include a picture of your mother with her mother (if you have one).

Settle into a peaceful, quiet space where you will not be disturbed.

On the first paper, write a letter to your mother. Include everything you feel she could not give to you in it. On a separate sheet of paper, write everything you feel your mother didn't receive from her mother. Compare the lists. Are there any similarities or cycles you can identify?

How did these wounds possibly show up in your relationship with your mother? How might they show up now in relationships with other women in your life?

Now, on a different sheet of paper, write out those things she could not give you due to her wounding and how it has affected you (and your mothering journey if you are a mother). Take your time and give yourself the space to sit with any grief that may be rising through you during this process.

Allow yourself to look at the pain. Are you willing to forgive her?

Now, take the last piece of paper and write how you can heal and implement change.

What will it take to bring closure to these wounds and stop the cycle?

Light all three candles and place them next to the photos. The candles represent you, your mother, and her mother (or the collective).

Sit in silence and meditate on what comes up for you.

When you are ready, take the first paper (the letter to your mother) and burn it in the fire-safe container. Now take the second one and burn it, then the third and burn it.

After, place one hand on your heart and the other on your womb.

Take about three deep, cleansing breaths. Say the following mantra:

"I release these wounds and cycles to the fires of redemption.

May I be healed and transformed.

And through my healing, may my mother be healed, and may her mother be healed.

May these ashes of pain be used for compost so the seeds I plant going forward will be fed with understanding and forgiveness.

May they blossom through acceptance and love and be pollinated by the bees for healing, transformation, and the benefit of all.

And so it is."

Now gather the ashes and the last piece of paper where you listed your intentions for healing and breaking any Mother wounds/cycles.

Fold it up as small as possible with the ashes inside.

When you are ready, bury it in your garden near some flowers or a pot with seeds. Nourish it. Water it. And as your plant or flower grows, may it represent new beginnings and new cycles on your mothering journey, whatever that may be or however it may look for you.

For we are all mothers, and as we heal ourselves, we also heal the collective and humanity as a whole.

And so it is.

Wendy House is a certified Reiki practitioner trained in the Usui method and incorporates intuitive energy readings with deeper divination and healing work. An earthy alchemist, sacred space-holder, and plant medicine creatrix, she offers a unique approach when working with clients through her business, Stillhouse Herbals. Wendy has been practicing the healing arts for almost 20 years, and she pulls from direct life experiences when working with clients, allowing her to establish a deep connection of trust, openness and understanding. She is a mother, an herbalist, an astrology geek, and a lover of all things mystical, ancient, and esoteric. If you would like to learn more about Wendy's magical offerings or to work with her directly, please feel free to reach out via email at stillhouseherbals@gmail.com or visit her website at www.stillhouseherbals.com You can also follow her on the socials at instagram.com/stillhouseherbals or www.facebook.com/stillhouseherbals for more of her story and services.

CHAPTER 13

INSTRUCTIONS FOR BEING BORN:

An Invitation to See and Be Seen

Dusty Rose Miller, PhD

"Turn sideways into the light as they say the old ones did…"

~ David Whyte, Tobar Phadraic

For Lauren — my friend and guide in this life and others.

MY STORY

I woke up in New York crying. I'd gone to attend a conference, a crunchy blend of science and sacred medicines. I heard, *open to this*. Though I hadn't expected much, my tears made everything precious.

Troy from the Sia Foundation spoke. I knew the name of his people's plant medicine, but he didn't speak it. He spoke of eagles.

He explained how Sia's feather repository serves his people by connecting them with the increasingly rare eagle feathers used for prayer.

Checking on a nest one day, he found the fledglings older than expected. But not quite old enough. Two fell from the treetop nest and plunged into the river below. Troy dove from the tree into the raging river and somehow got them back to the nest safely.

I felt the crystal grid of connection between them.

With Sia's help, the eagle population in the US quadrupled. Then, the country of Spain asked Troy for help with their national bird, the Spanish eagle.

"We've been looking for a way to repay Spain for the gift of the horse," he said.

I heard honor and freedom in his response. I could almost see him riding fast across the plains, making real what was in his heart because he didn't believe it impractical or impossible. Rather than begrudge the Spaniards to the tune of 1492, Troy chose to follow the eagles.

Sia Foundation is an act of resistance in its very concept. It receives funding from governments that want linear progress toward concrete destinations they can understand and therefore control—not feather repositories. I felt myself being held, swirling up on the wings of prayers.

After every other speaker, lines of people gathered at the mic with questions. After Troy spoke, you could hear a pin drop. I don't remember stirring, but I found myself at the open microphone.

"If I find an eagle feather," I asked, "would it be pleasing to you if I left it there, or sent it to you?"

Eyeing each other, I felt my matrix scramble. I saw something, just a flash. A flash of my boyfriend, Karl. But not of Karl. Dark, unboundaried, hidden mirrors and smoke.

I didn't think much of it. *Of course I would see Karl. I love him.* Now, I look back and see my moment of darshan that began a shift so big that even in hindsight I don't know if I made it through or if another soul walked in to continue a life that I could not.

"If you find a feather, it is for you, but you must leave it there." The vision broke. My foundation turned to sand.

Landing back home, I couldn't shake the feeling that I needed to go to Mexico to see my friend Marissa. But it didn't make sense—she lived in California.

We planned a visit, but on the day of my flight she told me not to come. She'd just had a baby, and I'd had too much Covid exposure.

Scrambling to reorient, I went to see my family.

While there, I found myself wanting to reconnect with Gail, an old friend from grade school.

"Can I tell you something weird?" she asked.

"Of course," I said.

"I named an eagle after you."

"You mean you named an eagle my name?" I wondered.

"No, I named it after you. There is a young eagle here, the first one in a long time. When I looked at it, I saw a flash of your face, playing as a child in the playground, so I named the eagle Dusty."

This is real, I thought. *Something is happening.*

* * *

I arrived in Mexico without a plan. Whatever I was looking for felt near, and yet I couldn't see it. I went to a medicine man to see if he could shift something into focus for me. He examined me and pierced me with needles, but it was not until the session concluded and he went to write my prescription that something shifted. I glanced at the carbon copy of the previous prescription, and the name stuck me deeper than all the doctor's needles—*Marissa*.

* * *

In Sayulita, I connected with my friend Destiny.

"There is this abandoned house on the beach," she beamed. "It's rumored that babies were drowned in the bathtub there, and the walls are covered with paintings of children. Wanna go?"

"Umm, I'm not really into horror movies," I said without a thread of curiosity.

A few days later, we went for a walk on the beach. Passing under a large rock archway, we saw an abandoned house on the bluffs. Flanked by spindled plumeria that reached up to the half-collapsed roof, the house emitted ripples of color and a gravitational welcome.

I led the way up the stacked rock staircase and was met by orange and green dream catchers twirling slowly in the sun. Inside, a landscape mural with whale and fox, lotus and little reminders: "*Yo soy un gran misterio.*"

It felt clear to me that a woman's spirit dwelt here, a woman who enjoyed telling ghost stories to keep people out of her house. She made me laugh.

Two days later, I came back alone. I felt myself opening and started singing, "*Ama, sonríe, vive,*" a song I didn't know I knew. Interrupting the song, I sang major scales, something I had never done. Although I couldn't see her, I felt her gaze upon me. "Okay," she said, "we have some work to do on your voice." I was shocked—shocked at the thought of another being singing through me and shocked again at her judging me for it.

* * *

I hitched a ride back to town with a boy in a golf cart named Max.

"Do you know anything about that abandoned house on the bluffs?" I asked.

"The haunted house?" he said with nonchalance. "A woman lived there. I never knew her. She went to school with some of my friends. Died in a car crash 10 years ago. *Marissa.*"

Bouncing in the golf cart, I looked back, and a knowing flooded me. She loved this place more than anything, even her own body, so when she died, her soul returned to this unique constellation of rock and sea to roam the beach and sing with the whales.

* * *

While in Mexico, I spent as much time as I could at Marissa's. I also started questioning and speaking up to my boyfriend Karl. We had been together three years, but I had never questioned, never crossed his invisible lines—until now.

"I spoke with Neem Karoli," Karl told me on the phone. "He said you're ashamed of how much you love me." And on command—shame.

My last day at Marissa's, I felt torn: I had never experienced anything so magical, but at the same time I had just received funding for the project of my dreams back in the States. I needed to make a decision.

If I chose my work, I had just a few days to book a flight and return to life in Tennessee. Was I running out of time, or did I, like Marissa, have all the time in the world? Was my life here now?

I called my most otherworldly friend, and she said, "It's okay to have boundaries."

I wanted to stay but felt myself closing. I would return for work. True, but a half-truth—I wanted to go back for Karl.

Whatever it is you want from him," Marissa oozed, "I can do better."

She had me throat-singing in the most luxurious ways and seemed to see right through me. My choice echoed in an enveloping voice not solely my own.

I gave my life a scan. I was healthy. Karl and I were having our first rough patch, but I wasn't under that much stress.

Was I losing my mind?

* * *

I went back, and Karl gave me an eagle feather. I didn't take it. I left it there and walked into my spiritual emergence.

The slip planes in my brain have offered me delightful merger with you.

I came to you to bow, to be moved, to not know.

But my love has grown

to see you beyond my reflection.

You want to follow me, but I leave you no trail.

Only presence.

You're mad. Your wanting hurts.

You like it the other way.

You'd prefer if I stopped this madness.

But nakedness does not make me stop.

I go slow,

But consciousness travels at the speed of light.

I am not moving.

I am being born.

To believe this,

Is to let seeing become irresistible.

Darkness seeped out of Karl, smoke that choked me when the mirrors could not reflect my gaze, sometimes leaving me on the floor, grasping at my throat.

Around the time I met him, a vision began of being drawn deeper and deeper into the forest.

I saw the forest now. I saw myself. Hypnotized, doing everything he wanted, raping myself younger and deeper till I broke.

* * *

The day of breaking, I sat across from my dear friend Drew, a chronic pain therapist. We were going to go for a walk, but instead words tumbled out of my mouth. "Why don't you see me? I know I've been hiding from you, but I'm right in front of you. Why don't you see?"

Years of training were behind him, presence his only tool. "What do you want me to see?" he asked.

"I want you to see what's in front of you," I shot back. "Why don't you see?"

I carried on like this until I sensed awareness enter him like a breath of thunder.

Only then did I let go.

The depths to which I saw opened up lifetimes.

I saw everything that was being done to me, with me.

I saw everything I had done.

Terror.

Bigger, higher.

I could feel myself pushing up, up, up.

Out past the stratosphere. No longer rooted in this earth.

Everything and everyone became as little planets, gravitational fields of karma. I began to pray:

Please, let me be drawn to love.

Densities and frequencies emerged like meteors in my flight path.

Love, please let me re-enter to love.

Like an octopus brain, I felt my way through, saying yes to the wet, the slippery. But I had to be careful; a moment's glance magnified densities and acceleration.

Drifting as a golden, sparkling cumulus mist, away from the singularity, passed the blackhole confusion of spacetime, beyond the veil of the event horizon and into the boundless, ever-expanding cosmos in which I knew I might rest a while.

I never went back to Karl. I want to say I stayed in the golden light, but that couldn't be further from the truth. The universe outside of the black hole was plenty dark, too. I exited one amnesia and entered another. This time, I couldn't remember ever being loved by anyone.

The memories of Marissa and the eagles gave me strength. I knew I had legions behind me. But the clarity of vision I had been gifted showed me every choice I had ever made.

There was no greater gift. But it was hard not to let the shame consume me. Sometimes out of sheer exhaustion, I believed I'd made it all up and returned to a great forgetting.

When I forgot, someone would invariably tell me their story. With loosely threaded transitions, words would fall out of their mouths. They would tell me their stories of abuse, and I would whisper silently, *It's real.*

It stung sometimes, to be a homing beacon for the putridness of this world. But I know every story has been medicine; every story has helped to make mine real. This is the story of my birth. Not just in this lifetime but for all my lifetimes, I have wanted to wake from this.

* * *

Slowly I woke through dreams. They were one of the few things that could touch me. One night, I dreamed of a blue grandmother; her mouth creaked open with a puff of dust. Another night, it was the singular note of blue surging through me so intensely I awoke gasping for enough breath to hold it all. Another night, all silver. These dreams felt more real than real, and I lay laughing and asking— *How can it be that every miracle is needed?*

* * *

I remember the first time I met Lauren, whose words you'll find in this book. It was in a dream. I had legions, but few that seemed to be both human and living.

In the dream, I saw Lauren's fingers gently touching the tar black sphere still lingering around lost parts of me. She didn't break the membrane, but the touch was enough to tell me there were humans out there who knew my orphans were still trapped inside, struggling to get out.

* * *

When I began writing this story, it ended here.

I had expected the writing process to be cathartic, but I didn't think it would change me. A new ending emerged:

I dreamed last night that a note floated down from the sky.

"Are you ok?" It blinked.

"Now?"

Backwards, I saw, to Lauren's fingertips resting the note on the threshold of dreamspace to flutter it down for me.

The note faded.

I found myself with sand in my toes, salty sea air at my back. On the shore, alongside sea anemone and purple-crowned hermit. I recognized this place as the gateway to Marissa's.

I was searching for the arched tunnel that I had passed through in waking life. Having checked the tide, I thought the passage would be clear.

Entering the tunnel, I remembered it bigger and saw the sands had shifted. The tunnel narrowed so that I crawled on my hands and knees until I could scarcely move at all. A faint wisp of fresh air came in from the other side, but I could no longer see the opening.

How had you passed through?

I pulled back and lay there in the cave, dreaming inside a dream.

Iridescent rainbows lit up the walls, turning into golden streams of light. Marissa stood over me.

I thought she was me.

She saw all of me, and I felt myself curl up, the way that shame makes me do.

But the love kept growing, getting more intense, filling me.

Blue, tall being.

Yeshua had come. He was standing behind.

A red cloak.

Mary Magdalene was weaving threads of my womb. A galaxy in place of her eyes.

In my dream, I cried. In every plane of existence, redemption. Orphans of my soul, home from the black hole that had held them beyond reach.

I know what it is to have shame. To have shame and not know how to get out; to have shame and have nothing that can reach you but miracles. Miracles and weavers that stitched the threads of my universe back together.

There are legions behind you.

How do I know? Because you are me.

No matter what you've done, or who you believe yourself to be, there is more at work than you know.

In the stories throughout this book, you'll find tales of persecution, abuse, even hospitalization for speaking up. For seeing. The instructions for being born are everywhere. Finding the tether to your intuitive guidance can serve as an essential resource when you find yourself in your own spiritual emergence.

Some people have visions, some dreams. Some hear words, others have knowings.

This is real.

Find your tether, your golden thread, your eagle, your Marissa.

Then, exercise your willingness to trust it and be guided by it.

We all need friends on this journey.

THE MEDICINE

There are eyes in your voice.

You can do this practice alone, but I find it most beneficial when working with clients.

First, notice when an energy arises that calls you. Perhaps there is something hidden that you don't want to sleep in relation to. With permission, set the intention to track the energy.

Begin toning into the energy. Without losing the thread to your client, listen to the tones you are making. Are they low and deep, or high and angelic? Go slow with the practice until the listening becomes effortless and does not distract from the sensing.

If it's wanting more form, begin bringing in rhythmic elements. Listen to the rhythms. Are they slow and fluid, or fiery and driving? Go slow with the practice until the rhythm ceases to be distracting and you can move rhythmically with what you are sensing. The energy expression may now be complete.

Let the sound flow freely. Don't worry about how it emerges. The energy you are tracking may come through as words, whole phrases, or glossolalia. It doesn't have to mean anything to you. Or it might mean a lot. Often, the meaning will show itself later.

Listen for when the energy is complete. Thank the energy for letting it be experienced and expressed, then give it back and return your awareness to yourself.

Go slow with the practice and ask your clients if what you sang was resonating for them. Be mindful of your projections in the field and have clear intentions. I have found a wealth of information that was living in my body but needed expression before I could fully receive it. I have found it to be an immensely helpful connective and expressive experience. My clients have really enjoyed it, and I hope yours do too.

I think I might be a janitor. If not that, I'm a gardener. I grew up in the California redwoods of Mendocino, Pomo land, where my grandmother taught me to garden and wild-forage huckleberries and mushrooms. Now, I run a small farm and work as an Assistant Professor of Chemistry at Vanderbilt University, researching the chemical composition of *Psilocybe* mushrooms. I offer individual and group work in presence and love. I enjoy learning about people's cosmologies and how they interpret symbols and engage with the hero's journey of their lives. I love to collaborate with and lift up those who work in conservation, community action, and along the River Styx, tending to the safe passage of souls. I'm a listener, a seer, a fire tender in a vast network burning around the world.

You can reach me via email: dustyrosemiller@gmail.com

Or visit my website online: dustyrosemiller.com

CHAPTER 14

THE LIGHT SHE BRINGS

Moving Forward with Grief through the Guidance of Ayahuasca

Kim Collins, C.C.H., Medicine Woman

"In the midst of hate, I found there was, within me, an invincible love.
In the midst of tears, I found there was, within me, an invincible smile.
In the midst of chaos, I found there was, within me, an invincible calm.
I realized, through it all, that...
In the midst of winter, I found there was, within me, an invincible summer.
And that makes me happy. For it says that no matter how hard the world pushes against me, within me, there's something stronger – something better, pushing right back."

~ Albert Camus

MY STORY

He slammed me down.

Held me down on the kitchen floor. He was twice my size.

His hands held firmly around my throat.

His knees straddled my midsection.

He even spit on my crying face.

I gasped for air in total fear, too fragile and frozen to protect myself against his substantial frame.

Why are you choking me?

What did I do to deserve this?

Did you know I'm pregnant?

I woke from this dream with a start, covered in sweat and tears, still trembling as if it were real. Indeed, it was a nightmare because I was in the early stages of pregnancy in my real waking life. I didn't think much about this dream beyond that day.

Two weeks after this nightmare, the fetus growing in my womb was gone.

I was diagnosed with an early sign of placenta praevia. It's a condition when the placenta is low-lying in the uterus and can be life-threatening for both mother and fetus. I was devastated to hear this news but knew it was not uncommon and could possibly be handled with extra care during the pregnancy. But I never got a chance to find out after the loss of my fetus at three months.

A year later, life seemed back to normal after my husband and I said goodbye to our unborn child. The loss was powerful, yet we rarely talked about it. We moved on with our lives and understood that the child simply wasn't meant to be. We weren't ready to be parents anyway, or so we told ourselves. Perhaps the child's soul wasn't ready either. Perhaps another soul would return and take its place someday when we all were ready.

I have all the time in the world to be a mother! I thought.

I was only 31 years old. Women were having babies well into their 40s. I trusted in the process of how my life unfolded and was always good at acceptance, going with the flow of life—gifts of mine I'd later need to call upon. But for now, all was okay.

This was 23 years ago. It wasn't until decades later I'd wonder what significance my ominous dream had regarding my pregnancy diagnosis.

Could it be possible?

Did I manifest the outcome?

Was my dream a premonition?

Did subconscious fear somehow play a role?

As life went on, my husband and I never had a child. We were professional musicians on the road most of the time and lived a very eclectic gypsy life. I couldn't imagine how we'd fit children into this scenario, yet I still assumed we'd have a baby together at some point. As the universe would have it, I hit early menopause in my mid-40s. This is just on the heels of healing through breast cancer. It was a lot on my body and my heart all at once. It toiled heavily on our marriage.

Being a biological mother was not in my destiny, after all.

My husband and I both came from the view of "when it happens, it will happen!" so when it didn't happen because it couldn't happen, well, that was another story. And it hit me hard.

Through my years of working on myself, I later realized I was allowing my husband's feelings to dominate my decision-making in a lot of areas of my life. I handed over the reins. This isn't to say he demanded we didn't have a child, but I knew the feelings he expressed over the years—he never really wanted to be a father in the first place, or he felt he wouldn't make a good father. Why would I want to bring a child into this world knowing this? I found myself catering to my husband's needs regarding childbearing rather than my own. I allowed his desires to dictate my own. I was afraid to have a child with him, end up alone raising our child, or that it would tear our marriage apart. I see now that I allowed my husband's fear to drive my own fear. That's my empathic nature. It was not his fault. I did not judge his feelings on the subject and was grateful he expressed them. He's a beautiful and caring human being still dealing with his own childhood trauma. Aren't we all?

It was no one's fault.

It just was.

Yet I held on to regret.

Why didn't I push harder to have a child?

Why didn't we talk about it more openly together?

Why didn't he want to have a child?

Why couldn't he meet my needs?

Did I truly even want to be a mother?

Over the years, that regret turned into resentment towards my husband.

And both those emotions and the loss of my child turned into a melting pot of grief in my body because I hadn't dealt with it or even identified it early on.

I stored that unknown grief for years.

My husband likely did, too, although I will not write on his behalf here. What I do know is the loss and resentment caused me major grief. I'd go back and forth, blaming my husband, blaming myself. Neither one of us talked about it. Ever. It was just easier that way.

This caused us to drift further and further apart until it came to the point of almost no return. We had to do something.

I have to do something.

I never grieved before, so I didn't know what that emotion felt like. No one close to me had ever died at that point in my life. I lived a charmed and abundant life. I was loved. I loved. The only true loss I have ever known was that of a fetus that wasn't meant to be.

How could it be grief? So many humans deal with much worse loss in life!

It all turned to grief for me simply because it was never dealt with. I didn't allow myself to sit with the pain. When emotions are left to simmer in the cauldron that is the body, it can create havoc if left unattended later down the line. Disease even. I let it simmer to a boiling point.

When it became clear my husband was having a difficult time handling my emotions and not dealing with his childhood grief, I decided to focus on myself and move forward with my grief.

Moving forward with our grief is not the same as moving on from our grief.

There is a background of melancholy that is never far.

A melancholy that sits in waiting for our healing, rebuilding, and moving on.

Loss sits and doesn't budge. It is and always will be.

We must learn to grow into ourselves. We learn how to grow around loss. We learn how to grow bigger than our loss. It's always there, though. Scars tucked deep into the corner of our hearts—wounds that never truly heal. Wounds that make up the essence of who we truly are.

We get a lot of advice on how to love and grieve.

Yet there still is no damn handbook and never can be.

Not even this book can do that.

And, if there were a handbook, it would simply say:

If you love, one day you will know sorrow.

Because what they didn't tell you is that to love is to grieve.

They come hand in hand, wrapped tightly around the heart.

Where there is love, there will be grief.

They come as a package deal.

What I learned on my path that changed everything is that pain doesn't have to be suffering. We can sit with sorrow. We can know grief. To allow suffering is where we have control. We must know and learn how to love ourselves to come out of the suffering.

I learned to move forward with my grief.

The best medicine I can offer the world is moving forward with the grief that is forever a part of the human I am now.

Meeting Grandmother Ayahuasca

I received many of these downloads and realizations by tapping deep within myself on a three-year journey of plant medicine healing. Being a medicine woman, I looked no further than to the jungle herself to find myself again. To heal.

I do not buy into the Western mentality of healing through pharmaceuticals or talk therapy. So, off to the Costa Rican and Peruvian Amazon jungle I went. I found my shamans and my freedom there. I was introduced to my indigenous healers of the Peruvian Amazon jungle via a very organic and intuitive course of events. The shamans (now my family) are of the Shipibo Conibo indigenous tribe from Pucallpa, Peru, deep in the heart of the Amazon—the gatekeepers of Ayahuasca.

In today's world, "Grandmother" Ayahuasca is widely known, so she likely needs no introduction, but due to the restrictions of this chapter, I won't go into too much detail (that's for another book).

This master plant has gained popularity because of its innate ability to heal a wide range of emotional and physical maladies. Ayahuasca combines two different plants from the Amazonian jungle, the Ayahuasca vine (which by itself is not a psychedelic plant) and the chacruna leaf (which contains the psychedelic compound DMT). When mixed in a certain fashion, this is the brew known as *Ayahuasca*, an entheogen, a psychoactive substance that induces alterations in perception, mood, consciousness, and cognition to help spiritual development, reaching deeper layers of the human subconscious.

I have sat with Ayahuasca well over thirty times now. It's been one of the hardest yet easiest relationships in my life.

Oh, the light she brings.

She shines the light upon our darkness, our shadows, so that we may sit with them and find a better understanding of our human being-ness.

Ayahuasca has the ability to open the space in between and allow higher conscious awakenings.

The liminal spaces, the in-between moments of a psychedelic experience, are a space of waiting and not-knowing and are potential spaces of transformation.

It seems most humans are disconnected from nature, the self, and one another. How can we feel the disconnecting elements limiting the consciousness within our own lives? Within our inner landscape? The health of our inner ecology requires going into the depths of our being. Stepping into the challenges of shadow work. It's vital for humanity's future and for our own healing.

So how do we do it?

We must be willing to leave the illusion of the ivory tower that is our ego, our comfort zone, and instead dive into the underworld that is our deeper self. Dive into those liminal spaces—the shadows.

I have gratefully found through my years of working with Ayahuasca that we can improve our inner landscape and embrace our shadows there to help towards healing in our outer world.

Ayahuasca taught me full surrender.

My grief lifted.

I'm grateful to fully live and love from the highest version of myself.

I'm grateful to know grief, how to sit with it, and how to move forward with it in my life.

My life's path as a healer and medicine woman continues to flourish and grow in ways I never expected. I now have more tools to help others and myself.

The irony is that *I am a mother*. I discovered one of my natural archetypes was, in fact, the *Mother Archetype*. I hold mother energy for many—my clients and my community. My mother's instincts came full circle. I didn't need to bear a child to love from the mother space within me.

And the child I lost? Well, she is always with me, with angel wings around me. I call on her at night to help me sleep, guide, and watch over me. She is and always will be with me. Oh, the light she brings me, too.

I'm consistently reclaiming who I truly am and what the future vision of my life looks like. It's been heavy, but it's been absolutely necessary.

It's my duty to speak my truth as divine feminine. I want to hold up hope for us all. It's for that quest of transitioning into the realm of higher frequency that some of us are rising into, fighting for. I've let a heavy, wet blanket lie on me for too long. No longer.

So, I challenge you to bare yourself.

Notice the pain that is repeating on your life's turntable. What wound do you have playing on repeat in your life? Skipping on the scar-like grooves. How do we break out of those grooves?

Dare to witness the compassion for yourself, see what's going on, but don't get caught in the trance. Instead, see where it hurts, be touched by grief, but do not get possessed by it. Rise from the ashes rather than staying small. Because you, my divine one, are *enormous*.

THE MEDICINE

1. Rise - The practice of finding the morsels of vibrant, abundant living:

I truly believe this planet is heaven on Earth. We have one life to live in this particular body on this Earth, so why not make it as blissful as possible? Even in the face of loss or grief, we have within us this birthright, the capability to live blissfully—the choice to not allow suffering to take over our lives. It's easier said than done, shifting a brutal mindset. But it can be done. Living in a state of abundance instead of lack and allowing pain and grief to be our greatest teachers. Reminding us how precious life is.

How can you live in your body more blissfully right here and now? In the present moment, regardless of your life circumstances? You don't have to die to experience heaven. Heaven is a state of being.

Death through rebirth here on Earth is possible.

We can shift our mindset to see that this can be a radiant world (heaven), yet so many of us have yet to experience it due to past conditioning and clouds of grief and suffering hanging over us. Don't we want to rise above those clouds? Notice the beauty around you in even the smallest areas of your life. Rise into your highest self where you can—finding the juicy morsels of your life and moving forward with your grief. Rising above the suffering. One day at a time.

RISE.

Every time you do something good for yourself—rise.

Every time you do good for others. Every time you let go. Every time you immerse yourself in nature. Every time you eat healthy living foods. Every time you share that food with others that have less. Every time you meditate. Every time you sing. Every time you have big belly laughs with a friend. Every time you love without fear. Every time you dance in the rain. Every time you watch the workings of a butterfly. Every time you travel with intention. Every time you smile authentically. Every time you feel abundance without having a thing. Every time you love yourself. Fully.

Rise into your life because no one can live this life for you.

2. The Cocoon - A self-healing transforming visualization:

Go inward to that safe place within. The softness of self you can fall into, like a down-filled chaise lounge.

Lean into your comfort zone today, your energetic cocoon, and allow the grief or sorrow to just be. No judgments.

Feel into the vastness of your energetic being—your body.

Noticing the subtle feelings.

The skin on your bones.

The tingling in the tips of your fingers.

The buzz of your third eye.

The place in your body that is screaming for attention. Nurture that unmet need wherever you feel it in your body.

Perhaps it's heartache.

Place your hand there.

On the heart.

Perhaps you feel out of control.

Place your hand at your center.

On the solar plexus.

Feel your power of healing with this one small gesture—this one small healing touch. Fall into your own arms as if you were falling into the arms of your mother.

We are all just human-ing, aren't we?

And it's not perfect.

It's chaotic.

It can be messy.

Yet we still rise.

And we fall.

Only to rise again.

That wave of *being human*.

Throwing out labels that limit us or others.

Throwing out trying to control everything instead of just BEING.

Creating the best versions of ourselves instead of getting caught up in stuff that is not ours. Forgetting who we are, only to bounce back and remember.

We rise. We fall. We rise again.

And it's okay.

Now, give back the stuff that is not yours, not clinging on to it and not drowning in it.

Say out loud, "It is not mine."

Give it back.

Then, go deep into the cocoon of the self.

The inner ecology of you.

Only there can we emerge transformed.

Be your own transformer.

No one else can be that for us.

Transform the missing light and shine it within yourself.

Be.

The.

Light.

Holding space for it.

Breathe it in.

Feel it in your body.

Your wholeness.

Breathe in the light.

It's in that light-filled space where we find our truth.

Where we sit with grief and transmute it.

Our cocoon.

Our true essence.

You are the transformer.

You are the butterfly.

You are the light you bring.

Kim Collins is a trained Curandera Medicine Woman, kambo practitioner, board-certified hypnotherapist, herbalist, health and life coach, holistic cancer coach, Reiki Master, intuitive energy healer, sound healer, plant medicine integration specialist, retreat facilitator, High Priestess and shamanic apprentice in the Shipibo-Conibo lineage. Her given Shipibo name is *Bidi Neraté*, which means "Goddess who walks among the space and stars."

Kim has studied natural health and nutrition for 30 years, including Ayurveda, herbalism, yoga, mysticism, and the Native American and Amazonian shamanic arts. She specializes in herbs, plants, vitamins, lifestyle, natural substances, and techniques for supporting good health. Her small batch herbal apothecary includes natural body products, herbal medicine, and spiritual accessories focusing on ancient herbalism. Kim focuses on the mind-body connection, where emotional, mental, and physical health are equally important. She's a retreat facilitator and ceremonialist and offers a variety of options at her Ajna Wellness Retreat (East Nashville, Tennessee) for personal curated rituals, overnight stays, ceremonies, and other retreat events.

Kim is also a public speaker, independent researcher, creative raw/vegan cook, juicing expert, Feng Shui interior designer (she can create a healing space for your home), and is an accomplished musician of 30 years touring the world with her husband and her band, The Smoking Flowers. She believes that her Native American roots founded her belief in the body's innate ability to maintain itself in good health when given an appropriate healthy environment provided by Mother Earth.

Connect with Kim:

Website: https://www.ownyourohmhealth.com
Instagram: https://www.instagram.com/ownyourohmhealth

Shop the Apothecary:
https://www.ownyourohmhealth.com/apothecary-products.html
Book Ajna Wellness Retreat for a personalized wellness retreat:
https://www.instagram.com/ajna_wellness_retreat
or email at info@ownyourohmhealth.com

To make an appointment (long distance Zoom or in person) email: info@ownyourohmhealth.com

Music: https://www.thesmokingflowers.com

CHAPTER 15

HOMEBODY: LOST AND FOUND

Using the Sensory Wisdom of Plants to Guide us Home

Lauren "Elle" Russell, MA LPC

"Forward, into the future, my child, my baby, with love, hope, faith, charity"

~ From Prayer of the Four Directions by Gordon Kuhne

MY STORY

My arms wrap tight around my body, slouched in the back seat of our family car, my head resting against the cold window. It is November 6th, my parents' anniversary. *Why aren't they doing something "anniversary-ish?"*

My 11-year-old sister sits next to me. I don't want to give my attention to her, but I sense her exaggerated gestures pulling at mine, so I avert my eyes toward the clear pane to avoid any temptation to break the unspoken older sibling code. Rapid rows of trees reach for me, but never fast enough. The painted lines on the gray road lull me with their too-perfect rhythm, like white-capped waves of a restless sea, the subsequent crashing on the previous ones' ebb.

My thoughts drift. *The last few years have been hard. Me and Dad fight all the time for hours. I'm pretty sure he hates me. Mom is too busy for me. Kids at school tease me—the quiet, awkward, homeschooled kid from California.* I sneak out at night because I love the quiet solitude small towns and southern nights give me and to smoke cigarettes on the high school's bleachers down the road with the guys. You know those guys. It's 1997, and half of their family is dead, drugged, diabetic, or in jail. I know they're not great for me, but I don't feel invisible around them, and that's enough to keep me showing up.

Mom turns off the radio, and the volume of my internal voices rise as they start chattering on their own station. "If you were my wife, I'd divorce you!" My dad yelled at me a few months ago after I did something that pissed him off. White-hot anger wells up in my eyes. I will not cry.

I think about how last year, I stole my dad's pills from his surgery so I could catch a break from feeling. Sighing, my breath leaves a heart-shaped fog on the window. *I think about dying too much for a kid.* I know I'm not supposed to think about dying like this, and I don't want to as it comes from a painful place, but the poetry of diving all the way into it helps me go somewhere else for a while. What is a life where thinking about death is an escape from living it?

A semi races past us, and my mind jumps to last weekend. My stomach tightens. I want to make sense of what happened that night at his house. *Did the drinking excuse what happened?* I didn't think I had that much. *Did I allow it?* I couldn't remember. *He was my boyfriend, I think, so does that make it okay?* I curl into a tighter coil tucked into the corner of the back seat and close my eyes.

Months later, during a group lecture, I learned the definition of date rape. I felt weird about it rhyming. My shame and confusion started to make sense, and the thumb of awareness pressed down hard on my sternum for years to come. A pothole jars me back into my body and inside the stifling family car. I cannot make myself care about this road trip.

After driving for hours on the pine-lined highways of western Louisiana, my dad announces, "We're going to stop and check out a place." I see my mom's jaw clench as I glance back and forth between them. Before we left our hometown in Mississippi that morning, I was told the plan was to go see my grandmother in Texas. But now, something else besides last weekend is stirring my gut, and I'm on high alert. My heart readies itself for action; my breath shallows, my hands sweat, and my body freezes.

This particular unknown is the most turbulent black sea. Another silent hour passes. Dad puts the blinker on; we slow down and turn right off the highway. Train tracks on the left side of the two-lane road are empty. The car moves up the hill of a tree-lined driveway to a clearing where I notice a scatter of log cabins spanning several acres of wooded and pasture property. Everything is moving so fast in this slow crawl. Every detail is retained through my eyes.

More pines. Tall, loblolly pines. We park in front of the largest cabin. Everything is a brown and green blur. My body is flotsam.

I'm not sure how my legs know what to do, but they take me to the largest cabin. It's the dining hall where I eat most dinners the following year. Rough-hewn log walls stiffly greet us. As we walk across the threadbare path on the red rug, I start to float a few feet behind my body. Disembodied. *It isn't safe here*, my body says to me. A man and woman, middle-aged, dark hair; he's tall, she's short, lead us to a conference room. Another blond one joins us. They speak. I glance inside periodically to check on my body. She's still sitting there. My hands clasped inside my hoodie pocket. The table is sticky and shiny; I press my thumbnail into the polyurethane, making a row of half-moons, letting my body know I'm here.

"Do you understand what that means?" they ask. My mouth said a word, but it did not feel like mine. The next time I check in to my body, I'm standing next to my parents' car, a single suitcase propped next to me. My sister, her face red and tear-streaked, cries in terror and wraps her wiry little arms around me in a relentless grip. I see her green and red eyes. *Did I hug her back?* I cannot tell. I hope I did. I feel the urge to laugh, but not at her. Thirteen-year-old me is frozen in incredulous shock. Our parents pried her from me and left.

When I come back to my body, everything is dark and muffled. I come to and notice the grit of sand in my teeth and on my cheek. In some poetic world parallel to me, my breath is heavy, belly down on the shore, waves lapping at my feet. Unsure for a moment if my body is my own, the proximity of my eye to the ground as I open it tells me it must be. Cold. Cold and rough is what I know now.

Shipwrecked. Marooned. It all starts to come back to me as my eyes come into focus. They left me. I feel the absence down to my marrow.

But I'm not in that world; I'm in Texas, surrounded in all directions by the pines.

Linear time lost importance that day, and the chilly, blue edge of the upper stratosphere became my home.

The bedroom they take me to is wooden and blue. They say things like, "This is your roommate, Sara," *Or is it Stephanie?* And "This is your half of the dresser." They seem nice.

I hang a curtain made out of an unused bed sheet and masking tape to keep out the security light piercing the blinds, and they give me three pills to take at night. Time passes without me being privy to its contents.

Now I understand what happened. My home had been a churning sea for a while, teenage tumult dredging up skeletal ships from the seabed of our ancestral psyches. Dad and Mom, overwhelmed with four kids and their own apostasy still ahead, became inundated with fringe advice and panicked. Or surrendered. The squall took over, and to lighten the load, someone had to go. I'm thirteen, and my scarlet letter is depth and sensitivity, anger and depression, sensuality, and my unwavering drive towards individuation. The dubious compass of Mississippi sweet-tea Christianity with the soothsaying marketers of the *troubled teen industry* steered them in their desperation to abandon me for a year, give or take, for the family.

The first few months are called "level one," and almost all autonomy is stripped. I have to ask for water, ask to open the fridge, to sleep, and go outside. I'm accompanied by a staff person everywhere except to the bathroom—they wait outside. This is only some of the kid's first time; for some, their second or third. Ross, Caroline, and Sarah—they have been here before. Taken away from home. We all deal with that grief later in life. For now, we flirt, make fun of staff behind their backs, and have not-so-subtle competitions about whether Wu-tang Clan or Tupac is better.

The medication they give me numbs not only my aching chest but also my heart's desires. I want to open up to new worlds and watch the world bend like my dreams. I want to go where my body becomes the wind and rain. My file says I have drug-seeking behavior, but I'm just curious and want to see a spark of sunlight that tells me there's a way out.

Caroline, my housemate, comes over and flops down on the living room floor in front of where I'm sitting against the couch, where we're all watching a movie. "Will you scratch my back, pleeeease?" she says in a lilting way. Her childlike laugh is disarming, and I comply. *Is this connection?*

There are several dozen young people in this program, and although the facility has strict rules for us, that summer, we all get to swim in the pond and sink knee-deep in mud, laugh, and pretend we aren't glancing at each others' bodies. *Is this friendship?* I smoke marijuana for the first time. It's strange, like putting on proper glasses after spending a lifetime nearsighted. I'm caught the next day and punished by something they call "restriction." The staff gave me an orange prison jumpsuit to wear for ten days while I picked up trash on the highway and pine cones in the horse pastures.

That East Texas July is hot. It's so hot and itchy, and I'm forbidden to talk to my friends during restriction, but I don't care; a cellular memory has been sparked. And I want to know more about this feathering awareness inside my chest of something alive. The fortitude of that remembering is woven stronger with each interaction with a plant, tree, the earth, or a friend. I can remember what is possible, which makes the sunburned shoulders and aching back worth it.

Even amid the blistering sun, thick air, horse-shit-filled pasture, and metallic insects droning, I find the easy bliss that recognizing one's interconnectedness with the essence of all life brings. I start singing in the middle of filling up trash bags with sweet-gum balls in the horse pasture. The next thing I know, I'm chewing on a sweetgrass stem while hauling trash. These plants want me to find my true home. I absorb the first lesson that "home" is a glittering pleasure and peace within the depths of my body, not a structure made of wood and stone that shelters me from the elements. That is a shelter or a structure. Home is a place where you sense your wholeness.

The more I court the plants, the more sparks appear, and constellations form in my mind's night sky. Dendrites branch out, and synapses fire, vibrating with animate consciousness. I didn't know what to call the feeling of *home* for some time, and the universe launched many more lessons at me when I wandered too far away from home over the years. Still, now I can identify that feeling with one glance towards a climbing sycamore or when I notice the first whisper of spring grass.

Though I do not follow my body home when I return to my family over a year later, the lesson remains buried in my soul like a seed in winter and faithfully calls me when I'm lost. Until I leave for college, the next two years are hazy chapters lined with gold-leafed lessons from near misses and the people who believe in me. Fortunately, the shimmer helps me remember my heart again, and with as many dreams as I can muster, I leave for college and find a home again among the creatives and misfits who know how to see me.

Years later, the reminder finds me again working among people who chronically live without homes because our society has refused to see them as whole. So those of us with open eyes witness them in full, broken, perfect brilliance. And seeing the world, the rivers, the vines, the soil through their eyes soothes my home-wound. Years later, the birth of my daughter cracks open the home of my body again, and she brings with her wisdom from the other side. Before her first words, she teaches me everything. Seeing life animate itself through her eyes brings me home again and again.

I do not blame my mother and father anymore. I love them. I forgive them and the lineage of stories that lead to mine. I understand their choice and release everything I do not grasp to the great mystery. I see the gifts handed to me through this story. I honor my experience and how it impacted me, how I struggled to come home to my very own body for decades after this, the bittersweet dance of golden resilience and suffering that has punctuated my life, and the sweet and resolute support of allies and guides in the material and non-material worlds that have carried me through life. Pursuing true beauty, I set my rudder towards the sparkle of water where the sun dances for her; that is my soul, and may I never forget her. This is a story of going home.

THE MEDICINE

This is my offering—somatic practice for when you are feeling lost, alone, and abandoned. By inviting the sensory wisdom of the plants to guide you home to the origin within, we create the opportunity to build our homes from a foundational truth.

First, let me define what I mean by home. Home is a place within you that feels safe, loved, connected, whole, and free. It is a sensation of warmth, being held, soft, and content. It is a place where we are creative, playful, curious, and compassionate without fear and apprehension. Some of us had this modeled for us in the constructed homes our child-selves were raised in, and others did not. Often, we experienced a range on the continuum with a bias toward one side. But we all have the implicit memory of it in our ancestral DNA because we are animated by the same force that electrifies all of life. This force seeks the sun and digs for the water.

I invite you into a meditative place where you take a step away from the world of thinking thoughts and into the world of being you. You can do this indoors or outdoors. If you are outdoors, find a place among the plants. If you are indoors, bring a plant or plant part to you.

Once you have focused on a plant, you can close your eyes or find a soft gaze.

Start to take mindful breaths at your own pace. Feel the breath enter your nostrils, move down your windpipe, and flow into your lungs. Visualize your lungs filtering, taking in what is needed for your body, and releasing the rest on your out-breath. What you breathe out is an offering to the plants, for they need what we release, and we survive on what they release.

Focus on this sacred reciprocity.

Find the seat of your inner witness. The inner witness is a place within the center of your psyche that says, "I notice myself feeling…" or "I feel my body sensing…"

Once there, allow yourself to experience the plant relationally. This means setting aside names, stories, and preconceived notions about the plant and simply noticing it. Notice it as if you are encountering someone for the first time and do not know their name or story.

Ask the plant how it wants to be touched, smelled, seen, or tasted. Allow it to ask you how to touch, smell, see, or even taste you back. When you touch it, feel it touching you back. How does your physical being feel to the plant? As you look at it, notice it looking at you. How does it see you without knowing your name and story?

Stay with this practice until you are complete. You will know.

You are fully immersed in the sensing experience in this place of no words—two beings encountering each other. This is a way to remember our true home within—the energetic core of our being underneath the layers of stories, protections, projections, and names.

There is nothing inherently wrong with names or protections; we need them to navigate and coordinate ourselves in the material world, but our instinctive reaction to trauma and grief can cause us to forget who we are underneath because we cling to the story in an attempt to survive. It's essential to practice remembering who we are so the world we create after grief and loss, both personal and global, is true to our original home.

Lauren "Elle" Russell, MA, LPC (she/her) is an artist, a healer, intuitive, and a compassionate tender of hearts. With roots in the Deep South, where she completed an undergraduate degree in Fine Arts, she spent the next twenty years showing up with equal parts creativity and compassion, guiding bodies and souls of all ages through difficult passages in life toward the home within.

An early career in community outreach, working with people experiencing homelessness, led to completing a Master's in Counseling. She runs a private practice and offers mindfulness-based, somatic therapy, transformational breathwork, psychedelic integration, and nature-based healing experiences. She also facilitates embodied movement and meditation groups for her community and aims to bring sun rays to the darkest corners. Her mission is to create safe spaces because the world doesn't guarantee safety, yet we need protection to feel our hearts and remember our medicine.

She is a story-weaver, a torch-bearer and threshold-keeper. Living close to nature is the constant thread that inspires her writing and healing tools for finding the way back home after it is lost. She loves and dedicates most of her time to creating body-centered experiences that develop the inner witness in her clients so they can build authentic connections.

She has traveled internationally for years with the most transformational connections to land and indigenous wisdom from her travels to Central America, walking with the wisdom keepers with deep roots in the plant world. The wisdom keepers are the people who keep the torch burning at the spiritual thresholds to welcome the wandering one's home.

Her grace, compassion, and strength define the bright energy she brings to the people she works with.

https://www.laurenrussellcounseling.com

laurenrussellcounseling@gmail.com

substack.com/@elleray

HUMMMMMM BEVERAGE RECIPE

Channeled from the Bees

~ Leah Benjamin

You will need any beverage you enjoy regularly.

Place in any vessel.

Before you sip, go ahead and gently inhale,

then hum on the exhale,

letting your chest and throat vibrate.

Notice it bouncing and changing between your chest and throat

as you give the hum attention.

Hummmm before each sip,

several sips in a row.

Give your attention to the bees as you hum.

Imagine how they are out all over creation humming, too.

Thank the bees for humming with you.

Thank the bees for humming with us.

Practice humming before a sip of anything,

resonating with what wants to bee.

Blessed Bee.

CHAPTER 16

PROCESSING PAIN THROUGH POETRY

Writing at Night Never Felt So Right

Lilly Emerson

"Instead of cursing the darkness, light a candle."

~ Benjamin Franklin

MY STORY

When did I stop singing silly songs?

Happy tears filled my eyes as my little girls and I giggled together. We repeated our playful jingle a few times, inventing a new rhyme each time. Of course, connectedness and presence with my daughters unlocked my inner joy after a miserable time in my life. I inhaled a long, deep breath of gratitude, filling my lungs and permeating my entire body; every cell came alive again.

It doesn't matter when or why I stopped. I'm singing again now.

Grieving, I've found, is never done. The bigger the love, the deeper the grief– and I love big. Whenever I think the sadness has all been purged, I'll uncover more. Or a memory finds me!

Keep it together. There's more work and mommying to do. Just make it to bedtime.

Once the girls drift off to sleep, I start writing at night. In solitude, I release the feelings held and hidden all day. The streams of consciousness rush to escape before my body collapses from physical and emotional exhaustion. Often, I wake up the next morning to sentences I don't remember. Whether poetic or nonsense, it's therapeutic.

I acknowledge that nothing about my writing half-consciously causes the world to change. But it puts my past where it belongs—behind me. Tears, memories, thoughts, and fears all surface instead of staying buried where they'd otherwise fester. Each day comes to a close like a book, so I fold and press it shut firmly. At dawn, yesterday's book is already put away—high up on a shelf in the library that chronicles my life. Every day is a new day, a chance to start over; blank pages wait to be filled with *endless* possibilities.

THE MEDICINE

About my struggles

It's not you, it's me
I didn't leave you
I left the old me.

I didn't run away
I found a new direction.

I didn't give up
I had nothing left to give.

My pain
My grief
My sorrow–

None of it is for you.
It is all for me and my girls.
They need a mother who is whole.
You see?
It's not you, it's me.

Looking back

seeing my beaming smile,
SO beautifully hopeful,
and unbroken
I miss that feeling.
It's painfully bitter,
yet still quite sweet,
to embrace all my memories:
the most wonderful
and the most unthinkable,
I must accept them all,
looking back.

Where I shattered

In the end, buying the big new house—
a huge investment,
the most expensive purchase of my life,
was the price to start over.
What a bargain.

I only remember the emptiness.
bare walls,

rooms unfurnished,
echoed by the emptiness in my heart.
Because all hopefulness of us together
vanished there.
We hosted nothing:
no celebrations of any kind;
not one holiday, birthday, or other meaningful gathering.
Never walked to my in-law's place down the block,
or to the pool around the corner.

We didn't take any bike rides in the cul de sac,
or go to any play dates at a neighbor's.
It took years of searching,
months of remodeling,
and then I lived there only a few days.
It was never my home.
Just a house
where I shattered.

Jealous
Yes, I showed up a little jealous
because I could not have afforded to throw this party myself.

Barely holding it together as I smiled
feeling immense loss
of a forever-cohesive family for my little girls.

I hid under the confidence of red lipstick,
held back tears behind big sunglasses,
and I walked on eggshells in my strappy high heels.
Trying my best to approach everyone
with optimism, kindness, and an open heart.
Thankful for anyone and everyone
who wanted to celebrate the birth of my daughter,
including those whom I had never met
and who did not want me there.

Showing up had to be enough.

Unfortunately, a warm, lovely summer day,
a day that could have been beautiful and healing
became anything but that.

Ultimately, jealousy was a gift.
True, I couldn't afford the material things for the party this year.
I could live with that.
I'll get back on my feet eventually.

Clearly, I had gained so much more than I had lost.
of all the important things, at least.
More breathing room for growth.
More peace going forward.
More joy in the long run.

So, by the end of the day
I felt better instead of worse.
My conscience harbored no regrets.
Now, who's jealous?

Alone
Exposed, stepping into the bright, hot sun
out of the shadows cast by a forest of shame and guilt
where I never belonged
and will never return.
This slow, agonizing escape (or emergence)
takes everything I am
to just. Keep. Moving.
Brutal light singeing every part of me,
sweating and enduring the scorching pain,
refusing the urge to seek comfortable familiarity
in the darkness from which I came.
Where you tried but failed
to hide me and my power,
to keep me for yourself.
Nice try.
This made me stronger.
Go back to the forest where you belong,
alone.

About my daughters

In case you didn't know
Since the first time I held a baby
when I was still a child myself,
you were a prayer in my heart
a dream in my imagination
a song my soul longed to sing on repeat.
Since I carried you in my womb
as my body grew
so did my love for you.
Your every move, miraculous
an angelic energy radiating
from
within
me.
It was and is the most spiritual
and sacred
experience of my life.
I hope these words,
too mature for you now,
will find you when you need them.
So you can know
how deeply
how completely
how without end
my love for you
flows through my body and soul.
And believe me when I tell you

God's greatest gift to me
was every day
I was lucky enough
to mother you.

Freely
Let her sweet curls bounce
and blow in the wind.
Dancing upon her head
with every skip and hop.

While she's still little and carefree
cute and messy
and in every way delightful.

Let her giggles sing,
watch her spirit flourish,
freely.

About my perspective

Rose colored
Glasses, loose on my face from years of wear
slip down my nose too often.
Vision through them less clear now,
perception, too, has lost my confidence.
Accustomed to my lifetime view
Through their pretty hue
True colors appear darker and dimmer now

For all the days in which the pink amplified joy
for all the beauty I saw,
and the ugliness I overlooked,
I am grateful.

Fearing I overlooked warning signs,
and minimized the problems I needed to face,
Realizing new lenses could add dimension to my life,
Might it be time for a new pair?
On the other hand,
What if replacements contain a different filter?
Change can be a good thing.

No.
I decide.
My glasses are fine,
they're the ones I choose,
just my style:
Rose colored.

About dating and break-ups

Something isn't right here
but it's not all that wrong.
The lyrics seem so perfect
but they're for a different song.

Do you envision our forever?
I used to see it clearly.
Now I'm so uncertain
and we're both growing weary.

A friendship—please, let's keep it!
No need to change much!
What a great thing we have here,
though we will miss each other's touch.

Maybe I'm just anxious,
altogether too uptight.
But I simply can't NOT feel it–
something isn't right.

To the guy who wasn't my future
I loved you
purposefully
with intention.

I hurt you
regretfully
without planning.

For a long time
I could envision our future together.
And then one day
I couldn't imagine it anymore.

Pretend for a while?
I considered it (sorry to admit).
It would have been
SO
MUCH
EASIER
to stay together,
accept the comfort and security,
indulge in your kindness
for a little bit longer.

But because I loved you
I could not do that to you.

Staying would have hurt you, too,
just differently.
So that's why I decided to be honest,
even though it sucked
to break up with
the guy that wasn't my future.

On a random Thursday
In April
spring rain looming
sunlight fleeting
open hearts beating,
I walked toward him
and he saw me for the first time.

I smiled and looked down at my feet,
wondering
if my wandering
brought me somewhere significant.
Admittedly nervous,
but not really shy
I greeted him with a hug.
We walked in together
comfortable, already,
hand in hand.
Live music, like Sinatra
the bird drink
was quite pink.
He was a gentleman
and a flirt,
vulnerable
and unapologetic.
Connecting immediately,
conversation flowed.
On the swing, he held me close,
made me giggle,
kissed me,
and it felt
nearly
impossible
to resist the urge for more.
So I didn't.

What if this is it?
I imagined,
pondered,
let my thoughts wander.
As I lay there,
in his arms.
Embracing him,
feeling cherished.
Emotionally entwined,
and cautiously certain–
enough to fearlessly
dare to think about
how my everything and his everything
might culminate in a
BEAUTIFUL
SHARED
JOY.
And, better yet,
I allowed myself to believe
we may have already started
creating our love story
together.
So I smiled.
I breathed him in.
Kissed him,
and indulged in the thought,
at least briefly…
"What if this is it?"

Searching for you
becoming the best me,
I keep looking and looking
believing soon we can see,
into one another's eyes
into one another's souls,
trusting each other's hearts
whatever the future holds.
We have chosen each battle
and earned every scar,
with courage
and patience
proudly proving who we are.
With purpose, I'm here
for "The One," it's true.
My heart is open, my dear,
I
am
searching
for
you.

About the friend I lost

You saw me fall
apart at the seams,
toward a dark abyss,
into the deepest depression of my life.
You watched and waited for a chance
to help me

to hold me
to free me.
But sadly, as much as I suffered
the waiting tortured YOU.

None of my madness
should have been your burden,
but it was.

None of my agony
should have caused you pain,
but it did.

You gave and gave and gave–
all you could
for as long as you could.
And eventually,
you did not have more to give.
I withered and withered and withered–
so I hid my shriveled self by lying.

I lied for so many reasons,
none of which are excusable morally,
but I hope this gives you some clarity.
You deserve clarity.

I lied to maintain the facade.
I lied because my soul filled with shame.

I lied because I didn't believe my truth mattered.

I thought it quite possible that I was not worthy of your loving friendship.

And I know I lost you, not because I was never worthy, but because I hurt you.

I hurt you by hiding past lies,

and by lying directly to you.

I hurt you by not seeing you fully,

and therefore not loving you the way a loving friend ought to.

Finally, after a lot of help and growth,

I think I get it.

I thought I was protecting you and our friendship from conflict,

but selfishly, I protected myself from the discomfort of facing the truth.

The truth you lovingly tried to show me.

Your truth-telling,

your pain,

and your fatigue of it all—

I think I get it now.

I think I can see you fully now,

and therefore, I think I can love you the way I wish I had.

If you're willing to speak again, even just once in a while, I can promise one thing: NO MORE LIES.

Here are a few truths I hope you can believe:

You are, and always will be, one of my favorite people of all time.

You deserve the fearless truth and love you give.

I have endless hope to reconnect with you at some point, someday,

when it will cause you no pain.

Because if you want me there for you,
I'm all in.
The way you were there
when you watched me fall.

The one with lyrics

Mothering

to the melody of the song *Lucky* by Kat Edmondson

Mo-ther-ing
Feels like this
Love, it comes ea-sy
There's a way
We sing and play
That brings me bliss dai-ly

So know my dear, I'm glad that you're mine,
and everything will turn out just fine,
I promise you… I promise you…

Life is beautiful
Mmmm mmm mmm
Beautiful
Beautiful, you see.

You are everything
Mmmm mmm mmm
Everything
Everything, to me.
…
Have you found
Walkin' around
You might feel lost at sea.

But every day
You'll find your way
Just find a song to sing.

Please remember every night,
When I'm not there to tuck you in tight,
I'm with you n' I'll love you AL-WAYS,
FOR-EVER

Life is beautiful
Mmmm mmm mmm
Beau-tiful,
Beautiful, you see.

You are everything
Mmmm mmm mmm
Everything to me.

In the end

I choose to forgive you
You didn't say sorry
Or say you were wrong
You show no remorse
And don't seem too long
For healing or mending
So keep on pretending
You don't care about me
You're blind, and you can't see
The pain and the sadness
From which I must break free.

I choose to forgive you.
Whether you're listening, or not
I choose to forgive you
Even if you forgot
All the things that happened
All the words you said
All the tears I cried
On my pillow in our bed.

I choose
to forgive you
Even though
I don't have to
I choose to let go
Of the past
But not FOR you.

You're the father
Of our children
They're miracles, all three
Made up of our genes
And they're as perfect as can be.

So, I choose to forgive you
And there's one other thing–
I choose to forgive me
What an amazing feeling.

Lilly Mathews Emerson is best known for how much she loves children. While not written for children, Lilly's poems often reference her daughters and the beauty of childhood.

As a young girl, she volunteered in the nursery during religious services and started babysitting at just 12 years of age after taking an infant care class at the YMCA. During her time at Emory University, working as a nanny helped prepare Lilly for her nursing career and her future as a mom. She now proudly refers to her daughters as her *greatest joys*!

Enjoying her career in Neonatal and Pediatric Nursing since 2008, Lilly is also an American Heart Association CPR instructor and entrepreneur. Through Harmony Children's Village, her first business venture, she devoted her expertise to caring for babies with medical conditions in her home from 2017 to 2021. Although Harmony did not become all she had envisioned, in 2024, Lilly returned to nursing school, paving a new path toward serving the same patients and families she loves so dearly. As a Pediatric Nurse Practitioner (PNP), she plans to pick up where Harmony left off, creating improved models of care that foster inclusion and community.

Lilly attributes her love for reading and writing to her grandmother, Virginia "Geda" Bradley Mathews, a published author of the Golden Book, *What Was That?* Although she has only known Geda on this side of heaven, Lilly feels a special connection to her due to their mutual love of books, fear of public speaking, and affection for the color red.

Connect with Lilly:
   Instagram: @pediatricnurselilly
   Email: nurselillyatlanta@gmail.com and her
   Website: https://www.nurselilly.com

CHAPTER 17

FORGED IN FIRE

A Heroine's Journey From Darkness to Light

Paula Martens

"Just like moons and like suns, with the certainty of tides, just like hopes springing high, still I'll rise."

~ Maya Angelou

MY STORY

Have you ever had a time in your life when your light went out? You know the spark that gives you life? After my relationship with Adam, my spark was gone.

It was a weird, uncomfortable feeling I never want to experience again. I was dead inside, yet alive on the outside, as I wandered around on this plane of existence. I wasn't able to engage with others. I could hear them talk, laugh, and move around, but when I talked, it felt like no one could hear me shouting out.

Hey! Hey! Can you hear me? Help!

I just wanted to be loved. Was that too much to ask? All because of the strong desire for intimacy, I stayed six and a half years in a relationship with a man who was not exactly Prince Charming.

In the beginning, I didn't care that he was kind of odd. I allowed myself to believe his character flaws made him more interesting. I wasn't in the best mindset for dating. I recently had a falling out with some friends and was left feeling isolated, lonely, and longing for affection. I was emotionally raw and vulnerable and the perfect target for Adam.

He and I had similar interests in art and photography. I believed he was genuinely interested in my life experiences and struggles. He responded in a way that led me to believe he understood what I'd gone through. He told elaborate stories that mirrored my own, so it felt like we had a Divine connection.

When I eventually learned there was an age difference and he was 14 years my junior, I paused the relationship; however, I decided to let the age gap go and continued to date him. After all, if the shoe was on the other foot and I was the younger female, no one would even bat an eye.

As time went on and our relationship evolved, so did Adam's peculiar behavior. Often, I caught myself scratching my head, wondering, *what is up with this dude?*

An off-handed comment here and there left me feeling uncomfortable and, at times, unsafe. However, I second guessed my intuition. *You're just reading too much into things. Let it go.*

Big mistake.

After a few years with this man, my sense of who I was slowly eroded. I completely lost myself. I lost my self-worth, trust in my instincts, compassion for other people, sense of adventure, and ability to function and make decisions I knew were best for me. I was a shell of a human.

The new me felt like this incredible embarrassment to Adam and to everyone. My anxiety was off the charts. I had this deep sense of shame for staying in the relationship, but couldn't make myself leave. *Just leave. Just walk away. You know better!*

As my awareness of Adam sharpened, I noticed things weren't adding up. His stories were all over the place. The lies—so many ridiculous, crazy lies. Many I had believed and trusted.

At one point, he told me he spoke French. Later, he explained that I heard him wrong and it was Spanish.

"Paula, you got it all wrong. I speak Spanish. My paternal grandfather fought with the Abraham Lincoln Brigade in Spain in 1938."

None of that was true.

He lied about his background, telling me all these fond memories of his maternal Irish grandmother, his Jewish heritage on his father's side of the family, and how they were Jewish Spaniards.

Absolutely *none* of it was true.

His lies also encompassed our everyday interactions. Adam did everything he could to convince me I was incompetent, selfish, foolish, crazy, oh, and his favorite, a whore.

He loved to attack me on matters of intimacy. My body was frequently targeted by his verbal assaults.

The names he called me burn through me to this day.

"You're a cunt! A whore!"

And the mind games were endless. I really thought I lost my mind.

Looking back, I can see how he worked to isolate and control me. It was like he enjoyed making up these elaborate lies to pit me against many of our mutual friends, to the extent that even his mom stopped interacting with me.

He hated my friend Suzanna. Once, he said, "I will never rest until I completely destroy her and see everyone she loves turn away from her."

I was an idiot to think he wouldn't do the same things to me.

There was so much projection. He accused people of doing things he was doing himself. If he was lying, I became the one who was the liar.

Before Adam was in my life, art was my passion. I loved painting and photography. My subject matter was rich in colors and textures of nature and people enjoying life—living.

When I was with Adam, my desire to create art vanished.

His paranoia about my time with friends pushed me to isolate more and more. What little bit I did work to create, he refused to acknowledge. He once said, "I don't want to see or know what you're doing with those downtown theater faggots. I know it will just piss me off."

When I finally decided to get out of the relationship, his emotional attacks got worse. He started a smear campaign against me among our closest friends and acquaintances.

He harassed me for nearly two years post-breakup—constant text messages about my age, my weight, and my ADHD.

My internal light blinked once, twice, then went out completely.

I wasn't suicidal, but if something had happened to me, I wouldn't have cared.

My art changed. It grew much darker.

One of the last exhibits I created during the dark days was a set of photographs of this Madonna figure made out of sharp metals. There was a rosary hanging loosely from her neck, and she was sitting in the middle of a circle of white candles. I didn't realize it at the time, but I see now that I think my soul was actually crying out to Mother Mary with the only bit of voice that remained. There were also photographs taken of a fortune teller's teacup encircled by white candles—my hidden light.

Several months passed, and I felt a shift. I began to feel better. Everything seemed wonderful. I thought everything was going to be just fine. I was excited to get back out and do fun things again with family and friends. But within this shift, there was also this raw, bitter side of me coming out.

I admit, I was a total asshole in those years. I guess I didn't realize exactly how angry I was. I teased my friends, thinking I was absolutely hilarious when, in reality, I was not.

Finally, one day, my friend, Louis, called me out on all my bullshit, and he said, "You're angry, and this crap's gotta stop!"

"I know, Louis. I know. I'm seeing a therapist, but I guess I really haven't been taking it seriously."

"Well, you know I love you. But for real, as your friend. You gotta take care of yourself."

That was when I finally started investing in myself and my mental health. It took a long time to recover, and by 2019, I was feeling much better about myself. I was stronger than I had been before.

November 30th, 2020, my heart suffered an immense loss. My dear dad unexpectedly passed away. He was 82 years old and had been suffering from health issues due to diabetes that led to a stroke earlier in the year. We had him cremated, and his funeral was at the same place on the same day, just 17 years apart from my mom's funeral.

I mourned him. Oh, did I mourn him. His death ripped out another huge chunk of my heart. I physically felt like a part of me died with him that day. He loved and encouraged me to be who I was. My sister Claudette and I were quite different from each other, but he accepted us both and never tried to compare us or pit us against each other.

We were close, and no matter what, he was always in my corner, whether he agreed with me or not. Growing up, he was dependable and knew what to do in any situation. There wasn't anything in the house he couldn't repair. He was a solid dude. When he died, I felt frightened and helpless, as if I was a small child again, even though I was a grown-up, capable woman.

My dad used to joke about how he wanted a Viking funeral, where his body would be laid on a barge and then set on fire and sent out into a lake. That would've been a fitting funeral for him. Unfortunately, the state of Arizona wouldn't see it that way, so we just had to settle for regular cremation. *Sorry dad!*

I was born and raised in Phoenix, Arizona, and ever since I was a little kid, the actual mythical bird of the phoenix fascinated me. Anywhere you go in the city, you see representations of the bird in a mosaic, painting, or stained glass. As a kid, I stared at that bird, mesmerized. The story of the phoenix is about a bird that rises up from the ashes. It symbolizes our ability to take our devastating losses and deaths and find hope and new perspectives that help us grow and expand into the joy and life that still surrounds us every day.

My life crumbled that day. As my dad was cremated, I felt like energetically I was burned with him.

That night, I had a strange dream. I titled it "The Day of The Burning."

The funeral was lovely. It was a dark but starry night. The moon lit everything up. The sky was showing off its bright constellations. My body was carried out on a board and set upon the funeral pyre by some women I did not know. They were the pallbearers. I heard them calling each other by name - Christina, Jennifer, Maria, Leslie, Cypress, Angelica. There was an air of familiarity. Though I didn't know who they were. I heard the sound of drums beating and a song about ancestors. They took a torch and lit the funeral pyre. Suddenly, I was engulfed in flames. The burning hurt, and I became nothing but ashes. The blonde woman named Jennifer told a story about Saint Brigid. Suddenly, I rose up from the flames. Though I didn't look anything like my human self. I was a fire bird of orange, yellow, and red! I became a Phoenix.

Growing up Catholic, I remember seeing the images of the Anima Sola. We were told it represented the souls in purgatory, but I felt it was something different. Fire doesn't just destroy; it also purifies and renews.

Soon after the energetic shifts of the dream, I began attending different women's circles in the Nashville area. Last Spring, almost exactly a year ago, I registered and attended an Imbolc retreat whose main theme was working with our dreams for emotional healing. During the retreat, Dasha led us through a tea ceremony where we connected with Mother Mary, the bees, and our deceased loved ones. Thinking back, I can see this was the circle of women who were already showing up in my darkest hour. The photographs I took in the past, the magic of my art, called me into this beautiful healing circle of sisters.

During the retreat, we honored Brigid and her sister Gobnait, both bringers of light. All of the women I saw in my dream when I turned into the Phoenix were living, breathing, real sisters who were present at this retreat. My mind was blown, to say the least.

Below is a poem I wrote in honor of where I am in life.

"53"

I want to tell you a story.

Many people may understand and many may not.

ADHD, age 53, post-menopause.

Brain fog.

I just cannot get these words out.

Loss of expression.

Do not count on the medical profession.

Dryness.

Loss of libido.

Invisible.

My mind feels like it is stuck. Stuck!

This fucking sucks!

Get nervous.

Tasks not completed.

The house is a mess.

They tell me I am lazy or that I am making it up.

Panic attack.

I never used to have panic attacks.

I forget words.

Is it dementia? Or Alzheimer's Disease?

Or is it just post-menopause?

Sometimes, I feel like I am encased in a plastic tube.

Can you hear me?

Can you see me?

I wonder.

Invisibility.

I can see and hear you.

Life is going on all around me.

I bang on the plastic to get your attention. Help!

Help! Get me out of here!

I am tired of this shit.

This fucking sucks.

I want to return to my old self.

ADHD, age 53, post-menopause.

Brain fog.

I am done.

THE MEDICINE

Many people are afraid to do any kind of art project because they think they lack talent, especially when it comes to drawing. Repeatedly, I've heard people comment that they're not artists and don't even try to express themselves this way. I understand their fear, having dealt with this myself.

Collage helps get the mind going and gets people to think and feel in imagery if they can't find their voice. Images can be found in magazines, online, or through our own personal photo collections. Other items such as fabric, plastics, and paint could be used as well.

"Let That Shit Go" - Collage Art

Gather your art supplies and an inexpensive piece of poster board. You will need scissors and glue, tape, or Mod Podge - decoupage paste.

Based on how you're feeling, turn on one of your favorite playlists.

Light a candle and call in Mother Mary and the bees to help guide your hand as you choose different images and words that symbolize those things that you need to release energetically from the body.

Try and completely fill up the white space of the poster board.

Call in the energy of the phoenix, asking her to help you transform your pain and sorrow.

You can burn the collage in an actual bonfire (if safe) or close your eyes and meditate on the thought pattern of watching it burn energetically.

Speak aloud "So Bee it So" to conclude your ceremony.

Paula was born and raised in Phoenix and Scottsdale, Arizona. Ever since she was a child, Paula loved creative expression through art, dance, and theater. She currently lives in Nashville, Tennessee, where she has her own art studio called Artemis Girl Studio. She was not trained in fine art and considers herself a folk artist. The themes of ADHD, mythology, death and dying, aging, older women, menopause, and religion often show up in her work. Her most recent endeavor is producing the rock opera musical Fix this spring in Nashville, Tennessee. Paula loves hearing about other people's stories and experiences and then encouraging them to create their own artwork.

CHAPTER 18

BEHELD BY BODIES OF LISTENING IN ALTARED STATES OF GRIEF

An Offering to the Mountains of Our Great Body

Leah Benjamin, LMT

"Embodiment means breaking apart and flying away."

~ Joshua Michael Shrei

MY STORY

Like so many of us, I am one that Covid wreaked havoc on. I began the pandemic excited about finding new ways to be together. Soon in, I found myself pummeled by multiple home displacements and seemingly never-ending, deeply traumatizing ordeals. Grief feels too pallid of a word for the multiple, world-shattering depths of deaths I experienced.

Sharing these experiences directly is not honoring the dignity of others and can compromise tender spaces. In this time period, I found myself fully losing hearing in one ear over the course of 24 hours. This felt par for the course and was honestly the least of the traumas. It's the greatest gift. Funny enough, exactly one year before losing my hearing, I had a prophetic experience being told I was to become "Listen." Hearing loss and extreme tinnitus catalyzed finding the new ways of being together I was excited about, yet not in the way I anticipated, nor who or what I thought I'd be together with.

Over the course of this journey, I surrendered to resonance and multi-sensory communication with animate forces that are all around us and move through us. Becoming a different body of listening took me on a wild ride. I also learned that when we lose our narrator who uses words and deeply listen, magic is bursting at the seams of the veil.

This story is alive. It has a body. This story kept me alive. The erratic pulses and stillnesses in our lives are generative. I'm sharing this story from the motions we go through in our bodies during traumas. I live in a magical forest and narrated this story to take you on a somatic journey with me, to feel your resonant being, and a new togetherness. Because our magical connections and hummm carry us through and feed each other's stories and bodies, together.

* * *

My body can't hold this story anymore.

Let's go on a somatic journey.

This faery tale is *real*.

Once upon a time—a tensile time held by sands bonding together for dear life, and people repelling from each other in a grasp for the same dear life.

In a lush land—where these desperately hugging sands form a great wall of rock.

It's a wall so tall that even if the long-settled, deeply-rooted umbrella magnolias below stood on each other's shoulders, they wouldn't reach the sky up top to kiss the sun the same way. Yet just like the people of this time, they dream of trying, of risking life to feel what it's like to touch each other above ground and fluoresce.

It's the shortest night and longest light this cycle—a gathering for summer solstice. A new togetherness since time began being held this way.

We're here, the oracle and I, Leah—or, called by my family—Woo. For several moons, the oracle continues to shake her head, telling me I'll be given a new name. Like much change spilling at this time, I resist hearing, dusting it to forget, yet only uncovering it further.

I do not want new sounds coming in to respond to—that's coo coo.

Call me Leah; call me Woo: A simple and powerful set I know how to use.

Not able to celebrate the highest sun, I approach the great wall and its shouldered twirling people with relief of the shortest darkness. Our soles press and swirl grit that can no longer be locked down. Our palms join—the oracle, the other, and I. We begin a dance, but not just any dance. We dance the body of grief, becoming one with the mountain, reciprocally giving this great wall our spaciousness. For this short night, the tensile time we've been in changes; everything a fluid body alive and together.

And SHWOOOM!

A lettered arrow soniferously pierces through the sudden threshold surrounding me, coming straight at the compromised and sensitive space between my right eye and ear; fletching with a lettered trail to another world.

"LISTEN," it spells and sounds clearly.

Is this my new name? Nooo! Dancing, denial.

The word comes at me again, entry point unguarded. "LISTEN," just as clearly.

This is the same place in the sky my son's name came from. I don't want a new spell-calling. Dancing, denial.

"LISTEN!" it undeniably imparts.

Now, more powerfully than before, LISTEN makes its way into my face, to my core, takes over, and swells out from the center of my body until my skin disappears.

Okay! I am LISTEN!

The great wall, the oracle, the other, and I, having become LISTEN, dance and dance until it's time to bow and turn away.

Calculatedly tossing bright sun spheres to rise and fall between body and sky, the other reveals himself as a juggler, carrying this form of alchemical dance to delight all around as we disperse.

I find my way back home to The Ridge.

The Listen.

It's five moons later, next door to the hole black snake and armadillo share. Lustrous white Ghost Pipe meets my gaze, and a conversation begins. A pull takes hold, stronger than any rescue rope that's saved me, yet I don't know of impending danger. Its tugging force is beyond familiarity and imperative to acknowledge. I begin driving to faraway places for no known reason other than to proclaim that I know I'll find out later.

I listen.

Sometimes, I resist, then the body blow happens, and I propel— the timing aligning perfectly. I am collaboratively birthing new patterns of suspended time, strings of web, for unquantifiable dimensions for the greatest listening. The web is casting a network of deific synapses to facilitate one of the biggest rearrangements of my consciousness. It grows. I feel it grow in places in my body and don't yet know what it's connected to.

I listen.

Whispers. Whispers. ScURRRRRpPH!

The signal comes. The Listen is vital.

Here is where I protect another's story. I can share what happened in my body.

The white blur drops down, deranging my vision. A throbbing WONG WONG WONG envelopes me, barring any usual modern human sense from taking my attention or keeping me from not solely deliberately moving in this multi-sentience form of creature. My hands reach out to grab supplies because I know I won't be back, but I can't feel touch to grab, nor visually identify physical objects and register utility.

I'm now part of a period outside of time. Every moment fully relies upon my inhabited alternate form of many bodies and allies, listening to and with the most finite life forces, nuances, tedium, and magnitude than perhaps imaginable. It's the impalpable place where life and death are dancing in such untethered flight that only unimaginable creatures can fly the winds of.

Time is not still long enough to stay one thing.

They say knowing is becoming, and I become them all—flash by flash by flash.

A different confluence refracting each pulse. A swish of syncopated chaotic metronomic body of nearly deafening listening. Tumbling quartz pebbles and lucid glass lens.

I fully become another. It is life dependent.

And this is how we stay alive. Together.

The crows come. It has been ten days.

I am called to The Valley.

So what happens when we return from time outside of time? My bodies are confused. I viscerally urge to shake them all out and be held, but I may need to keep some. My flesh body clenches. My other bodies—some need incubation, some are left wandering, some need to be fed, and some need new homes. Some need new families and worlds. Flesh needs to be held in touch, but humans still need to stay apart.

I'm led into The Cave with emeralds for the dragon. A miles-long path is made with the lover, only tending what I'm touching. Yellow dock is swirled into hurricane eyes, secured with antique suture thread, hung to ferment and dry. I birth bodies of art with black snake and armadillo's bones as bees land on the cave miso patina, creating new veils with the dragon's eyes. I try to find ways to allow my clenched flesh body to be held.

The path has made its way to The Goddess. The anemones come up. I care. We make kaleidoscopes.

I listen.

Mmm, braaaaaah. The Earth has made it around the sun one more time. It's summer solstice and we gather again. In this faraway land, tensions are tides. The ground is soft to give and receive. Electric waves of song are condensing and evaporating time through the great lake waters and pools of people. New life blooms bright algaeic greens and purples. The turbidity refracts, illuminating the great-grandmother pines, congregated and anchored in harmonic shedding, sharing, and shaking above and below.

Ready to entrance, the lover and I are directed to a stairway beside a stage. We nestle in, forming the sternoclavicular magic booth meniscus of the observatory with kaleidoscopic treasures to breathe new stories with others. Wake and sleep hours become molten.

Here, the whoosh of enraptured bodies launching and landing begins to change the rib-like rafters back to dark stardust shrouds, replacing the air. Each wet breath cycle forms pining sap on our vocal harps, rerouting our resonance through shake bark of collective lungs.

Is that—How can it be?

The juggler is here, ritualistically tossing bright sun spheres into the sky. This Litha, as each radiant, increment-eating sphere descends, their consuming fires extinguish; gasses left in centrifusion and confusion, instigating dangerous shapeshifting. Spikes shoot from their seed centers like sweet gum balls, relinquishing the juggler's hands before they can make him let go. Suspense-fully making way with forest floor fodder, flying like confetti from the feet of ravenous dancers, spiked spheres slyly penetrate the bio-rich valves of my ecstatic state breath, swindling their way into town to begin a Covid circus in my body.

Let's head home. Let's rest in The Valley.

Imagine you're underwater, eyes closed. Your body is able to be in every direction at once but pause nowhere. You hear nothing around you, yet the loudest undecipherable, multi-colored laser chirps, sounding from inside your head, in continuum. You're a new kind of insect, hatching and trying out every stridulation that ever could be to find your sound. Wait—you still have one human ear, and it's making everything about embodying your exoskeleton woozy and confusing.

I've lost auditory hearing on my starboard side between dusk and dawn. I've gained beaming sound zings between my right eye and ear. My eighth cranial nerve declares rest.

Any sound coming through my port side, innervated cochlear, increases volumes of alien soundscape from the other side, disturbing my place in space. Dizzied to immobility, I pray the muscle memory of my flesh to let my bones walk. Misshapen, remnant cellular fabric patterns from The Listen hold me in gravity now. I loomingly know I need to unravel this physique of experiences on some timeline, but that is too bad for now.

It's not some weird wrong or right will—it's everything.

I try to listen while deafness is resounding.

I must get myself to a place to be held with nothing to hear.

That's different when your body is an instrument of strange cacophony with no recognition of proprioception. That's different after humans have to stay apart for so long and now make words and sounds vibrate painfully.

Get low.

The Cave.

I crawl into the belly of our momma, a body also built by coquina of echoing calcified shell fragments. The piercing audio signals calm here. I'm met with felt drips and echoes of time; cold clay met by my cheeks. At last, I'm beheld by an ancient soirée I innately know how to hear. The musk is mountain veins. We share our bones. The dragon shares its new eyes. This conch is safe. We sound waaaaaatooooooor together.

Semi-primed, I breach, tracing the body of the path leading to The Gore—the sail shaped land between the quartzite sinkhole breasts of The Goddess. A place of life that pulses up through limbs as The Goddess feeds the mountain. I can hardly traverse vertically. My steps pitter-patter: prayer-struggle, prayer-struggle. My grief-laced sinew alone is unable to support my sacrum and spine. My crooked boning deforms my under-bust, restricting my womb and diaphragm. I pitter-patter, prayer-struggle toward home.

Will this body reform?

With no force to despair, I land on the long velvet couch. Between horizontal respite, I cathartically craft conductive, bejeweled, barren borosilicate vessels to glow in the dark. Despite, home cultivates incongruous clamor. I can't be anywhere.

Get lower.

An un-podded whale fleeing sonar, I make broad movements back to submerge in the limestone-encapsulated cocoon of dry ocean. Safe nowhere else, long resigned to endless danger, I collapse, following streams of erratic melody that my strange body and The Cave render me. I don't care if anything is generative; I simply can't hold on. The songs of the bodies from The Listen are screaming to be heard through me. I resound. I stay until I can bear to listen to anything other than this mountain singing back. Let's crawl out of The Cave.

Time's been gone awhile. Covid comes and goes again in my body, this time with glimmers of alliances. With reluctant reach, I'm called back to the magic chambers with the lover to craft kaleidoscopes for the sol journey. My glittered hands can barely grip to fold the mirrors. Even thinking in words misaligns my body. I must be careful. My body is an altar: viscous silica stirring to refashion a world. I want to try one more time to make it. I want to care.

I listen.

Summer solstice whirrrrrrrrrrs. We retrace our thread to the faraway land of tinseled pine; neon tidings of magpies and lit beings making sky. The giant trans body throbs. The magic booth is rebuilt by the thumping sternum, a nest from which to leave all of these bodies until one knows not who one is, yet who WE are becoming. Colloidal cave dust meets shedding snake skins to grow new grandmothers. When we fall apart together, the world won't stop. I'm here to fly further out and come back part of a greater body.

Across the electric forest, my eyes lock with steadily hovering orbs set amidst a mysterious creature of erect neck hair and seaweed frock. This orb nymph sails the wave in. My skin ripples with the coolness of the deep ocean from their clammy body. My growing nautilus eyes mirror their swelling pearlescent orbs in a deep-sea stare. We're in the same tide.

"I have a gift for you," they say.

Their lips shore into my auditory hearing ear, piping in other-worldly wordless song, each coo matching my sounding inner world from the other side. I'm hearing the same sounds in both ears.

Is this real?

Colorful sound strings connect inside my skull, beaming in and out each side into forever. Salt streams down my cheeks with this generously continuing current.

This may never happen again.

My entire body listens, tastes every twirrr, and savors the spectra of symphonic phosphorescence in equilibrium—the first time since the scorched orbs fell last Litha.

The orb nymph's song changes to a worded whisper, "Dweller of the cave. Take people underground. Carry messages." The Orb Nymph ebbs away. I'm struck.

This is real.

We are magic chambers resonating through all time and life and Earth and space, continuously fragmenting and birthing a Great Body.

The lover and I dance our loose bones back to The Valley.

I stumble and rumble in exhaustion and excitement with The Valley. Our zinging generates heat and rattles cooling sweats that clank like bones that can't settle.

I clench to keep them together. The form doesn't fit. Protection shifts to deep contraction.

Each night, upon the pillow, my head begins an uncontrollably deliberate unwinding; my neck a conductor's soft and thrashing baton to the cranial orchestra. Sleeping dreams change. This morning, I wake still interlaced with the veil, bones flying from the back sides of my head; flesh body, and the beyond aligning, expounding words that I can at last integrally encompass,

"MY BODY CAN'T HOLD THIS STORY ANYMORE!"

I must go to The Cave. I crawl in and ball up. My clench of fascial chainmail, with a true and present chance to serve, makes its protraction, turning the prophetic arrows to the mountain body I'm inside that demands my attention.

Grrrrrrunts, grrrrrrrrrowls, rrrraaaaaawrrrrrs, howwwwwls, turn to quivers and quakes.

Imagine you're naked in a blizzard. Each snowflake that pangs your stinging skin strikes off a chord in the core of your bones, splitting them into shards,

shaking and splicing,

shivering and splintering,

separating and shooting,

sending them into space.

You're so frozen you're burning. You fall into a faery tale rest, held by a mountain you've fed everything that's been keeping you standing. The guardians of The Goddess consume what'd become your perilous armor with pure ecstasy. You sensually merge with land, becoming the throbbing Great Body. You're feeding a new story.

I'm awake in The Cave as cave. Every crevice of my body is every crevice of the mountains, kindred allies; resonant fountains. Fluids and gasses and altered states purrrrr in the dark. My body is an instrument; the echoes of the mountain make form, my womb and diaphragm rhythmically heave and heavy-breathe words out,

"Frwa fwa weh.

Muh maaaa maaaaayk.

Weee maaaaaaaake it.

WE MAKE IT!"

I listen.

I sense Ghost Pipe's floral, musty tickle of deep tendril time innervating the reciprocal tension membrane of my glacial-formed mountainous spine.

A draw to the bottom of the exhale at the peak of the plateau at the other end of these mountains. A further away land where I first entered the belly of our momma as a child, sharing eyes with the dragon, expanding chamber beyond chamber, beyond chamber.

Why journey now?

To write this very story.

My sacrum may unhinge.

Whispers.

I trace the full length of the plateau over and down, over and down, knitting bones of greater story, pulsing my cerebrospinal fluid with the swish and wish of our Great Body. A body whose amorous armor feeds and breathes and weaves—beech to beach to breach.

I'm deposited in a town atop a mountain of sands, sordidly sifted to spaciousness, whisking whirs cavernously connecting our stories. Gathered graveside Yuletide, we jubilantly pipe the ghosts humming heralds; hearts hungry for hollowness.

Transient trills carry joyously jumping thrills—ancestral kin to kin to kin. We're saving each other. I never want it to stop.

We break for saunter to the red and white twinkle-lit, peopled village green where a crowd marvels in merriment. I Pan the intermediate space, an upright hair in jeweled breath.

Whispers. Whispers. ScrrrrrUUuup!

Kindred allies I've felt the singing bones of but never met in the flesh appear, of the mountain's ongoing prayer.

How are they here?!

The signal hits. The Listen is vital to our Great Body.

The cave of my womb and diaphragm expand and contract, this time flooding waters with its sounding love. Receded oceans returning through mine and the dragon's salty eyes. Wails from the depths of primordial ocean leaving new formations. A glacier peers through tears as a new lens to know The Plateau.

Cries echo new relationship with our ever-changing, miraculous Great Body.

This is how we make life—together.

Beheld by our Great Body.

One that holds and feeds and devours and echoes our changing story.

Above and below ground.

We MAKE it. WE make IT. WE MAKE IT!

THE MEDICINE

Grief doesn't only change our relationship with something lost; it devours us and generates our great body.

"The more hollow a heart, the more resonant it can become."

~ Kathleen Dean Moore

YOU are part of this story, generating our Great Body with your resonance.

FEED THE STORY!

Choose parts and add to them. For example, say aloud, "I am the ashes of the juggler's fiery spheres."

Listen to Leah tell this story and engage in the resonance deeply here: storytelling

Leah Benjamin, LMT is fortunate to live intimately with a body of land that has her floored and consumed. Held in the Sequatchie Valley by the most wondrous caves, falls, and bluffs that, if you follow the sounds of, all the way up the plateau a thousand miles, you'll find her home sand.

Raised on the salty shores of the North Fork of Eastern Long Island, falling off the end, she heard mostly waves and the calls of seagull flocks. She still won't do her hair.

She lives rather ferally, crawling out of the forest to visit Marrowbone and community farmers' markets she is honored to run in Nashville. Please engage in your local food networks!

Enthralled by ferments for ages and the sacred honor of food play and offering, she invites you to please play with your food and please feed the spirits.

She's a voice of Amanita Muscaria and tangled in Smilax. She is a devout hiker and ecstatic dancer, building paths and story with the land.

Leah is a multi-medium artist giving bodies to that which want them. This includes adornments, paths, myths, words, sounds, plant medicine, food, community and culture, and her favorite—her son Jonah. She works with copper electro-forming to compose amulets of whispered stories of plants and stones, as well as kaleidoscopes.

She's a skilled bodyworker, listening intently and deeply to languages your body and subtle bodies share, honored to be in the space with whatever change is ready to take place during integrative sessions.

Bodywork and land experiences are shared in The Valley.

She travels for retreats, sacred gatherings, transformational festivals, and music venues to share bodywork, art, food, and workshops.

Explore her ever-changing offerings:

https://www.ritualridge.com

https://www.instagram.com/flourishwithleah/

https://www.instagram.com/ritualridge

https://www.instagram.com/feedthestory

Photographed on a walk deep grief with alamesser.com

CHAPTER 19

ESCAPING THE BELLY OF THE BEAST

Finding Your Way Through the Nightmare of Traumatic Grief

Carrie Elizabeth Wilkerson, M.A., M.MFT, O.M.

"Where there is ruin, there is hope for a treasure."

~ Rumi

MY STORY

"I, I think I need somewhere to go. I can't take care of my child right now. I can barely take care of myself. Do you know of anything like that around here?" I was stammering into the phone, my holistic doctor on the other end of the line. He had been a traditional medical doctor until the diagnosis of his wife's cancer when he decided to expand his expertise to learning anything and everything he could to help heal her. But what I was suddenly dealing with was new for him.

"I...don't actually know, uh—let me look into it, and I'll call you right back." He knew my need was urgent, and I heard the concern in his voice. The next day, I checked myself into a no-frills, specialized branch of one of our local hospitals, what they called a *low-level* psychiatric ward, reserved for anxiety, depression, and suicidal clients who required the least amount of intervention. It was an absolute turning point in my life, one I had unknowingly been waiting for since childhood. Finally, someone was going to help me. The dam burst inside me, and I gave in to receive it.

In life, all of us will know loss. All of us will feel grief. We will all suffer failures, broken dreams, and disappointments. At some point, we will all have our hearts broken. We'll have acquaintances and loved ones get sick and pass away. We, too, will get sick. Eventually, our bodies, too, will die. These things are incontrovertible facts of life on planet Earth. They are painful and life-altering, and acceptance of their inevitability and universality is part of how we learn to cope.

My story is about a different kind of loss. For some of us on planet Earth, there can be moments of loss that are qualitatively different. These losses are more complex because they also involve trauma. In the therapeutic world, we call it *traumatic grief*, or *complicated grief*.

Traumatic grief can come in one of two ways: either you suffer a loss that involves some trauma, like a violent death, the passing of a close loved one in a shocking or developmentally interrupting way, etc., or you suffer a trauma that involves major losses to grieve, which most traumas do. Traumatic grief is a loss multiplied by a shock; it's a whole lot to process, and many people get stuck there for a while. Post Traumatic Stress Disorder can be a part of this experience, which can look like intrusive thoughts, fixations on death and dying, persistent fears that others will die or leave, avoidance of triggers, trouble moving forward with life after a period of grieving, or even an absence of feeling or any sense of grief at all.

In my case, I had the trauma of being sexually abused by my father for about the first ten years of my life. As soon as he began to be my abuser at night, I lost him as a father. I lost my childhood in that moment, my sense of safety, innocence, and trust. And yet, during the day, my father still did show up regularly in my life as a caretaker, nurturer, provider, and mentor. The paradox is mind-bending. Because of this split in realities and the inducements to keep the secret, I was able to repress my knowledge of the abuse until I had my own child and began my own healing journey at 32. This is not an uncommon age for repressed memories from childhood to surface—often because we have the resources to deal with them by our early thirties, and our own children begin to reach the age when our abuse started, our memories are triggered. And then it's through dealing with childhood trauma that we can lose our family all over again.

By the time my first child came along, I had already hit several walls in my life. I knew something was *off* for me, but I had no idea just how far away from my true self I was—I had no idea who that woman could even be. I certainly couldn't have ever designed the twists and turns my life would take as it guided me from where I was onto my authentic path.

Up until that point, I followed in my father's footsteps as a professional academic. I was completing a Ph.D. program at Vanderbilt University in Community Psychology, a highly masculine, competitive, internationally renowned milieu, and after four years, I crumbled under pressure. I interrupted the accepted timeline by insisting on having a baby. But my postpartum body suffered from symptoms of chronic stress, and the medical doctors at Vanderbilt didn't have a solution for me. They addressed my complaints, one by one, with prescription medication that had side effects and with little hope of actual resolution.

As a trained systems thinker, I knew something larger was going on in my body than just these coincidental constellations of disparate symptoms. I grew up with severe illness and food allergies, and I already had a base of knowledge about holistic healing. I began to learn more and apply what I learned. I began to do cleanses and detoxing. I began working with a local holistic doctor. I also began meditation for stress relief in a small, local *sangha* (or practice group) of women.

My mind and body responded well to the changes I made. Many of my physical symptoms began to resolve. I became able to witness my own internal dialogue and emotional states and realized I had many layers of false, egoic protection around my true sense of self in relating to the world around me. As I progressed in healing and awareness, I had more congruence between my inner experience and my outer engagement. But even as I solved some problems, I found others puzzlingly emergent: I woke up every morning unexpectedly at 3:33 am on the dot; my overall sense of anger remained a major stumbling block and, at times, exacerbated by the healing process.

And still, other areas of myself remained entirely hidden. During a guided visualization with my holistic doctor in which I was to enter rooms in my inner *home* of my own design, an entire section of the house remained in the dark, unable to be consciously seen or known by me. My provider found this curious, as he had never encountered an experience like this when using the symbolic, exploratory tool in the past. Regardless of the anomalies, I persisted in my treatments.

One afternoon, as I was searching through online resources about anger processing, I stumbled upon a piece of artwork done by a woman whose father had sexually abused her. Her artwork was how she processed her feelings. As soon as I saw her artwork, my heart rate exploded. My thoughts scattered. Sweat prickled on my forehead. Because of my meditation training, I stayed present with my thoughts and sensations, and I began to ask myself: Why am I having this reaction? Did something happen *to me?*

My body told me *yes*. My heart raced faster. I felt a sense of cold-hot terror rising from the depths of my guts, through my solar plexus, chest, and heart, and continuing up my body. Later, I'd understand that this excruciating, unmoored experience was a panic attack, and I'd have several, even visiting the emergency room once when I mistook the event for a heart problem.

I asked myself, *who?*

If someone did this to me, *who was it?*

I searched my mind for possible answers, any male teachers, babysitters, coaches, or relatives who might have had access to me. No response from my body. Could it have been my own father?

My body's response was off the charts. If I felt terror before, now I became completely afraid of losing my foothold in reality. My world spun. I lost my breath.

I had enough presence of mind to calm down, focus, and call my husband home from work with a shaky voice. Once he arrived, he found me in a heap by the front door, waiting for him. I collapsed in his arms there on the floor, in the throes of a full-bodied flashback from the abuse.

When the hallucination subsided, we called my holistic doctor for help. This was beyond what any of us knew was possible. Luckily, he was able to refer me to a place to go where my real healing journey could begin. I spent four days in that in-patient facility and received a diagnosis of PTSD and a low dose of an anti-psychotic they typically used to treat PTSD hallucinations. From there, I began three weeks of an intensive outpatient program that introduced me to psychodrama and my inner child, coping skills for trauma, anxiety, and panic attacks, and family dynamics education. I was referred to a local counselor for weekly sessions after that and received EMDR (Eye Movement Desensitization and Reprocessing). I began going to a women's only group of a 12-step program, Survivors of Incest Anonymous (SIA). All of this was the initiation of a massive life transformation. My very existence was at stake—I felt I had no choice but to move in the direction of healing, and I clung to it.

As my childhood abuse memories came to consciousness, my mind opened to older, more ancient memories and understandings. I began to have psychic experiences, past life remembrances, and contact with spiritual guides who walked me through the darkest moments of my journey. I had dreams and sensations of healing energy pulsing through circles of light in the palms of my hands. I allowed myself to leave behind my strict academic background of the scientific method and began to learn as much about this new metaphysical world as I could from the most reputable sources available and from my own experience. Opening to these aspects of my journey brought me tremendous peace and refreshment. They enlivened me and gave me a larger sense of wholeness and understanding about the great personal tragedy I was walking through. It felt very much to me like a near-death experience—in facing some of my most brutal memories and shattered realities, I revisited moments in which I had thought as a child, that I very well might be killed. I also made contact with a much more profound level of reality that some might call Heaven; I was able to know my spiritual source and support. These weren't one-off events, either; they were spiritual revelations that expanded my sense of identity and became foundational for my new life that was carefully unfurling.

These years of transformation were a crucible for me, in which my old life and reality had to go through a horrific burning away so that an entirely different me could emerge. Almost everything had to be changed, inside and out. I had to surrender. I went through many different chapters of this alchemical process, one of which included confronting my father and disclosing the abuse memories to my family, ultimately losing a relationship with half of them. My father and I never spoke again, and he recently passed away last Christmas. We both had choices around how we navigated the truth of our relationship—none of them were easy. The grief over my father began long before he died. I lost a father, and I lost my father.

Although some days still feel complicated, I have an overriding sense of peace about it all. What my childhood abuse and its reconciliation brought me was ultimately a life of great purpose and passion in helping others to heal from the pain of trauma and in my connection to Spirit. Everything I have faced has led to my own wisdom, courage, and compassion for the darkest chapters of others. Now, I get to carry a torch and help them find their way through. I have made it to the other side of creating a new family for myself. I have also found an incredible, authentic community with others who understand the walk of profound transformation. These have been the gifts of a lifetime for me. They are also my path to forgiveness.

THE MEDICINE

My biggest medicine for living through traumatic grief and making it out the other side comes from my time in the 12-step program, Survivors of Incest Anonymous. You can learn about the program here: https://www.siawso.org.

I found the 12 steps to be a powerful spiritual program, tailor-made for our times of mass consumption and addictive stimuli so built into our daily lives. The first three steps are the foundation for everything after. They are about admitting our powerlessness in the face of our challenges, making the decision to offer everything over to the Higher Power of our understanding, and then doing it.

Let me acknowledge that spiritual connection or realization is no small feat—there are rituals and traditions thousands of years old from around the world designed to assist individuals in having mystical experiences of union with their sense of the Divine.

So, what I'm proposing now is perhaps overly ambitious, but it truly is the centerpiece of medicine that I would offer for anyone and everyone who finds themselves in a place of intractable devastation. Whether you have ever known it or not, there is a force greater than you that can carry you, develop you, and has your soul's best interest at heart. And through a moment of brokenness, you may finally be willing to lay aside your own grand schemes and give in to the ultimate source of all.

This medicine is most likely not enough on its own to heal someone of their traumatic grief. In fact, it may take many more interventions, treatments, and years for the healing to organically take root and flourish. But this medicine may be enough to help get us out of the deepest, darkest moments and to begin to connect us to our sense of direction, guidance, and nourishment to continue on our authentic path.

Often, a posture of humility is recommended for this first "moment of contact" with the Divine. That might look like a very traditional form of getting on our knees to pray. I would never recommend against that posture. But I do want to advocate for anyone who finds themselves in a place of traumatic grief where the load is simply too big to carry any further. What has been given to me is the idea of what we call in the West a *Lazyboy* recliner chair. So, I'm calling my medicine *God's Lazyboy.* If the word *God* triggers you, find a word that feels at least neutral or hopefully friendly. Spirit. Universe. Higher Power. The Tao. Universal Life Force. Creator. The Divine Mystery. Goddess. Love. The name is not as important as the sense of trust, goodness, and openness that could happen here for you.

For people who have been through any kind of trauma and grief, our bodies and minds have been stuck in fight/flight/freeze mode for weeks, if not years. We are exhausted, beaten, and bruised. We lack the ability to trust and feel safe in our own skin. We have been alone in our pain for as long as we can remember. We just need to *be held.*

So, at this moment, if you'll please indulge me, find the comfiest seat in your surroundings. If that's your bed, that's just fine.

You may want to grab a cozy pillow or a fuzzy-soft blanket. Get yourself really snuggled in somewhere.

And once you're in that seat, it's time to *relax.*

Because I want you to begin to realize that in this very moment, where you are sitting, God has got you. Love has *got you*.

Take five nice, slow, deep in-and-out breaths. Let time start to slow down. Notice the growing sense of calm around you.

Let that cozy, warm, snuggly, stable, solid, well-cushioned seat be the loving hand of your Divine Creator. Let it be a felt expression of benevolent energy that's just for you. Let yourself really feel held and supported. Let your body finally release all the burdens it's been holding so loyally. With each breath, let your muscles melt a little more into the seat holding you.

See if you can begin to *just let go*.

Now, if you're really feeling ready, as you're in a place of deep release and trust, you can even allow yourself to verbalize what your intention is here because it will make this relationship you are establishing even more powerful. Try saying something like:

I'm handing everything over to you now, Creator. It's all yours to order as you see fit. Just for today, I'm giving everything to you. Please show me the way, Your Way, and give me the courage to follow.

Even more, you can speak out the list of burdens or problems you want to hand over and get help for. Go ahead and call them all out as you let them go.

Now, for all survivors of traumatic grief, this is probably plenty to challenge us. So, after such a brave extension of trust and surrender, see if you can go back to 5 nice, slow, deep breaths to just relax again.

Let that seat where you are just keep holding you so strongly. See how it never lets you drop? Maybe there's even some love and uplifting energy that you could imagine is coming up from out of the seat as it holds you. It's the truth of our universe, the very fabric of our existence, even underneath all of the illusion of loss and pain. There it is. We just have to begin to open to it and realize it in safe moments. In God's Lazyboy. Here, we can relax, connect, and just be held.

Carrie is the owner of Back in Touch Wellness Center, a holistic healing community for body, mind, and spirit, since 2012. She has also been a hands-on healer and intuitive counselor since 2009, and is now a marriage and family counselor finishing her prelicensure phase. Through her teaching, consulting, writing, and healing, Carrie has been assisting organizations, communities, and human beings in their transformation processes for over 20 years. She has a Bachelor's degree in Psychology, cum laude, earned her Master's degree from the Human and Organizational Development Department at Peabody College, Vanderbilt, and her Master's degree in Marriage and Family Therapy from Lipscomb University. Carrie is also an ordained minister in the Universal Life Church.

In 2008-9, she experienced a profound awakening and began to have spiritual visions and energetic healing abilities as a result of her healing journey from childhood abuse. Since then, she has studied and apprenticed with a variety of healers to develop her hands-on technique working with the chakras and her intuitive skills. Most recently, she has deepened her clinical abilities through her therapy training program and added EMDR as a tool to work with trauma. She has a wild and wonderful family of four children with her loving husband, including one wolfdog and a leopard gecko. In her spare time, she loves to go adventure in nature, dance, meet up with her women's circle, or just be still and daydream out the window.

Connect with Carrie:

Website: https://www.backintouchwellness.com

Website: https://www.carriewilkersonhealing.com

CHAPTER 20

SAFE IN THE WORLD

Heal Ancestral Trauma and Free Your Magical Child

Kristin Clark

"There is a place of imagination and it is entirely real."
~ Robert Moss

MY STORY

The rowans and willows are weepin'. The roll of the hill whimpers on. I'm silent as stone—a bird with no song. I'm telling the bees that you're gone.

"This is who you are," she said. "A shapeshifter. A wild daughter. A traveler between time and worlds. You change the future and the past. You play and imagine and make worlds new. You make all things new."

In whispers, she told me my secret stories. She told me where I've been and who I am. I fell in love with her during the summer storms that blew through our woods—*the Wind*.

Sitting in our garage, on my tiny, green lawn chair, my dad and I watched her bring in the storms. She shape-shifted before my eyes. My heart mirrored her moods, filling with sorrow and wild longing, then bouncing joy as I watched her dance with a lady birch or weeping willow.

My dad was staring out at something too. I followed his gaze and saw two ravens. They were catching the wind beneath their wings to play and frolic. I wanted to laugh in wonder, but my dad looked so sad. He seemed almost translucent. There but not there. So, I stifled my laughter and joined his energy. *I'll be sad with you.* She became a mad gale that soaked us and sent us inside.

Later, the summer breeze was nuzzling my face. I couldn't stay awake. The night sounds were swirling into my dreams. *Crickets begin to crawl up my chest. Hundreds of honeybees circle around me. I slide down a twisting ladder of rope and wood. It's a 3-dimensional spiral, like a double helix. The bees begin to sting me again and again. I see myself through their eyes. I'm a beautiful blue peony. They sting me once more.*

I wake, gasping.

My parents were still out. I was waiting for them to be home, watching for their car lights to creep up my bedroom wall. After that, my mom would be in my room in minutes to kiss me goodnight. But there were no car lights that night. I heard footsteps running outside on the gravel driveway. The front door opened and shut. I soon felt her presence in my room, then her weight sag into the bed as she leaned in and kissed me, bringing the cool night air with her. And a little wine and garlic from the party. She was breathing somewhat heavily, but she was smiling and snuggling me. My Faery Mama. She left the room, and I heard the car come down the driveway, the engine revving and then screeching to a halt. He mumbled a few swear words as he slammed the car door and came into the house. I knew the drill. He was drunk. But I wouldn't learn for many years what had happened that night. She told me much later how my dad had gotten drunk at the party and drove home crazy. She told me she was screaming at him to stop and let her drive or just let her out. It made him drive faster and more crazy, nearly missing trees and mailboxes. He finally stopped long enough for her to get out. He watched her walk down our long, winding driveway, waited long enough for her to make some distance between them, then revved the engine and tried to run her down. She ran for her life into the woods. He ran into a tree.

Silver my veil in the twilight—funeral black for the hive. The humming is strong. The spirits have come. I'm telling the bees that you're gone.

My dad loved *Monty Python*, steam engines, and old pipe organs. He was given up by his 15-year-old mother at birth and adopted at a few days old. His adoptive father told my mom that when my dad was a baby, he had a mastoid ear infection, and when they couldn't take the screaming, they put him in his crib and left him to cry alone.

Sometimes, instead of bedtime stories, my dad told me horror stories from his childhood—stories of abuse. I knew he was a sensitive boy. He played violin and built beautiful things out of wood. He made my brother and me a life-size puppet theater, a three-story playhouse in our woods, and just for me, he built the most beautiful dollhouse I've ever seen. He carved every brick, and my mom, an artist, painted them the perfect variation of brick colors. Most of these gifts were kept secret and revealed on Christmas morning. He promised he wouldn't, but every year, he got drunk. As the day wore on, he'd become more sloppy and unkind. Berating us. Belittling us. One year, he laid into my brother extra mean until he finally broke and ran to his room. He had already crossed that threshold where boys stopped crying freely, which just made it feel worse. I glared at my dad as he started singing along with Handel's Messiah, oblivious to the wreckage. Then he noticed me.

"Kristin," he said, sounding alarmed. *It was my turn.* "Did you just kiss that dog on the head?"

"Yes," I said. *Oh, no.* I pulled our Sheltie tighter to my chest.

"Little girls who kiss their dogs on the head die." He drew out the words, incredulous that I could be so stupid.

I stared at him. My heart was pounding. He stared back, keeping up his joke, looking alarmed, like I'd drop dead any second. *Am I dying? How long will it take me to die?*

"Where's Mom?" I asked.

He was silent for a minute. He gazed at the little snow village he made, then back to me with a somber expression. The wind wailed and keened outside.

"She's left us, Kristin. She's packed her bags, and she's left us." Tears started streaming down my face. I knew my mom would never do that. But I couldn't take anymore. Maybe it would've been a funny *Monty*

Python skit. Maybe that's what he thought. Maybe he was a little sadistic. I just knew he was not a safe place.

It was snowing too hard to run out to the faeries, so I ran to my room to cry into my pillow. I let it out, the same questions running. *Why can't he love us? Aren't I precious?*

After a bit, I got up, wiped my eyes, and headed out to find my mom. Walking down the hall, I stopped to gaze at the large black-and-white photograph of my grandfather from the 1930s. It hung in the library loft with lots of other old photos of our ancestors. He wasn't smiling in the picture, but my mom said he had been a kind man. I stared into his face, wondering who he was. His people came from County Meath, Ireland—the land of the Celts. I got my faerie DNA and biggish, pointy ears through this line. I could also see my own reflection in the glass staring back at me. I'd play with letting my reflection come forward, then his. Disappearing. Reappearing.

Then, I'd hold us both in my vision at the same time. A kind man. I could almost feel it. And then, suddenly, I did feel it. It felt like everything was love, like when my mom beamed her light at me, her obvious and uncontainable joy in my existence. I felt his presence. I knew my grandfather was there, had been there with me, my mom, and grandma all this time. I knew that besides the faeries, besides my brother and my mom, besides raven and the wind, I had another guardian to keep me safe. Safe from my dad. Safe in the world.

Please, don't fly away. Stay. Stay with me stay. Singing your secrets, dear as the sun. I'm burning the oak leaves. Winter has come.

The night terrors started after my dad tried to kill himself. I'm not sure how hard he tried. He drank himself into oblivion, breaking things and then begging my mom not to leave him. She wouldn't appease him this time. He peeled himself off the floor, said he would do it, and ran out the backdoor into the dark woods—*my woods*. We stared at the door for a long minute. Then my mom decided that my brother and I should look for him. We grabbed flashlights and headed out. I felt myself disappearing. There but not there. We finally found him passed out in a sacred grove of white oak trees. The faeries could have danced him into a long sleep—100 years of sleep. I wish they would. I prayed they had. *Please, keep my dad for a hundred years and heal his sadness.*

I don't remember how we got him home. That night, I woke up screaming. I had nightmares every night for a year.

Then, at some point, despite everything, the dreams began to change. The nightmares stopped, and I began traveling into my father's story and the origin of his darkness.

I'm in my grandparent's home, standing in the shadows, looking at a crib. I know my dad is the baby crying. I look down. I'm wearing a white flowing dress, and smell like lilacs and green things. I'm a mother goddess of the spring with blooms that seem to be sprouting from my head and body. I walk to the baby. I pick him up tenderly and hold him to my heart. I croon and sing and dance him gently around the room. "You're safe," I say. "I'm here. You're safe."

I had many dreams like that over the following year. They were lucid and often repeated. It took me years to understand and embrace what I had been given in them. It was my kind grandpa who whispered to me from beyond the veil, "Go back to the dreams." I knew which dreams he meant, but it wasn't until the news came that my father was dying that I followed his guidance.

By then, I had already lived out the darkness I absorbed from him with drugs, alcohol, and stunning self-sabotage. By then, I had been healing for a long time through songs, art, and dreaming. I married a kind man of music and poetry and had two baby boys, all of which helped me heal my wounded child and bring forth my magical child as Queen of the Realm. The one who hadn't had much chance to reign before the wounded world crept in as a fearful place.

I didn't know all the times my dad was hurt, but there were a few I knew I needed to visit. The night before I flew to say my last goodbye to him, I journeyed into a memory he somehow had enough discernment to hold off on as a bedtime story.

I'm a little fox girl—wild and tender. My dad's eight-year-old figure is walking towards my hiding place in the woods. He's carrying the body of his cat, Blackie. She's big with kittens. All dead from the cold Wisconsin winter. He had begged his father to widen the cat door so she could get her expanding belly through and inside to warmth. But he wouldn't. That morning, he found her frozen by the back door. I watch as he circles aimlessly, holding her tight, weeping. There's no one to comfort him. I step out of hiding and approach him gently. He knows me from other journeys. We're friends.

Sobbing, he spoke, *"I'm so sorry. It's my fault."*

"It's not your fault. Your grown-ups are ghosts. And their grown-ups were ghosts. They don't have all of their soul. So they hurt you when they meant to love you."

I lead him deeper into the pine trees. I put my arms around him and let him cry on my shoulder. I think of St. Francis of Assisi, and he appears. He takes Blackie from my dad's arms and anoints her with love. He holds his hand over the ground, and a pink glow melts the snow and softens the earth. We bury her and the kittens in the black soil. We sing a song to Mother Earth, to take sweet kitties and hold them in her womb. The wind assists the pines, and they lean in to embrace us—*arms around arms around arms.*

"I wrote a song about you," I tell my dad, sitting on the side of his bed.

"Uh oh," he says.

"It's about the good times. Remember when you took me swimming in Lake Michigan during a thunderstorm? I loved that. It's about that." Tears stream down his face.

"I'm sorry," he says.

"I know," I say. "I forgive you." *I forgive you.*

Dripping like gold from my fingers. The trumpets and celandine sigh. You are the one on the tip of my tongue. I'm telling the bees. I'm telling the bees. I'm telling the bees that you're gone.

After he passed, I felt my little one tugging on me. It was her turn now—the one who walks in curiosity and wonder. The one who knows the wind and faeries and moss-covered land is in love with her. The one who knows she creates real worlds when she plays and imagines. It was time to go back and bring love, safety, and magic to all the moments it seemed to be missing.

I go back now to my little self at about seven. I see her staring out the window in wonderment as the March wind calls.

She's a madwoman. She knows every way into the house, and she is screaming and whistling through my room. Outside, she conjures a frenzied dance of falling leaves. It's a celebration day—a jubilee. I don't know why it's so exciting or why my heart feels so achy. But I know she wants me to come out and play. I know they are all waiting for me in the woods. As soon as I bust out the door, she's all over me, whipping my hair up like a mermaid in a watery cavern, bundling me with such urgency down the path that I'm tripping over my feet. I get to the deepest part of our woods and lie down on a pile of leaves. Laughing and breathless, I spread out like a five-pointed star, a soft smile on my face. My breath deepens and slows.

"Caw, Caw, Caw," says raven from an invisible perch. Goosebumps rise all over my skin, and I don't know if it's from the chill, the sound of his voice, or the feeling that he is singing from a deeper world, a world behind this one. Everything goes still. Her madness softens to match my breathing. She gentles herself and trills tenderly. A wild mother now, she encircles me with love, tickling a tiny troop of faeries and honey bees on my bare legs. I begin to hear their song. First, it is a deep hum beneath me, then a lifting to strings, bells, and a feather. Tones of ecstasy echo and bounce through time and hemispheres, through the hallway of a thousand doors, and into every one of my dreams. Faery music, the song of the Earth. Infinite layers in one note. Layers peeled back for me, like pages in a book of soul. My heart breaks a little in awe and wonder, and my pages begin to write themselves. Stories of selkies and dragons and green buds, of raven boy and the Queen of the Faeries, of wild mothers and little boys. I sing out loud with the trees. I am cherished and adored. I am safe in the world. I write myself as a love story in the faery woods, in the in-between, by bedsides and passageways, in the terror of the night, in the cradling and keening, the welcoming and farewells, in the hum of the bees and on the shores filled with wandering ghosts. I am not afraid. I came to play. I am safe in the world.

THE MEDICINE

The poem woven throughout my story are lyrics to a song I wrote called *Telling the Bees*. Bees are psychopomps, like ravens, who connect us to our beloveds beyond the veil.

Consciousness is the source of all creation, and what we do with our imagination and our dreams can change reality as we know it. Returning to my father's wounded one as a healing agent has brought tremendous healing for me. It has spun a thread of love and forgiveness and sent out a curative ripple through time in all directions. I embarked on these journeys only after I'd moved through lots of pain, rage, and loss.

When you're ready (and if you choose), I invite you to journey back to your little one or to any family member who was not able to free themselves from patterns of abuse in their lifetimes.

To Begin…

Set your intention. Which memories or ancestral stories come forward that most need to be reclaimed in love? Where has soul been lost?

Feel into the sacredness of the mission, remembering that everything is connected, and the experience you have in the imaginal realm may bring change to the physical.

Create a safe sanctuary conducive to magic and privacy: a room with sacred objects and candles, your bed, the woods…

Choose a portal: secret door, soul tree, cave.

Allow your imagination to flow wild and free. You're dreaming it up and receiving it from spirit.

Don't edit what appears. Trust the wisdom of your imagination and the journey.

Allow your loving intent to bring light to the dark places.

When you feel complete, return to your body and journal your experience.

In my journeys, I ask divine love to express through me.

Let this love guide you.

So that all the stories we inherit and pass on that hold us outside of love may be re-known.

 **Kristin Clark** is a singer/songwriter, award-winning fine artist, and certified dream coach. These artistic expressions all began as explorations into self-healing and have now become life-long passions.

In the art world, she has studied with renowned artists Dawn Whitelaw, Pat and Jody Thompson, Anne Blair Brown, James Richards, and Peggi Kroll Roberts. She is a signature member of the American Impressionist Society. Her paintings hang in private collections throughout the United States and Europe.

In the world of dreams and Shamanism, she has studied with Wanda Burch, Udana and Solarum, Sandra Ingerman, Gaia Sisterhood, Dasha Bond, Dana Micucci, Karen Renée Robb and New York Times best-selling author Robert Moss. Robert Moss has been a true guide and mentor, sharing Kristin's music with his readers, students, and fellow dreamers.

She also finds great inspiration from Paul Selig and the Guides and feels their teachings have influenced her work and visions.

In 2020, she released her debut album, *River of Mist*, produced by her husband, Bryan Clark. Most of the songs on the record first came to her in dreams, whispered by the faeries and other holy helpers. Poetic and mystical, they offer a portal for healing journeys in magical, inner landscapes. Her songs have been featured on the Shift Network, at festivals honoring the Celtic Turning of the Wheel, concerts of healing sound, moon circles, and recently in the Faery Glen of Rosslyn Chapel on the Summer Solstice. She shares her performance schedule, paintings, and other offerings on her websites and social media platforms. Her record, *River of Mist*, is available on iTunes and Spotify and is the perfect soundtrack to this chapter.

Connect with Kristin:

https://www.kristinclarkmusic.com

https://www.kristinclarkartist.com

https://www.facebook.com/kristinclarkart/

https://www.facebook.com/riverofmist/

Instagram: @kristinclarkmusic

https://music.apple.com/us/artist/kristin-clark/1486250876

BEE STIRRED RECIPE

Channeled from the Bees

~ Leah Benjamin

You will need a soup or beverage that can be stirred.

It does not have to be something that needs to be stirred.

Simply something that can be stirred.

Perhaps you'd like a special spoon.

The bees stir for many reasons.

Sometimes for a short time and sometimes for a long time.

Sometimes faster, sometimes more slowly.

The bees stir when something has their attention.

They also change,

stirring in a different way,

giving something else their attention.

Begin to stir your beverage or soup.

Notice what has your attention.

Does the stirring have your attention?

Or does a thought have your attention?

Does the thickness or thinness have your attention?

Does the stir stick or spoon have your attention?

Notice that you can change what has your attention.

Notice you can change how quickly you can stir while being gentle.

Blessed Bee.

Chapter 21

FOLDING TIME

Our Stories that Heal Lineage Forward and Backward

Sonia Fernández LeBlanc, M.Ed

*"May we forage our own stories,
gathering from them the medicines that will heal us,
all the way through and back again."*

~ Sonia Fernández LeBlanc

MY STORY

What if I could show you how to fold time to heal yourself and your lineage forward and backward? Our stories live in reality yet rest on the precipice of liminality, and clarifying inside our dreams can entwine to become our very own curative elixirs, healing us through time and space. As a medicinal storyteller who guides those who feel called into their deepest stories, I share my own as a prescription.

On the pages to follow, I offer a layered personal story of generational mental illness, forgiveness, cyclical endings, and healing through the long lens of soul kin. We can overlay our stories upon this template if we feel called to the journey. This is a communal practice in grief, joy, and getting the damn thing out from inside so you have room for the stories to come. Let's get to it.

* * *

I dreamed of us not so very long ago.

We were both little but near the precarious age when grown-ups began to condemn playing make-believe because it was time to get serious. In my dream, we are both perched upon the thick, twisty limbs of the beloved mango tree at La Finca. You are a solemn, dark-haired child whose eyes have a sadness not your own, which you carry inside your bones, and I recognize my child self with all the lightness and delight I have always exuded.

The tree we are in is your solitary respite for lounging, eating mangos, and imagining. I am welcome there because I am your imaginary friend. You tell me about the children in every generation of your family and their imaginary friends who are, in fact, their own future children. You tell me that someday I will come into physical existence as your child, and so on. I already know that, upon my embodiment, I, too, will have an imaginary friend—two who will eventually embody as my children. This is the way of our family line.

I awake to realize that, rather than a dream, this is my soul's remembering of a friendship stretching back through time, returning to me in the realm of dreams, a reminder of who we are to one another. This story will bear witness to the healing powers of remembering. I want it to exist for us both in this earthbound realm, not because I want you to read it but for the story to be a medicine for more than our lineage alone.

It begins for me the night both your birth family and your chosen family died to you. Do you remember that night? I can still close my eyes and return to my 11-year-old self, waking to the sound of a phone ringing in the dead of a cold December night 35 years ago. I can feel myself rising from my cozy four-poster antique feather bed with the rocking horse comforter I adored. With all my history between that moment and now, I can pinpoint when the tight weaving of our lovely little family snagged and the slow unraveling began. Let me tell you our story, Father.

Back when phones only lived in homes and not in our hands, a call in the middle of the night was either a wrong number or something terrible. When it woke me, I waited and listened to hear if my parents would go back to sleep. But their light came on down the hall and didn't turn off. Then came murmuring and movement from their room. When it was clear they were very much awake, I left the warm comfort of my bed and crept down the hall to discover my father packing a suitcase. I crawled into their bed and learned my grandfather, my Papa Rufino, and my Uncle Anibal, my father's older brother and only sibling, were dead—their lives taken, just like that, in a car accident. Every bone of my grandfather's body was broken. The back of my uncle's head was severed. It's one of those horrifying stories you hear as a child about your own beloved family, and it lives inside your DNA forever. You would still remember it even if you heard it and didn't know the people involved.

When my grandmother, my dear Mama Lina, received the news, her heart literally broke—a massive heart attack. My father was leaving for the Dominican Republic, (his birthplace) and family home on the first early flight to attend to the tragedies that had befallen his immediate family.

Before this moment, life for me was a beautiful, steady-flowing stream. Loving parents, a very connected and involved extended family, the cutest two-year-old baby sister, a good school, lots of friends, and my most sacred practice of ice skating, where I spent most of my waking time outside of school. It was a lovely existence.

And it all changed with that ringing phone.

When my father left early on that dreadful December morning to bury his father and brother, nurse his mother back to health, and attempt to run and then sell the land that had sustained his family for over 50 years, it was the last time I saw him as the beloved, devoted father he had been to me for every day of my life thus far. I got him for 11 years before his unraveling began. An inward madness, which I later learned had been lurking in his genes and building up from a lifetime of unacknowledged heartbreaks, broke free inside my father. This latest upheaval was his undoing. Not even his lovely family, my wonderful mama, baby sister, nor I could save him from the void he dropped into that day and from which he chose never to return.

All the while, this devastation led to one of the most poignant experiences of my life because we moved to the Dominican Republic shortly after that. I lived abroad at such a pivotal coming-of-age time, attending an international school with kids from across the globe. I spent weekends, holidays, and summers at what we called La Finca, our cattle ranch, whose house was nestled in a grove of giant fruiting shade trees. Most notably, I developed deep, lasting friendships with my father's family, especially my Mama Lina, *with whom I remained very close into my adulthood as she lived to be 92. Although all these wonderful experiences shaped who I am today, my father was the collateral damage.*

We only lived there together for two years before political unrest forced my mother, sister, and myself to return to the States. Another two years passed before my father could sell the ranch and return to pick up where we left off. But he was already lost to his madness and tangles by then. He abandoned us and never spoke to or saw his own mother again.

When I had babies of my own, they helped me remember that I, too, can unravel in order to reweave. That our familial lineage can be healed.

I could go deep into what happened as you tore yourself from our family. The ultimate villain for the first 25 years after you left us, I shaped you as an adulterer, a thief, a pathetic and insane excuse of a man who abandoned his family. And honestly, that is an accurate description of the facts of your indiscretions. For years, I made a joke about how there was someone crazy in every generation of the Fernández family, and you were the one in your generation.

A decade ago, my already precarious inherited mental health began to crumble, confirming I was most likely the crazy one in my generation. Just as I became a mama to the two most glorious humans I have ever encountered, lifetimes of unresolved trauma layered upon my very own life's worth and threatened to sink me to the bottom of the well. But I had made a pact with myself long ago that I would never be like you. I couldn't let my babies, nor their father—my most beloved—down.

In my work to understand your story, I know you struggled your whole life with much of your own trauma and abandonment and that when the sadness and darkness of generations fold themselves into the crevices of our being, it's so hard to unfold and realign to a new timeline. You could only manage it for so long before the darkness reclaimed you. But it is possible to crawl out of the well where you remain trapped. I know because I did it and saved myself—and I think I saved a part of you, too.

I had been surviving on the story of how you broke us for 20 years before I became a mama myself. In order not to perpetuate the madness of the previous generation, I needed my energy to be clear so I could be fully present with my own children. But 20 years is a long time to manage unresolved trauma. I realized I wasn't equipped to continue to create the energy needed to maintain my lifetime of anger, bitterness, and the constant expectation of further abandonment, nor was I able to ferment it into the hatred and anxiety I had been churning out at you for decades. It slowly began leaking out onto all I loved: a spillage site needing immediate remediation.

The clean-up began with a simple question.

"Mama, do you have a Papa?" My six-year-old caught me by surprise on a regular day.

It was inevitable that they would wonder about you. My mama has always lived with us since they can remember, and my husband has a mama and papa who, although they live far away in the Caribbean, are engaged and connected to our family. I knew, eventually, my children would wonder why you were missing. But I wasn't expecting what came after my response, which began the reweaving.

"Yes, Elena. Tía Clara and I have a papa, but he left us long ago when Tía was very young, and I was a young teenager. I haven't seen him or had any contact with him since I was in high school. Tia has no memory of him at all."

Elena thought about this for a moment and spoke with the wisdom of the elders. "How could anyone miss out on being with you and Tía? How sad he chose to miss out on you two. Y'all are the best."

Listening to the truth of my child's knowing response, all the rage and anxiety began to slowly release, offering space for my long-suppressed grief to surface. I understood at that moment I had learned how to be a devoted and loving parent to these young babies because, for the first 11-and-a-half years of my life before your own devastations broke you beyond repair, you and Mama were the best parents anyone could ask for. When you fractured before us, it disrupted us at a cellular level, which I have only recently been able to begin to repair, thanks to the two human souls who chose me to be their Mama.

I knew who they were before you came to me as your child-self in a dream to tell me I was your imaginary friend, further confirming how time is a revolution folding in and over upon itself. We're all tethered together in this reality, in the liminal realm beyond, and inside one another's dreams. All of us. I was your imaginary friend, as my own babies were mine. I understood then we are all just healing one another through the long lineage of our interwoven souls.

But how can this be? The medicine is the story.

Not so long ago, I learned a little trick about time. In deep contemplation of my childhood, I wondered why my father had been so devoted for the first 11 years of my life. What was so special about that time which allowed his mental capacities to remain healthy enough to be the best father a girl could imagine having? And then it clicked. It was this very contemplation of a 45-year-old grown woman remembering her bright childhood and her beloved father. This current iteration of myself is the reason he was healthy enough to be devoted to me for 11 years.

His once imaginary friend, his first-born daughter, and the grown woman I would become were all rooting for him to be the best father for as long as possible—and all that love created the conditions for it to be so. Circumstances unfolded, and layers of unacknowledged trauma broke free, only allowing us 11 years. But for a short span, I can say with certainty, time folded us in, and all the stars aligned to heal the long existence of our souls; right now, remembering my child-self and our shared relationship is what allowed for those 11 lovely years to happen in the first place.

Humans are powerful time travelers who realign time in ways we don't even know how to discuss yet. I don't even know if I'm making sense here. But realizing the clarity of how setting one's attention to a time long before can bring our energy to that point in time and offer support inside that previous timeline was the craziest and truest knowledge I have ever encountered. A peace settled in me knowing the current version of me, who had done the deep mental healing my father never had a chance to go through, had walked alongside him during my childhood, offering him energy and strength to be mentally sound and devoted to my own child self. It was a profound witnessing.

My recent understanding is that I did this in the same soul capacity that brought me to him as his imaginary friend so long ago in his childhood: The same soul capacity created the conditions for my children to whisper in my ear when I thought I had broken beyond repair to get up and do whatever it took to heal so I could be there fully for them. This is the same soul capacity that supported me in my decade-long healing journey, which has rewoven all the unraveling of my lifetime, including past generations and those to come.

My embodied contract with my father for this lifetime is complete. Our relationship continues in the liminal and dream realms, healing from our earthly complications in order to know better and do better in the next iteration. I find comfort in all our higher selves tethered to one another through time and space, offering support and walking us through life on this planet. I believe we all can tap into this time-folding experiment and find the medicine we need to heal ourselves and our lineage from our very own stories.

THE MEDICINE

What is a story in your life from which you still hold deep unresolved trauma that you are ready to transmute into medicine? What is a story with which you are ready to cross over into the liminal and back again, to fold in and outside of time and space so that it may be cleared and so that you have room for new stories?

I bet something came up for you as you were reading mine. Go with the one that is whispering, "I recognize us in this story." Remember that all our stories are simply a mirror for one another.

- *Write down or voice-record your story.*
    - Dump everything that you remember about it onto the page. Get the whole thing out of your body and bind it in ink or in audio somewhere other than inside you. That is a spell in and of itself. If you go no further than this step, you will have made a little room in there for more stories.

- *Focus on the magical, joy-filled, simple, quiet, or sweet parts of the story.*
    - Those are the memories that we can fold into our hearts. For me, it was the life I had with my little family until I was 11.

- *As you are in your "now" moments, walk back into those memories and actually see your current self playing a role in why these memories are magical and sweet or why you found a strange inner strength and wisdom to survive a horror.*
  - This is when our past and future selves are supporting us all along our timelines. Where could you be showing up for your previous and future selves? Where were you bringing light through the darkness, helping your "then" self through a difficult or traumatic experience, or being the reason you survived?

- *Trust your story in all its iterations and through the realms, including how it's healing you and your lineage forward and backward in the now.*
  - Believing all the iterations and the multidimensionality of our stories is a story trust-fall practice that slowly heals the heartbreak because it helps the love and joy we hold at our core grow around the trauma. I fully forgave my father for all the brokenness because I had been broken, too. My only work has been to heal myself. I'm neither here to heal him nor here to use my energy to hate him. Targeting where we have our own healing work to do and beginning there is the only trickle-down economy that actually works. We ripple that energy outward to everyone we encounter, healing ourselves and all our ancestors and descendants as we practice this unraveling and reweaving.

Remember, this practice is a template. Hopefully, my story can be a guide for you. The key is simply choosing to open yourself to the reality, the liminality, and the dream realm where our stories exist. Begin where you are. Time is not a measurement. Your story is now.

Sonia Fernández LeBlanc, M.Ed (she/we) is a medicinal storyteller, a magical realist, an interSovereign community connector, and a scholar of ancient futuring and the imaginal.

She serves as a guide, teacher, and fellow traveler for those who feel called to journey with her in becoming the elders our vastly changing society needs and deserves through her imaginal space, Revolutions Imaginarium.

Within this realm, Sonia can be found…

- writing and self-publishing stories, essays, and books.
- facilitating workshops and retreats on writing, liberation, personal lore, becoming elder, expressive arts, and ancestral archiving.
- leading communities offering tarot and human design experiences.
- serving as spiritual guide for individuals and organizations wanting to connect more intimately to a balance of political, spiritual, and creative homemaking through a liberatory lens.
- leading the Root to Rise Contemplative Community, where she curates and creates learning opportunities around secular works as sacred text in the lineage of wisdom traditions, intensive study on a cycling curriculum of topics around deepening connection to our embodied divinity, which roots us to the Earth and raises us into the divine, as well as expanding the possibilities for liberation for ourselves, our ancestors and descendants.

She is a devoted mama to her two human loves, a trio of fur loves and a jungle of plant loves; a pretty impressive spouse to the coolest human she knows; and a damn good friend from what she has been told by those who call her so. Finally, and maybe most importantly, she throws one hell of a dinner party!

Connect with Sonia:

https://www.linktr.ee/soniafernandezleblanc
https://www.soniafernandezleblanc.substack.com

CHAPTER 22

WISDOM OF YOUR MOTHERS

Weaving Ancestral Grief and Hope into Your Own Story

Shelby Reardon, LMFT

*"Trauma was not being
able to get the hands
of the clock off me.*

*Healing was learning
no one has ever laid a fingerprint
on the part of me that's infinite."*

~ Andrea Gibson, You Better be Lightning

MY STORY

"Do you ever choose a word or a phrase to focus on at the beginning of a new year? This year, mine is *consistency*."

I intend to. Sometimes, I do.

I usually choose something to help me focus on my goals for the new year, but I don't always remember to check in with myself to see if I'm on track.

"What do you want to focus on for 2024? It can be anything! Don't overthink it."

Ha! Don't overthink it! Right.

"Be bold. Be brave. Be authentic."

"Perfect! Why did you choose those words?"

These words reminded me of a path that first appeared after my divorce—a path toward healing. I turn 50 this year, and I am truly ready to grieve and heal, to be bold, brave, and authentic. My journey toward healing has been generations in the making.

OCTOBER 30, 2022

Día De Los Muertos Ceremony

"Lay down and get comfortable. Cover your eyes, listen to the music, and let our voices guide your journey to the underworld."

Nothing will happen. I never see any visions when on a shamanic journey.

Don't be so negative. Be open. Let your mind wander.

Okay, okay.

Soon, I'm floating, drifting amongst swirls of golden light illuminated by the voices of chanting warriors. My body, senses, and soul are consumed by the rhythmic beating of native American warriors banging on their drums, chanting and wailing; the air pulses with the vibrations of the bass, enveloping my body like a warm, loving hug with swirls of golden light guiding me into a visit to the underworld.

Welcome, my love.

I sense, more than I see, the faces of women surrounding me, whispering.

Welcome, my love.

These ethereal spirits invite me into their realm. These enchanting women, whose bottomless brown eyes look deep into my soul, are parts of me. It seems impossible, yet they all hold my gaze, allowing me to see and feel their collective consciousness, how their souls weave into the tapestry of my own story. These women are my mothers. These women, born of their wombs, are the souls whose experiences crafted my existence.

Listen, my love. Feel.

Pain.

My soul drifts amongst waves of anguish, pain, loss, and grief.

My mothers engulf me, a lifeline, as the golden light was eclipsed by darkness.

Their pain is everything.

I scream out their pain.

I cry for their loss, their grief.

Their anguish guides me, taking my hand and inviting me to understand and weave their story into my own.

This infinite tapestry of trauma that weaves itself from generation to generation.

Scenes upon scenes of women's lives trapped by poverty, violence, restrictions, and expectations. Fabric ripped by anger, fear, pain, and violence stitched back together with love and hope.

Their stories.

My story.

A majestic grey owl emerges from the darkness, swarmed by golden bees whose nectar creates trails of light following its flight. With a nod, the owl invites me along as the bees illuminate a path toward healing and hope through the pain.

Be Bold. Be Brave. Be Authentic.

The chorus of my mothers' voices chant these words, and I feel an urgency, a command to listen.

What do you mean?

In the distance, I heard Stephanie and Jennifer calling me. Their voices gently summoned me back to the present, signaling the end of this shamanic journey. I opened my eyes.

What the fuck was that? What just happened?

I've taken part in shamanic journeys before, usually left disappointed that I didn't see or feel anything magical. This time was different. I was awake; I remembered their faces and love; I still felt their pain and believed in the hope of their words.

Be Bold. Be Brave. Be Authentic.

These seemingly simple words from my mothers guided me toward the path I'd been searching aimlessly for my whole life: the path to myself. Ironically, this wisdom was always with me; I just had to listen.

I had to sit with these words.

What did they mean? How would I ever figure this out?

How was the pain of my mothers a part of me?

Could grieving their pain help heal mine?

How do I even do that?

The Universe provides angels to guide us. Stephanie and Jennifer, my soulful sisters who hosted the Día De Los Muertos ceremony, were planning a Dream Weaver's Journey to Oaxaca, Mexico, in the spring of 2023 for women to connect through community and facilitate healing. This was perfect! I'm so grateful I decided to go.

Be Bold. Be Brave. Be Authentic.

Could this be what my mothers meant? I boldly and bravely signed up for a week-long journey to Mexico with women I barely knew, excited and hopeful to learn what '*be authentic*' meant for me. That trip was transformative, crafting a space to connect with my ancestors, feel at home with their culture, and embrace that part of me.

So, what drew me to Mexico?

My maternal ancestors descend from the Yaqui, an indigenous tribe from Sonora, Mexico. Fleeing from war and persecution in the 1800s, my great-great-great grandmother Maria immigrated to the United States, married a Yaqui man, and settled in a rural, impoverished area in California. Being a brown-skinned woman from Mexico in the 1800s, there were little to no opportunities or resources other than to marry and have children to survive. The cycle of violence, poverty, and persecution followed her to the United States.

Could she even conceive of a life where a woman could choose what her future looked like not based on her gender or the color of her skin nor live under a man's rule? I don't believe she saw that for herself or her daughters, but I hope she saw a glimmer of hope for her granddaughters.

The trauma my mothers experienced from the constraints of denied freedoms and discrimination was passed along to each generation, daughters carrying the collective pain of their mothers. My great-great-grandmother Theresa, my great-grandmother Custodia, my grama Freda, my mother Dania, and my aunt Cassy all felt the burden of this trauma.

My great-grandmother Custodia, born in 1906, felt particularly burdened by the weight of this trauma and chose not to teach Spanish or native traditions to her children, especially her daughter Freda, with the hope of easier assimilation into the mainstream white culture of the 1920s and 30s in Monterey.

"Why didn't Grandma Cass teach you Spanish, Grama?"

My grama Freda learned from her mother that her native roots were a burden and her white heritage from her Scottish father was the key to opening doors of opportunity and a way out of poverty. Freda never fully embodied this idea and had a strained relationship with her mother for most of her adult life. She spoke of something missing in her life, a yearning for a connection to her ancestors, to her mothers, that she was denied. She never felt like she belonged anywhere or identified with any group, a soul out of place and time. I know that feeling.

Freda spent a lifetime collecting books, reading, and learning about everything she could, especially about her native culture, which she celebrated with me and her grandchildren. She passed that inquisitive nature, love of learning, and cultural knowledge down to me, and I'm eternally grateful.

"Mom, did you realize that the women in our family are all divorced, had strained relationships with their daughters, and some sort of addiction?"

"Really?" my mom asked. "I wonder why."

"Most of them married young and had at least one baby in their teens or out of wedlock. All chose to divorce, many multiple times. Addictions ranged from alcohol, drugs, smoking, and excessive spending. They grew resentful and angry after failed relationships and dreams lost, inadvertently directing that anger towards their daughters. The cycle continued generation after generation."

"Damn. You're right."

Unbeknownst to them, my mothers developed ways of coping by numbing and distracting from the pain through failed relationships and addictions. No one taught them how to feel or name that pain or even how to understand it. They were brave, resilient women who did what they knew to survive, react, and cope.

I feel the burden of this trauma, too. I didn't know what it was, how to name what I was feeling, or even know that my pain was woven into theirs. Before I understood the root of this trauma, I repeated many of the same behaviors and patterns of my mothers.

Now, over a hundred years after my grandmother Maria fled her home village, I'm the woman best positioned to finally heal and break these generational chains so my daughters will not feel their constraints.

Am I too late?

No. Show them. Teach them by example.

Be Bold. Be Brave. Be Authentic.

Two words. *Be authentic*. Perhaps the most challenging two words for me to understand for myself.

It took me almost 50 years to begin to understand what being authentic means for me. The wisdom of the words from my mothers broke through the noise of my pain with divine timing, and I began to feel, to grieve, to heal our trauma. Through this process, I'd understand how to be bold, brave, and authentic.

Two life-altering moments illustrate how the trajectory of my story shifted—each moment held the opportunity to be bold, brave, and authentic. The first, I was not ready. The second, I was.

APRIL 24, 1994

My mom is calling.

Fuck.

"It's time," my mom murmured as soon as I answered the phone. "You need to come down here and see your grama now."

My grama is dying. She fought bravely through her second round of cancer, and she's tired. She has decided it's time to pass over.

Fuck.

How am I going to navigate my world without her?

I need her. I want her. She can't leave me.

"I'll be there tomorrow," I mumble over the phone, my voice barely audible as fear and grief overwhelm me.

Fuck.

My grama Freda left this Earth two days later. I know she waited for me before letting go, succumbing to the cancer that ravaged her body. She wouldn't leave without sharing one more moment together. We were incredibly close, sharing a soul connection others didn't understand. She saw me, heard me, and supported me in the unique ways I craved.

When she left me, I was just 19 years old, in my second year studying marine biology at the University of Santa Cruz. I felt broken and lost, hating myself for unknown sins. I knew I was incredibly smart and going to save the world somehow; that was never in question. The self-loathing permeated that knowing, and I often found destructive ways to avoid feeling it.

One way was finding solace in drug-filled trips with friends to raves in San Francisco. I'd take ecstasy, acid, and smoke pot and escape into a world of pulsating beats, bright lights, and hundreds of strangers turned best friends on the dance floor. For those few hours, it was bliss. I felt present and connected to myself, my friends, and strangers in a spiritually profound way. I knew it was all temporary, but I didn't care. I wasn't ready to face that pain.

I drifted for years, avoiding feeling my emotions, choosing instead to remain numb and disconnected from my life. I accepted behaviors from others, feeling I deserved nothing better, which further diminished my light. Life didn't stop. I graduated college, moved to Washington, DC to fight the "man," earned my first master's degree, got engaged, had my first child, moved to Tennessee, married, and had two more children. Thirteen years flew by. I didn't feel bold, brave, or authentic. I still felt broken, lost, and now angry.

DECEMBER 2011

"I want a divorce," my ex-husband declared late one December night after a particularly tense holiday season. This was not the first time I'd heard these words. We had separated once before.

"Okay," I responded flatly, feeling numb.

Here it is. I expected this. I want this. He simply chose to ask first.

"Really? You're okay with that?" he asked, perhaps confused that I didn't resist the idea.

"Yes. I want a divorce."

This time, I knew I would follow through with it.

That was a watershed moment. I boldly asserted myself and bravely stuck to my decision to leave an extremely unhealthy relationship. This, I realized later, was being authentic to myself.

After my divorce, to be authentic meant choosing to change careers to fulfill my soul's purpose to help people heal. I earned my master's degree in marriage and family therapy, and as a therapist, I now guide others to explore their path to healing. Sometimes, I forget to keep moving along with mine and need reminders. I really need to listen to those reminders.

"Your body holds your trauma."

What the hell does that mean?

My body warned me time and time again, and I ignored it.

I spent years trying to figure out why my body hurt, and years of not finding anything that accounted for my fatigue, systemic pain, and inflammation.

"There is nothing wrong with you."

"Your blood work looks great. I can't find any cause for your pain."

"Let me prescribe…"

Whenever I left a doctor's office, I felt ignored and defeated.

I'm in pain! Don't tell me there is no reason for it!

I'd finally had enough. There had to be another way to heal.

What was that?

"Your body holds your trauma."

There are many ways a person can manifest their pain, and my body took the brunt of mine. With all that trauma stored in the cells of my mind and body, it's no wonder everything hurt.

Not until I embraced the exploration of my generational trauma and began to grieve years lost to anger and fear did my body finally begin to feel safe. Safe to feel and celebrate the joy and passion of embodying my spirit and to feel present and alive. I started exercising and running to celebrate my body, challenge myself, relieve stress, and help move the stirred-up emotions out through my body. Remarkably, my body began to feel better.

Allowing myself to grieve the trauma my mothers experienced felt courageous and transformative. I acknowledged the pain and emotions deep within with patience and growing self-awareness. To understand, I must sit and feel all the emotions— anger, fear, sadness, and confusion (without numbing or hiding). By allowing the pain to surface, my path toward healing emerged, and I continue daily.

Seek those who heal. Show them who you are.

Many of us need guides to help navigate the seemingly dark muck of our thoughts, memories, dreams, and the deepest parts of ourselves we keep hidden. My grama guided me through my youth. During my shamanic journey, the owl and the bees led me to my mothers. Now, my mothers are my guides.

"Welcome, sister."

The owl and bees also led me to a community of beautiful, badass women offering themselves as spiritual guides, creating and sharing rituals and ceremonies that help me grieve, heal, and grow. Like my grama Freda, I felt on the fringe, never truly fitting in anywhere with anyone. These women see me, accept me, and invite me to witness their lives and share my story.

Who are your guides?

THE MEDICINE

WEAVE HEALING INTO YOUR STORY

Telling your story is essential to understanding your trauma and pain. Writing is a deeply personal and therapeutic process to explore and craft your story. As you begin, allow your guides to support you as you grieve. Let your words weave hope into your tapestry of trauma.

Create a safe and sacred space to honor this exploration. Reflect on your guides. Bees appeared for me during my journey, gentle guides through my muck. Perhaps they'll appear to guide you.

Ground yourself by breathing deeply, grab your favorite notebook, find a cozy nook to curl up, and begin to write.

Below are some journal prompts to help.

REFLECTIONS ON CHILDHOOD

What memories do you have of your upbringing? How do these memories make you feel?

How did your parents' experiences shape their parenting style? In what ways do you see these patterns continuing or breaking in your parenting (of yourself or your children)?

What emotions come up when you think about your mother's or your father's experiences or your own experiences as a parent?

How have these emotions affected your relationships, self-perception, and overall well-being?

IDENTIFYING PATTERNS

Reflect on any recurring patterns or behaviors in your family that you find challenging. How might these patterns be linked to generational trauma?

Are there specific events or situations in your family history that have a lasting impact on generations?

UNDERSTANDING BELIEFS AND VALUES

What beliefs or values were passed down from your maternal or paternal lineage? How have these influenced your own beliefs and values?

Do you want to challenge or redefine beliefs or values for yourself and future generations? Reflect on ways to do that.

SELF-COMPASSION AND FORGIVENESS

Practice self-compassion by acknowledging the challenges and pain within your maternal and paternal lineage. How can you be kinder to yourself in light of this awareness?

Reflect on the possibility of forgiving yourself and, if applicable, forgiving your mother or father and other parental figures.

Reflect on cultural or familial practices. Do any resonate with you as a source of healing and strength?

BREAKING THE CYCLE

Reflect on ways you can consciously break negative generational patterns. What intentional steps can you take to create a healthier, more nurturing environment for yourself and future generations?

Journaling is a powerful way to explore your emotions, connect with your pain, reflect on your strength, and move toward healing. This process often dredges up suppressed emotions that can feel overwhelming. Here's a gentle reminder to consider seeking professional support or therapy to facilitate this process.

Shelby Reardon, LMFT, MMFC/T, MPA, CYT200, is a licensed marriage and family therapist in Tennessee, guiding people toward healing their relationships with themselves and their loved ones. She is a published author whose works range from poetry, nonprofit fundraising and healing. After working over 20 years in the nonprofit world, advocating for justice and equality, she shifted direction and now advocates for her clients' by empowering them towards healing and growth.

Always exploring and learning, Shelby is a Usui Reiki Master, a certified yoga teacher, and a health coach. As a healer and an advocate for change, she finds creative ways to incorporate her passions. Being an ultrarunner passionate about the healing benefits of nature and running, she's an ambassador for a nonprofit striving to provide free counseling to people in the trail running community, sharing their mission and educating about mental health issues. Shelby also offers energy healing sessions, educational resources, and empowering workshops for personal growth.

When not helping others, you'll find her running through the woods, training for an absurdly long race, sweating in a hot yoga class, dancing with strangers at a concert, or curled up on the couch drinking tea and eating dark chocolate while looking up new vegan recipes to try.

Connect with Shelby:

Website: https://www.shelby-reardon.com

Instagram: https://www.instagram.com/shelbyreardontherapy

Facebook: https://www.facebook.com/shelbyreardontherapy

Free resources to explore:

https://www.shelby-reardon.com/resources

CHAPTER 23

TWO MOONS

A Mother's Journey

Hope Kernea, Author and Mother

"Some of us are here to be the change makers in our family system. We're here to end generational trauma and start passing down love instead of pain."

~ Sheleyana Aivana

MY STORY

Toddler: a concept the new mother could neither fathom nor accept.

Her son's chubby legs would stagger around the mess of a house, digging through old beer bottles and crushed cans, never opting to play with his hand-me-down toys, just trash. Like mother like son, she thinks bitterly, tapping the ash from her cigarette into the empty beer can. The ashtray was broken courtesy of a fight between the woman and the child's father. Her son would bring her an empty can or a cigarette butt. He would flash her a toothy grin she felt should melt her heart, but her heart is a stone, and she has lived too long, so she sighed and peeled the can from his thick, sticky fingers. Gives him a stern 'no' before sending him on his way.

She tries to ignore the writhing ache in her gut. The ache that tells her it's no coincidence he brings her trash with hope in his eyes. Like mother, like son.

When it's time for bed, he screams and screams and screams. It's all she can do not to pull her hair out, so she digs like mad through her purse to find some piece of a pill that might make things less. It all seemed too big to carry. She was trying to sleep-train him, but his wails were a heavy thing. Too heavy some nights. She feels a wave coming on—feels herself beginning to spiral and thanks a god she doesn't believe in when she finds enough to hold her over. His screams die down in her head, and if she knew better, she wouldn't call it peace. All she'd done her whole life was break.

She was afraid because she felt her heart burst and cave in and shatter all at once.

He was beautiful.

Now, he clings to her for dear life. He follows her around, eyebrows furrowed, bottom lip jutted out, blubbering nonsense, jelly roll arms reaching up. His mother digs through the foul refrigerator for something to feed him. (Old milk, empty orange juice carton, moldy leftovers, case of beer.)

She can't look him in the eye anymore—his father's eyes.

Every chance she gets, she pawns him off on her mother, neighbors, and anyone who can take him so she can just breathe. Because love is suffocating, and the girl is selfish and chokes beneath his hopeful smile.

When he's gone, she cries, and she cries. The house is empty and full of clutter. Her throat burns with chalky grit. She wishes for one savory moment she was half the mother she knows he needs. And every time he screams and twists and kicks as toddlers do, she hates his father a little bit more.

Once upon a time, she was thriving in destruction. Going nowhere fast. Bourbon was her lover, Scotch was her friend, all others were expendable, and she was okay with that brutal truth, lonesome as it was. She accepted her sadness, accepted her sickness. After all, she'd been sick since the beginning. And rounds of treatments, rehabs, and therapies hadn't made one goddamn difference.

But then the boy's father came along. Before she knew it, her belly was swollen with life she didn't understand; with no way to do it alone, and there was no way he would stay (the white-hot searing truth).

The back door to the clinic was dingy, to say the least. She placed her hand on the doorknob and felt herself cracking beneath the weight of the silence. Late October proved to be colder than usual. Or maybe that was just the bone-chilling indifference. The man caught her just before she stepped in. With a sweaty palm on her shoulder and a yellow smile, he offered her sweet promises of family and love.

What 'love' was to her at this point, she doesn't remember.

But that didn't last, and she was left beaten, bruised, and forgotten. Bourbon never tasted so sweet even as her baby cried in the room next to her.

It became harder to look at him every time his father left. Guilt is a funny thing. It festers. Quietly. Builds calluses from the inside. It's not that she avoids his unconditionally loving blue orbs because she resents him. It's because she resents herself for bringing this innocent child into her wreck of a life. When she knew, driving to that hole-in-the-wall clinic, he didn't deserve this wreck. This child would one day be a man. He'd have a future he had no choice in. He'd be a victim of her circumstance, and that wasn't fair.

She prays every night to a God she's not sure exists that love doesn't find him in the bottom of a warm bottle of bourbon.

Like mother like son.

She loves him. She loves him, so she doesn't look at him. She loves him, so she stays away as much as possible. She loves him, so she leaves him be. She loves him the best way she knows how- by building a wall. So he doesn't love her.

Because love is pain, and her son deserves better.

She will try to remember she did the best she could in a drastic situation; His father had tried to take him at gunpoint. She was trying to protect him. "The right thing," they all said to her, though that never staunched the bleed she felt inside. She will not see him grow, she will not hear his voice change, she will not be there for his first date, and she should be glad of it. The tears fall and bloom on the letter she leaves with his grandmother. An apology that can never be enough. She wants him to know she loves him. And she prays and prays and wears her shame like shackles.

Penance, she thinks, when her shame is so great she can't breathe. Tells herself he's in the safest possible place he could be. Pushes away the part of her that wants him back. That want will only hurt him more. She was in no condition for mothering and sound enough to know it. *He is safe*. She says this like a prayer when she wakes up on her way to work before bed.

The boy no longer reaches out to her for comfort; he spurns her attempts at communication and reconciliation, and she can't blame him for it.

Love is sacrifice. This is what she tells herself between bouts of madness and grief. On the floor of the kitchen, she can't see through her tears, but she can feel the long vertical ridge of scar tissue on her arm. One attempt at suicide while he had been sleeping. It wasn't right. She couldn't mother him like he needed, but that didn't mean he couldn't have a stable, loving home. She rocks back and forth, feeling his absence like a crater ripped from her chest, she can't even say his name. She looks up to see a photograph taken years before when she was still sound of mind and body. He's holding creek rocks, dimples showing, and she smiles despite herself.

She would pick herself back up. She'd make herself worthy enough for him. And so began the venture out of the darkness. There amongst the yawning abyss of her mind was the tiniest pinprick of light. It takes years of work. It takes learning and lessons hard fought. But the light beckons her to follow. Over time, it will become larger, clearer, and in that light, she will find her son, smiling dimples showing and creek rocks in his hand.

THE MEDICINE

THE INTERNAL

Above all, be kind to yourself. Many people will look at your situation as if they know your story, but they don't, and their opinions are not worth your time.

Your time is valuable; you are valuable. Start a journal, one for yourself and one for your child. They may not be with you, but you can feel closer to them by writing down your thoughts and things you'd like to say to them.

Let the tears come. It may be painful, but do not mistake guilt and penance to get back to your child if possible; guilt will get you nowhere fast.

Remember, everything is temporary; the pain will dull and pass.

You are not alone. You are not the first woman to walk away, and you won't be the last. The world will hate you for it, but you know that you are protecting your child and that is the most important thing to do as a parent.

Accept that you did what you had to do with the information you had at the time.

Listen to mindful meditations when you begin to spiral. It's amazing how the brain works. Instead of trying to force your brain to stop spiraling, just switch gears, listen to meditation videos and your brain will have something else to gnaw on, pulling you out of yourself.

Learning to reorient the spiral will enable you to be the parent you know you could be.

THE EXTERNAL

Find things to work on. If you are unable to work, find a hobby that isn't doomscrolling. There's no worse feeling than realizing you spent the whole day on something you can't even remember.

Try to take care of your body. This can be as simple as taking a shower. I use skincare as a way to focus on something else. Work also helps.

Reach out to them when possible. The little phone conversations a small child can have might seem like nothing to you, but those memories will be the difference between a child who knows you and a child who doesn't feel comfortable around you.

Recall why you had to leave. When you feel that emotion that you want to push away, sink deeper into it. Feel the very bottom of it and integrate it into part of yourself. The more you resist, the more the negative feelings will persist. Feel it, and then let it go.

Lean on the people who love you if you can. Listen to them.

Feed yourself good food; you have to take care of yourself so you will be ready when your child is ready, too.

That's the whole point really, to use the time away to get better. Think of it like that, and you might be able to remember you did your very best with what you were given. Nothing is written in stone, and time does heal.

Hope Kernea is more poet than storyteller, but she hopes her words will touch any mothers or children of these mothers. She went to school for esthetics but found her passion with writing and is on the long road to healing.

When she isn't writing, you can find her in her little camper scribbling away in her notebook. Newly published, she is excited to see where this journey will take her, as it's always been her dream to help others, and it seems she's finally found a way to do that. Hope isn't very involved in social media, so you most likely wont find her on the socials. Instead, you'll find her helping to tend her lifelong friend's garden, learning to make bread, and finding out just who she is underneath the skin.

CHAPTER 24

INRAVELING

Finding Your Way Through the Shadow Maze
of Trauma and Addiction

Batsheva

*"A good life is like a weaving. Energy is created in the tension.
The struggle, the pull and tug are everything."*

~ Joan Erikson

MY STORY

Trauma is a knot. Healing requires us to unravel these knots, examine the threads that make up our identities, and weave ourselves back together into something new. These three stories describe recent experiences in which I found myself unraveling the intertwining knots of trauma, addiction, and grief to create something more meaningful.

UNRAVELING #1

"I'm taking too much," I told my therapist. "Even though I was prescribed 60 milligrams a day, I'm taking more like 90." I was talking about Adderall and, in reality, it was more like 120 or 150. "The morning and afternoon doses wear off by 3 pm," I explained. "I still have a whole second shift to attend to—making dinner, bedtimes, and the kids' whining." I emphasized "the kids whining" and how I didn't have the emotional capacity to deal with them unless I took another dose.

"You need to see a psychiatrist," my therapist strongly suggested. She worked with them for many years, and I agreed, somehow under the impression that this psychiatrist might prescribe me 90 milligrams a day (30mg over the daily dose recommended by the FDA for this controlled substance).

A consummate professional, I scheduled the appointment swiftly and even wrote up my own brief psychosocial assessment with a list of questions:

I have been in individual psychotherapy consistently since 2006, the last eight(ish) years with Dr. B. I have a history of childhood trauma, substance abuse (sustained remission since 2006), and bulimia (sustained remission since 2013). My history of substance abuse is important to consider. Although I explored many substances before I went to college, the substances I used most were alcohol and amphetamines, with an acute period lasting two years from age 23-25.

QUESTIONS:

1. *Can I benefit from a stimulant dose that is higher than the maximum recommended dose? If so, what are the risks to consider?*

2. *If the high-dose stimulant I am currently taking is not sustainable, how can I decrease to a lower dose without too much discomfort? What medications and behavioral strategies can I use to reduce and maintain a lower stimulant dose?*

3. *Though I have been in remission/sober for nearly 20 years, how does my substance use history relate to my current stimulant use?*

I stepped into her office suite and immediately noted how it fit the bill for a New York City psychoanalyst's waiting room—dark, narrow hallway, noisy radiator, beat-up leather couch, and few mismatched chairs piled high with copies of the New Yorker, Vanity Fair, and National Geographic. I felt totally at home, inhaling the dust-tinged air and staring at some inscrutable comic strips taped to the wall. When she called me a few minutes later, I saw two chairs facing each other and her Mensa certificate balanced on the lower tier of the bookshelf. *She must know,* I thought. *My therapist must have told her I admire intelligence, which will be a good tool to gain my respect (and obedience, perhaps).* She wore a face mask and had another one set out for me. *Most people are no longer wearing covid masks,* I thought. So, without thinking twice, I tried to ameliorate the uncomfortable silence with a standard question: "Have you had COVID yet?" She aptly redirected the question with a vague response and asked, "We're all hanging in there, aren't we?"

She conducted a skillful psychiatric assessment, and when I left, I felt we had a plan going forward. I'd bring my old medications to the pharmacy and start a new, longer-acting medication as soon as possible. "I'll speak to your therapist and nurse practitioner about the plan," she said. Later that day, I wrote to my care team—the nurse, therapist, and the consulting psychiatrist to confirm the plan. I received a response from all copied that the plan would change. They wanted to add an addiction medicine specialist and have me take my meds in front of someone every day. I felt the pit in my stomach filling up with a powerless rage. I felt naked and impotent. *They're all laughing at me; they're all pitying me.*

The 15-year-old in me dashed out an angry response:

No. Let's wean me off all controlled substances. I'm done. There's no way I'm going to put myself through that so I can stay on a stupid fucking drug I don't need anyway. Sorry to be so vulgar, but I'm honestly mortified to find myself in this place - it's been humiliating enough.

The whole rest of the day, I cried—I sobbed until my eyes were swollen shut. I felt like a failure—like a danger to myself. I couldn't be trusted to take my own medication. My judgment was assumed to be so damaged, despite the many steps I had already taken to address my Adderall addiction, that I couldn't make decisions for myself. It all ramped up so fast, and I wasn't ready. I felt my need for agency wasn't respected, and the power of the stigma of addiction wasn't acknowledged. But there must have been more to this—*why am I so very broken by these straightforward suggestions?* The emotions rushed out of me like an erupting volcano, like a cyst under pressure. I couldn't contain them. I could barely speak. I tried to put words around the experience. Still, nothing seemed to capture what was happening inside me—the trauma of losing control, being addicted, losing all respectability, feeling small and humiliated, and being seen for all my flaws and weaknesses.

Then I received an email from my nurse practitioner:

I'm here for you. None of us have perfect lives. I also have to navigate through shameful and humiliating parts of my story, so I feel your pain. It can feel very unfair and overwhelming. Try to give yourself a little grace through this intense phase of recovery and healing. I have time this week if you want to meet earlier.

It was a light at the end of the tunnel, a life preserver in the sea of darkness, and I grabbed it. I was a little scared because mental health providers usually won't reach out to you in that way. We connected later in the day—really connected. I felt safe. She was attuned to my need for agency and respect, and we devised a plan together.

UNRAVELING #2

Still, my therapist urged me to see an addiction medicine psychiatrist. I reviewed some websites, and the first one that looked interesting to me was a doctor who described being able to "taper people down to a manageable dose of Adderall." *Amazing, so I don't have to quit and get sober again?* That's what I wanted. That night, we did a 15-minute discovery call. It almost felt like he was yelling at me. He lectured and explained Adderall addiction to me, while meanwhile, I lived it. "Misusing your stimulant medication is the best way to get dropped by a psychiatrist because you signed a contract with them at the beginning of treatment not to abuse the controlled substance," he warned. I felt confused about why he was sharing this. *Is this a threat to abandon me someday?*

He didn't seem to understand that I just spent 18 years completely sober and learned a little something during that time. I mean, I'm the one who lived with this disease, active or dormant, every single day of my life. I was born into addiction. Both my parents were addicted to heroin, and they've both been on methadone for as long as I've known them. Since birth, I bathed in the shadow of addiction and the stigma it carries. I heard his assumptions about people with addictions not being trustworthy and having a tendency to bite the hand that feeds them. The very fact that he seemed so uncurious about my experience betrayed his lack of respect for me as a person in active addiction. *Why isn't he more curious about my experience? I mean, I could teach him a thing or two.*

His words and their implications struck that deep well of shame within me, and the grief erupted once again. I felt totally alone. Both physicians suggested I was becoming a little problematic and displaying high-risk behaviors. They turned off their humanity and turned on their inner robot doctor, running checklists and covering their asses. They stopped listening (or weren't willing to listen) to evade a deeper encounter with the emotional truth of addiction. This is the type of clinical connection I'm always trying to avoid by being the good girl, the model patient who always progresses and is never a problem.

Look, look, Mommy, look how well I've done. Aren't you proud of me?

UNRAVELING #3

I ran out of Adderall and had no prescription for more. "Can you send me a few pills?" I asked a friend from Houston. Supposedly, he overnighted them to my parent's house (so my husband wouldn't see the package), and Western Union'd him $200 (so my husband wouldn't see the bank withdrawal). The package never arrived, so I have to assume this friend of 20 years ripped me off, most likely driven by his own raging Xanax addiction. I probably deserve it, but I'm still unsure if I can forgive him. Realizing the package would never arrive precipitated the Adderall detox. Sickening waves of fear and self-loathing swirled around inside me. All my inner resources to self-soothe were depleted from months of Adderall abuse. When I shared what was happening with my husband, he was understandably angry. "Can you please try to understand?" I asked him for compassion and flipped when I didn't receive the tenderness I needed. With closed fists, I slammed my face and legs—like when I was a child, and my mom was scary and raging. I hated her, so I beat myself up.

THE MEDICINE

Reason, Magic, and Crochet

Human beings need a balance of reason and magic to thrive. Too much reason and we become stiff and stressed; too much magic and we become grandiose and unrelatable. The medicine that restores me is a debate of reason and magic. Chaos magick is a modern magical tradition that subverts traditional hierarchies, even hierarchies of idea. In this tradition, anything can become a sacred ritual if it's imbued with magical meaning and intent.

If trauma is a knot, then trauma work is a process of unraveling. Unraveling can be painful, but when you take things apart, you can put them back together with greater intention. I have used psychodynamic psychotherapy to slowly reason through this process of unraveling. My therapist and I have poured over my history to identify sources of trauma and apply them to current tendencies. Developing analytic insights has been hugely beneficial. However, the process of intense unraveling described in these pages happened outside the confines of therapy. It happened on two planes. In the mundane, it appeared I was losing my mind and falling apart; in the magical realm of the spirit, I was breaking apart the old and welcoming the new. Unraveling trauma must be accompanied by a parallel creative process of examining the threads and weaving them back together again. I have been weaving a richly meaningful tapestry into myself.

Anything can be a source and tool of magic. What makes something magical is the meaning and value we assign to things. Meaning works on the mind and the heart and on the spirit. As social beings, we create and assign meaning in a process with others—in connection. We need each other's help to hold space for unraveling, to review the threads that are left, and to imbue them with new meaning. We weave new realities together.

Addiction can be a manifestation of trauma. I'm certain that for me, there's a combination of nature and nurture at work. I was born into a household where people used substances to cope with their emotions and the ordinary stress of life. As a result, my emotional needs were neglected. Neglect is a very difficult form of trauma to identify because it's about what *wasn't* there.

In Unraveling #1, I felt that my providers were misattuned. But there's another interpretation. As a child, I never felt taken care of and never had boundaries to keep me safe. The massive outpouring of emotion reflected my grief at never being cared for adequately. I was grieving that as a child, no one really saw the pain I was in and how badly I needed help.

As an adult working with mental health providers, I felt separate, naked, and vulnerable but cared for, while as a child, I felt separate, naked, and vulnerable but uncared for. The distance between these two states was the size of my grief.

During this time, I started crocheting, which has been hugely comforting. There's a crochet practice of taking scraps of yarn from previous projects and weaving them together into *granny squares*, each unique, nostalgic, and beautiful in its own way. Like healing trauma, the new work is sturdier because it's imbued with meaning. Just like you can pick the stitches and patterns the threads will take, by healing trauma, you can examine the threads and decide which you want to keep and restore. Many trauma-informed beliefs are no longer relevant. New beliefs, values, and priorities can be woven into a rich inner life that comforts and provides meaning and direction.

Crochet and knitting have been seen as domestic arts situated in the domain of women's work. Reclaiming this practice as one of connection and self-care is a contemporary take on this traditional art form. Women's practices tend to prioritize connection and relatedness over individualism. Healing interpersonal trauma happens in the context of relationships. In my case, the lack of attunement I experienced with physicians intensified my unraveling process. Yet, my friends were there to pick up the threads with me, meet me exactly where I was, and take turns leading. With my friends, I felt safe enough to explore, play, and make mistakes. By listening with empathy and reflecting, my friends helped me work the threads of myself back into something stronger and even more beautiful.

PRACTICAL MEDICINE: STITCH AND BITCH

Try knitting, crocheting, or just crafting with friends. I've included brief instructions on crocheting a *granny square* and engaging in empathic communication.

THERAPEUTIC FRIENDSHIP PRACTICE:

When with a friend, take turns asking, "How are you?" and really listening. Listening isn't passive. It requires active engagement. Listen to the details, but also listen for feelings (sometimes these are unsaid or expressed between the lines). Humbly reflect on what you hear them saying, "It sounds like you are concerned about…" make sure you understand what they're trying to express by asking as many open-ended questions as possible "Can you tell me more about what that means? Validate their emotions: "I understand why you'd feel that way." Once you have a good understanding of your friend's situation on both a practical and an emotional level, you may offer suggestions. But always ask first, "Would it be helpful to you if I offered a suggestion?" Sometimes, people just want to be listened to and comforted.

CROCHET A GRANNY SQUARE:

Materials:

- Worsted weight yarn in three different colors (Color A, Color B, Color C)
- Crochet hook (size appropriate for your yarn)
- Yarn needle
- Scissors

Instructions:

R1:

1. With Color A, make a magic ring (or chain 4 and join with a slip stitch to form a ring).
2. Chain 3 (counts as first double crochet): work 2 double crochets into the ring.
3. Chain 2, 3 double crochets into the ring, chain 2. Repeat this sequence twice.
4. Join with a slip stitch to the top of the beginning chain 3.
5. Fasten off Color A.

R2:

6. Join Color B in any chain—2 corner space.
7. Chain 3 (counts as first double crochet): work 2 double crochets in the same space.

8. Chain 2, 3 double crochets in the next chain—2 space, chain 2. Repeat this sequence in each chain—2 space around.
9. Join with a slip stitch to the top of the beginning chain-3.
10. Fasten off Color B.

R3:

11. Join Color C in any chain—2 corner space.
12. Chain 3 (counts as first double crochet): work 2 double crochets in the same space.
13. Chain 2, 3 double crochets in the next chain-2 space, chain 2. Repeat this sequence in each chain—2 space around.
14. Join with a slip stitch to the top of the beginning chain—3.
15. Fasten off Color C.

Finishing:

16. Weave in all loose ends using a yarn needle.
17. Block your granny square if needed to ensure it maintains its shape.

Initially drawn to academia, **Batsheva** found herself facing unexpected challenges when she grappled with amphetamine addiction. As a person in recovery, she's navigated the complexities of healing with a pragmatic approach. Batsheva's commitment to well-being goes beyond her personal journey— she's become a dedicated guide for others seeking their own paths to recovery. Her experiences have given her a unique perspective on the multifaceted nature of healing. Her narrative is one of overcoming challenges and finding meaning through simple, meaningful pursuits. Away from the academic and healing realms, Batsheva finds joy in simple meditative activities. Crocheting, gardening, cooking, and yoga serve as physical and spiritual practices that foster a deeper connection between mind, body, and soul.

CONCLUSION

*"Share your truth, so others have
the courage to share their own."*

~ Shambia Ananda Prem

While writing these sacred stories, all twenty-four authors reported experiencing notable shifts in their lives. Magical mentors from our pasts reappeared. New opportunities knocked on our doors. Little hints and winks from our deceased loved ones became more evident. Our physical bodies felt lighter, and our voices were uplifted. When you read our words, you bear witness and activate the medicine attuned to the healing power of the community.

We would love to continue working with you. Our authors have all included a practical medicine section following each story. Many have also included links to their individual websites, where you can access a wide variety of healing modalities.

Reach out to our dedicated Dreaming with Bees website, where you can find access to additional tools, workshops, and events. We're helping to create safe spaces for all to share and care as responsible, mindful, conscious beeings.

As a final note, please check out Aluna Bridge nonprofit at the website below to learn more about this amazing organization and ways you can help continue to support our mission.

http://www.dreamingwithbees.com

http://www.alunabridge.org

"Come back. Even as shadow. Even as a dream."

~ Euripides

POSTSCRIPT

Only a few days after all the stories were placed together as a collection for this book, I received a dream vision that insisted it be added as a message from the book itself. Below is an excerpt pulled directly from my Dream Journal.

January 27th - In this dream I was lucid. I felt like I astral projected into the dream, landing inside the body of my cousin. It was like I was her ghost body, so I could feel my own presence but also hers, like we were traveling together.

We were inside my Aunt and Uncle's ranch style home, standing inside what had been my cousin's room when she lived there. Subtle light is filtering in through the windows from the setting Sun. As the minutes tick by, the house is growing darker. We move to walk out of the room and are startled by the shadowy presence of my Uncle who is standing in the dark hallway. He is holding a shotgun with the barrel pointing up. I feel a wave of sickness push through my body and the energy body of my cousin. Our hearts are pounding against our chests. Flash of cold sweat. Mouth is dry, and we are unable to breathe or make sounds. We watch him move the barrel into his mouth.

I am lucid so know that I am in the space of the Dreamtime, yet this is all too familiar. I think within the dream of my own pain suffered when my Father took his life. I feel my cousin's fear building within our hearts. We move back into the bedroom and stand with our backs pressed hard against the wall just on the other side of the hallway.

In the window on the opposite side of the room, we see the reflection of a fire-truck and ambulance pulling up. However, it is oddly a reflection of what is happening in the room itself, even though we do not see these vehicles in the room. I felt my cousin notice my presence within her. It was as though we could finally see each other and know we weren't alone, we in fact were the same being. I felt her hands clasp mine, and we began to pray to Mother Mary and the bees to please help us.

"Please help us stop this violence. Please help us save our Uncle, and all our children, from these ancestral cycles of abuse, addiction and harm to self and others. Please free us all from the chains of ancestral shame and guilt that hides and feeds these cycles from within the shadowy places of our souls."

Our tears and prayers turned to pleading as we heard the gun cock to ready.

"Please don't do this! Please! We need you to stay! We need you to know we love you! You are so loved!"

We begin to smell the scent of wild roses. The light outside the window brightened into purples, rose gold, and amber.

We felt our Uncle's shaking hand reach around the corner from the hallway and grab hold of us, pulling us to him. We embraced as he sobbed through what felt like lifetimes of pain.

We went into his bedroom where a small child sat playing on the floor. He appeared to be around the age of nine or ten. His face was shifting between the faces of my Uncle and Father when they were this age, and then also the faces of my cousin's son and my own son, Avery, when they were younger. I could see this linking of ancestral DNA.

We settled onto the edge of the bed just above the boy. There was a small toy toolbox that the child had received as a gift that was still wrapped in it's plastic packaging and sitting off to the side. I asked, "Why haven't you played with this yet? What are you waiting for?"

The boy replied, "I don't know. I was saving it for the right time."

I was sliding off the edge of the bed, so pushed myself back up. In the process, my foot accidentally kicked into the toolbox and popped a hole in the plastic wrap.

The boy smiled and said, "Okay. I guess the time is now."

We watched as he finished ripping all the packaging off and opened up the different drawers and compartments. Inside, he found a bright blue hammer, several rainbow colored screwdrivers, a yellow tape measure, and a little green handsaw. Beneath those tools, he also found a purple carpenter's pencil, paper and a little jar of honey.

I looked deep into the eyes of the boy, and felt the gravity of his simple words ground into me. "Thank you!"

Dream Wisdom

I see my Uncle's house as representing the whole container of traumas experienced throughout my lifetimes and the lifetimes of my ancestors. I see the darkness of the house representing the buried, hushed up, secrets that continue to lurk in the corners and hallways of our hearts and minds.

Connecting with my female cousin in this way, brought to mind the collective wound of the Divine Feminine and our need, as daughters of oppressive Fathers, to have our voices, our words, our prayers and lamentations heard, so that our sons and daughters may be released from the chains that bind us.

Seeing the reflection of the firetruck and ambulance feels like the dream was saying, "You are the ones that will rescue them. You are the ones that will put out the fires and resuscitate the living dead. You are the siren's warning and call to action."

The prayers to Mary and the bees and the smell of the roses symbolized the power of the Divine Feminine to still find love and mercy, even in the darkest hour. Showing up in the fullness of love and mothering this world and remembering our sacred connection to each other is the medicine that will save us.

I'm reminded again of Mary Magdalene at the foot of Yeshua at the scene of the Crucifixion. So often the story is sold as one of sacrifice and suffering in the name of the great Father. If for only a moment, we turn our focus instead to what was happening at His feet, we see Mother Mary and Mary Magdalene, with hands clasped in solidarity and in utter grief and love, praying for the madness of violence to our beloved ones to stop.

In this dream, I love that it was my bare foot that ripped the plastic off the new toolbox, breaking the ancestral binding that has prevented our children from having the access they need to new brighter tools and perspectives. New tools that can help their lives grow and flourish. New tools that allow them to rewrite and create their own stories and dreams.

You're welcome, little one!

ARTIST STATEMENT

Artist **Ryan Davis** completed the gorgeous cover art for this book. Ryan is a Sophomore at MTSU studying animation. He has had an interest in art for several years. He enjoys sketching and painting and also creating digital 3D animations.

"My favorite part about this creative hobby of mine is transforming what starts out as a little idea in my head and being able to share the final, finished piece with others!"

The links below will take you to Ryan's portfolio where you can view his current work and contact him for your own creative graphic design projects.

https://www.behance.net/ryandavis51

Ryan@jdavisphotos.com

Made in the USA
Columbia, SC
02 June 2024

36515219R00167